Nickel

BEFORE RELIGION

BRENT NONGBRI

Before Religion

A History of a Modern Concept

Yale UNIVERSITY PRESS

NEW HAVEN AND LONDON

Yale University Press books may be purchased in quantity
for educational, business, or promotional use. For
information, please e-mail sales.press@yale.edu (U.S.
office) or sales@yaleup.co.uk (U.K. office).

Set in Janson Oldstyle and Futura Bold types
by Westchester Book Group.
Printed in the United States of America.

Library of Congress Cataloging-in-Publication Data
Nongbri, Brent, 1977–
  Before religion : a history of a modern concept / Brent Nongbri.
     p. cm.
  Includes bibliographical references (p.   ) and index.
  ISBN 978-0-300-15416-0 (alk. paper)
  1. Religion—History.   I. Title.
  BL430.N57 2012
  200.9—dc23   2012020811

A catalogue record for this book is available from the
British Library.

This paper meets the requirements of ANSI/NISO
Z39.48–1992 (Permanence of Paper).

10   9   8   7   6   5   4   3   2   1

For Janet and Govanon Nongbri

CONTENTS

ACKNOWLEDGMENTS

One does not write a book like this one without the help of numerous generous and intelligent friends. To my colleagues over the years at the University of Texas, Yale University, Oberlin College, and Macquarie University who have endured me pestering them with questions, I offer my sincere thanks. Funding for the research that has resulted in this book was provided by Yale University, the Mrs. Giles Whiting Foundation, the Catholic Biblical Association, and Macquarie University. I owe a special debt of gratitude to those intrepid souls who read all or part of the manuscript at various stages of preparation. As an editor, Jennifer Banks provided a wonderful combination of enthusiasm, expertise, and patience that helped to see the book through to publication. An earlier incarnation of several of these chapters benefited from the critical eyes of Harold Attridge, Adela Yarbo Collins, Ramsay MacMullen, and Wayne Meeks. Dale Martin, who somehow manages to be a role model in both the seriousness and the humor of scholarship, read more than one draft and made this a better book. Edwin Judge read the whole and saved me from a number of errors. The anonymous referees for Yale University Press offered insightful feedback and helped to improve the clarity of the argument. Jessie Dolch performed an admirable jargonectomy on the text and has made the following chapters much more readable. To all these people, I am deeply grateful. The infelicities that remain in this book are due to stubbornness on my own part, not a lack of charity or effort on theirs. There is no really adequate way to express my thanks to Mary Jane Cuyler, both for providing wise feedback on just about every aspect of this project and for making each day something to be enjoyed. Finally, this book is dedicated to my parents. It's a small token of my appreciation for decades of love, encouragement, and laughter.

INTRODUCTION

My father grew up in the Khasi Hills of northeastern India. The Khasi language is today spoken by roughly one million people, mostly in the state of Meghalaya. When I was in college and just becoming aware of the complexity of studying religion, it occurred to me one day that I had no idea what the Khasi word for "religion" was. I owned a small Khasi-English dictionary, but it did not provide English-to-Khasi definitions. Faced with the usual number of deadlines for various projects, I didn't immediately try to track down an answer to the question and soon forgot about it. But a few years later, the topic came up in a conversation with my father, and I asked him about the Khasi term for "religion." He replied that it was *ka niam*. By this time I was a graduate student in religious studies, and I was curious to learn more about this word. I dug out my little dictionary and looked it up. I found it could also simply mean "customs," that is to say, not necessarily anything particularly or especially religious. More intriguing, though, was the asterisk beside the word that directed me to a short note at the bottom of the page. It turned out that *niam* was in fact not an indigenous Khasi term at all but a loan-word from the Bengali *nijama*, meaning "rules" or "duties." My father's language, it seems, had no native word for "religion."[1]

For much of the past two centuries, both popular and academic thought has assumed that religion is a universal human phenomenon, a part of the "natural" human experience that is essentially the same across cultures and throughout history. Individual religions may vary through time and geographically, so the story goes, but there is an element that we call religion to be found in all cultures in all time periods. Introductory textbooks supply us with competing definitions of religion ranging from simple, confessional definitions (belief in God or belief in the supernatural) to more universal-sounding definitions (belief in an Ultimate Concern), but regardless of how they define religion, these books assure us that the institution of religion is ubiquitous. This ubiquity prompts different explanations. Some religious adherents claim that there are many false religions but that a "true" form of religion was revealed at some moment in history. It has become more common recently to hear that all religions (or at least the "better elements" in all religions) point to the same transcendent reality to which all humans have access. Or, as a number of authors from the scientific community have argued, it is possible that religion is simply, for better or worse, an evolutionary adaptation of the brains of *Homo sapiens*.[2] For all their differences, these groups agree on a basic premise: religion appears as a universal given, present in some form or another in all cultures, from as far back as the time when humans first became . . . well, human.

During the past thirty years, this picture has been increasingly criticized by experts in various academic fields. They have observed that no ancient language has a term that really corresponds to what modern people mean when they say "religion." They have noted that terms and concepts corresponding to religion do not appear in the literature of non-Western cultures until after those cultures first encountered European Christians. They have pointed out that the names of supposedly venerable old religions can often be traced back only to the relatively recent past ("Hinduism," for example, to 1787 and "Buddhism" to 1801). And when the names do derive from ancient words, we find that the early occurrences of those words are best understood as verbal activities rather than conceptual entities; thus the ancient Greek term *ioudaismos* was not "the religion of Judaism" but the activity of Judaizing, that is, following the practices associated with the Judean ethnicity; the Arabic *islām* was not "the religion of Islam" but "submitting to authority." More generally, it has become clear that the isolation of something called "religion" as a sphere of life ideally separated from politics, economics, and science is not a universal feature of human history. In fact, in the broad view of human cultures, it is a strikingly odd way of conceiving the world. In the ancient world, the gods were involved in all aspects of life. That is not to say, however, that all ancient people were somehow uniformly "religious"; rather, the act of distinguishing between "religious" and "secular" is a recent development. Ancient people simply did not carve up the world in that way.

In the academic field of religious studies, the claim that religion is a modern invention is not really news. The major (and still highly influential) study in English is Wilfred Cantwell Smith's *The Meaning and End of Religion: A New Approach to the Religious Traditions of Mankind*, which first appeared in 1963 and continues to be reprinted, most recently in 1991.[3] Smith famously argued that we should stop using the term "religion" because it has come to refer to systems rather than genuine religious feelings. He preferred to use the designation "faith" to describe what he believed were the universal, authentic religious feelings of all humans. As part of his case, he narrated a history of religion as a story of what he called "reification," that is, "mentally making religion into a thing, gradually coming to conceive it as an objective systematic entity."[4] For Smith, a committed Christian with a sincere interest in religious pluralism, this process of reification was not a neutral development:

> This much at least is clear and is crucial: that men throughout history and throughout the world have been able to *be* religious without the assistance of a special term, without the intellectual analysis that the term implies. In fact, I have come to feel that, in some ways, it is probably easier to be religious without the concept; that the notion of religion can become an enemy to piety. . . . In any case, it is not entirely foolish to suggest that the rise of the concept "religion" is in some ways correlated with a decline in the practice of religion itself.[5]

Thus, while Smith was ready to dispense with the concept of religion, he had no doubt that all humans throughout history have been able to "be religious." What was troubling for him was that this religiousness had been systematized over the course of the centuries into religion. Many in the academic field of religious studies have followed Smith's lead on this point.

3

My initial curiosity about the history of the concept of religion is in large part due to my first reading of *The Meaning and End of Religion* more than a decade ago. Yet, I have come to think that his focus on reification, a focus shared by many in the field of religious studies, tends to confuse more than it clarifies. After all, ancient people systematized. Ancient people had "concepts." The real problem is that the *particular* concept of religion is absent in the ancient world. The very idea of "being religious" requires a companion notion of what it would mean to be "not religious," and this dichotomy was not part of the ancient world. To be sure, ancient people had words to describe proper reverence of the gods, but these terms were not what modern people would describe as strictly "religious." They formed part of a vocabulary of social relations more generally. In Greek, for example, the word *eusebeia* frequently occurs in contexts referring to the proper attitude to hold toward the gods (as opposed to its opposite *asebeia*, the wrong attitude). Such words, however, were not limited to relationships involving gods. They referred to hierarchical social protocols of all sorts. Thus, near the conclusion of his *Republic*, Plato emphasizes the rewards for those who display *eusebeia* and punishments due to those who display *asebeia* "to gods *and parents.*"[6] The ideal Roman held an attitude of *eusebeia* "toward the bonds of kinship."[7] What is modern about the ideas of "religions" and "being religious" is the isolation and naming of some things as "religious" and others as "not religious."

The anthropologist Talal Asad has characterized the modernity of religion in a way I find much more helpful than that of Smith: "I would urge that 'religion' is a modern concept not because it is reified but because it has been linked to its Siamese twin 'secularism.'"[8] It is this simultaneous birth of religion and secularism that merits attention. That said, I want to stress that I am not interested in the so-called secularization thesis (how something called "secularism" encroached on a religious world and slowly rooted out religion until stalling at some time in the twentieth century as religion experienced a "resurgence"). Instead, one of the problems this book addresses is how we have come to talk about "secular" versus "religious" at all. These two words grew out of Latin predecessors, and the ancient words did point to a dichotomy, but *not* what is typically understood as the modern secular/religious dichotomy. In late medieval Latin (and even in early English), these words described different kinds of Christian clergy, with *religiosus* describing members of monastic orders and *saecularis* describing Christian clergy not in a monastic order (the usage persists among Catholics to this day).[9]

It is also unhelpful to think of ancient cultures' dichotomies of sacred versus profane and pure versus impure as analogous to the modern distinction between "the religious" and "the secular." Roman temples, for example, were sacred sites, but they could host a wide variety of activities, many of which modern people would not describe as "religious." In addition to their role as sites for sacrifices or festivals dedicated to a god or gods, temples in the Roman world functioned as meeting places for governmental bodies, as repositories for legal records, as banks, markets, libraries, and museums.[10] Even ancient statements that appear to self-evidently proclaim a religious/secular divide to modern people ("Render unto Caesar . . .") seem to have been understood quite differently by ancient readers.[11] All of this raises the question of how and when people came to conceptualize the world as divided between "religious" and "secular" in the modern sense, and to think of the religious realm as being divided into distinct religions, the so-called World Religions.

Asad's suggestion to think of ideas of religion and secularism as conjoined twins is both helpful and troubling. It is a useful metaphor in that it stresses the codependence of religion and secularism, and the metaphor of childbirth is useful because a birth occurs in a particular time and place. Like all metaphors, though, this one has its limits. Historical discussions are rarely so clear-cut that one could isolate a particular moment when something like religion was "born." Nevertheless, I do think one can posit a certain range of time and a particular historical context in which the ideas of religion and the modern secular nation-state began to take shape and in which the world came to be conceptually carved up into different religions.

In the wake of the Protestant Reformation, old arguments over which form of Christianity was "true" took on a new urgency as some Protestant groups were able to garner enough political support to seriously challenge papal authority throughout Europe. A result of this situation was the civil unrest in the conflicts now known as the Wars of Religion. Since these hostilities not only brought much bloodshed but also disrupted trade and commerce, prominent public figures such as John Locke argued that stability in the commonwealth could be achieved not by *settling* arguments about which kind of Christianity was "true," but by *isolating* beliefs about god in a private sphere and *elevating* loyalty to the legal codes of developing nation-states over loyalties to god. These provincial debates among European Christians took on a global aspect since they coincided with European exploration and colonial activities in the Americas, Africa, and elsewhere. The "new" peoples whom Europeans discovered became ammunition for intra-Christian sectarian disputes. European Christians arguing about which form of Christianity was true drew comparisons between rival Christian sects and the worship practices of the new "savage" peoples in Africa and the Americas. Europeans' interpretations of the newly discovered peoples around the world in light of Christian sectarian strife at home led to what the historian Peter Harrison has quite appropriately described as "the projection of Christian disunity onto the world."[12] This projection provided the basis for the framework of World Religions that currently dominates both academic and popular discussions of religion: the world is divided among people of different and often competing beliefs about how to obtain salvation, and these beliefs should ideally, according to influential figures like Locke, be privately held, spiritual, and nonpolitical. It was only with this particular set of circumstances in the sixteenth and seventeenth centuries that the concept of religion as we know it began to coalesce.

This basic story has emerged somewhat haphazardly in the work of historians, anthropologists, philosophers, theologians, and others.[13]

Their treatments of isolated historical episodes are insightful, and their arguments are often compelling. Yet, even though the notion that religion is a recent invention has been percolating for several decades now in various academic circles, it is still common to see even scholars using the word "religion" as if it were a universal concept native to all human cultures. In my own area of specialization, the study of the ancient Mediterranean world, every year sees a small library's worth of books produced on such things as "ancient Greek religion." Part of the reason for this state of affairs is a lack of a coherent narrative about the development of the concept of religion. This book thus provides a (not *the*) history of that concept, drawing together the results of diverse fields of research to show, first and foremost, that religion does indeed *have* a history: it is not a native category to ancient cultures. The idea of religion as a sphere of life separate from politics, economics, and science is a recent development in European history, one that has been projected outward in space and backwards in time with the result that religion appears now to be a natural and necessary part of our world. This appearance, however, turns out to be a surprisingly thin veneer that dissipates under close historical scrutiny. The following chapters are an attempt to offer such scrutiny.

The first chapter, "What Do We Mean by 'Religion'?," introduces the problem of defining religion and provides a context for the historical analysis that constitutes the bulk of the book. Although most people have a vague sense of what religion is, scholars have had (and continue to have) an extremely difficult time agreeing on a definition of religion. Struggles to find an appropriately inclusive definition have led to seemingly endless debates about whether Confucianism, or Marxism, or Nazism, or any number of other "-isms" ought to be considered religions. I confront this complicated morass by following the lead of Ludwig Wittgenstein and taking a pragmatic approach to the problem of defining words and directing my attention to how terms are actually used in speech. From this perspective, what most modern people appear to mean by religion is a kind of inner sentiment or personal faith ideally isolated from secular concerns. In this common framework, the individual World Religions are thought of as specific manifestations of the general phenomenon of religion. I do not necessarily agree that these are good definitions of religion, but it is the emergence of this conception of religions as apolitical paths to individual salvation that I want to chart in this book.

The primary purpose of the second chapter, "Lost in Translation," is to begin to dispel the commonly held idea that there is such a thing as "ancient religion." One reason the idea of religion seems so universal is because key terms in ancient texts are frequently rendered as "religion" in modern translations. I look at the early histories of some of these terms: the Latin *religio*, the Greek *thrēskeia*, and the Arabic terms *dīn*, *milla*, and *umma*. I show some of the range of meanings these terms had in ancient contexts and point out the ways in which their translation as "religion" both excludes some key valences of the ancient terms and simultaneously smuggles in modern assumptions of the sort outlined in the first chapter.

In the third chapter, "Some (Premature) Births of Religion in Antiquity," I examine four historical episodes that have been portrayed as the birth of the concept of religion in antiquity: the Maccabean revolt in Judaea in the second century B.C.E., the so-called religious dialogues of the Roman statesman Cicero in the first century B.C.E., the writings of Eusebius of Caesarea in the late third and early fourth centuries C.E., and the rise of Muhammad in the seventh century C.E. Each of these moments has been claimed as the inception of religion. I suggest that such terminology diverts our attention away from actual ancient strategies for conceptualizing difference among peoples.

The fourth chapter, "Christians and 'Others' in the Premodern Era," further explores the tactics that some "orthodox" Christians employed for managing difference in antiquity. As these Christians began to encounter groups of people whom modern scholars would designate as members of other religions (such as Manichaeans, Muslims, and Buddhists), they developed ways of interpreting "other" peoples, none of which involved the category of religion. In some cases, these "orthodox" Christians incorporated people they regarded as somehow alien into biblical frameworks in which all others (that is, both different kinds of Christians and what most modern people would call non-Christians) were deviant Christians, or heretics. In this light, I examine the phenomena that modern scholars have come to call "the religion of Manichaeism" and "early Islam," descriptors not often used by premodern "orthodox" Christians, who by and large regarded followers of Mani and Muhammad as Christian heretics. Beyond this heresiological discourse, Christians had other means for conceptualizing worshippers perceived as somehow foreign, which I illustrate by tracing the history of the wildly popular tale of *Barlaam and Ioasaph*, a story that might be called Christian, Buddhist, Muslim, Manichaean, or all of the above. The legend represents another way medieval Christians incorporated and internalized what modern scholars would call "another religion."

The fifth chapter, "Renaissance, Reformation, and Religion in the Sixteenth and Seventeenth Centuries," picks up in the late medieval period with ongoing discussions of what constitutes *vera religio*, or genuine worship.[14] I follow deployments of this notion through the writings of certain influential Italian Neo-Platonists of the fifteenth and sixteenth centuries and into the milieu of the so-called English deists. I then trace these debates through the fragmentation of Christendom resulting from the various reform movements in the wake of Martin Luther. Although Christians had never been a wholly united group, the political power of the breakaway groups in the centuries following Luther allowed them to have a much greater effect on the intellectual landscape than the dissidents who preceded them. Growing violence among Christians in the sixteenth and seventeenth centuries created a space for different ways of thinking about dissent and approaching the question of *vera religio*. It is in this context that I read the works of authors usually regarded as political theorists, such as Jean Bodin and John Locke, who began to conceive of religion as a distinct, privatized sphere of activity that should support and not disturb the affairs of the newly emerging nation-states.

In the sixth chapter, "New Worlds, New Religions, World Religions," I begin to shift the focus outward to Europeans' struggle to come to terms with the variety of "new" peoples they were encountering in the Americas, Africa, and India. I draw upon the results of recent scholarship on the encounters between native peoples and European colonial administrators, missionaries, and academics from the sixteenth to the nineteenth centuries in order to highlight the ways in which these colonial exchanges generated the idea of the world being divided into different religions. These new peoples were clearly not Christians, but neither were their ways of life wholly foreign and unintelligible. There were perceived similarities. The inhabitants of these distant lands venerated invisible beings similar to saints or demons; they had stories not completely unlike Christian scriptures; they had people who somewhat resembled clergy; they had buildings that were sort of like temples; and even though the native peoples did not group these items together, Europeans did do so for comparative purposes. Such comparative acts resulted in the generation of new religions. This is not to say that indigenous peoples lacked a voice in constructing these new religions. European missionaries, travelers, and colonial administrators relied heavily upon native informants to collect information, and scholars eager to translate new texts received crucial aid from natives. I examine three cases—religion in India, religion in southern Africa, and religion in Japan—to highlight some of the different colonial forces that are visible in the production of the religions. I close by surveying some of the modes of classifying these new religions that Europeans developed beginning in the seventeenth century and concluding with the emergence of incipient World Religions models in the nineteenth and early twentieth centuries.

The seventh chapter, "The Modern Origins of Ancient Religions," examines one of the mechanisms through which religion has come to seem so universal, namely, the continuing discourse on "ancient religions." This chapter thus folds the preceding discussion back on itself by showing how the concept of religion generated by the long historical processes outlined in the fifth and sixth chapters is applied to ancient texts and material remains to produce "ancient religions." I begin by observing that from the Middle Ages until the sixteenth century, most people who thought about the gods of Greece and Rome regarded them as demonic minions of Satan (once again understanding the objects of "pagan" worship in a biblical, Christian framework). It was only during the seventeenth and eighteenth centuries, largely as a result of comparisons drawn between practices described in classical literature and the practices of newly discovered American and African "pagans," that ancient pagan religion, or, more properly now, *religions* came into focus as legitimate objects of academic study. Once "ancient" Greek and Roman religions became viable entities in this way, scholars were able to create other ancient religions as archeology and manuscript hunting brought evidence of other ancient cultures to light. I take as an example of this phenomenon the creation of ancient Mesopotamian religion in the nineteenth and twentieth centuries. I observe how scholars, by arranging newly discovered texts and artifacts according to fashionable theories of religion, have created and re-created ancient Mesopotamian religion. The chapter concludes by reflecting upon how and why, despite the fact that many scholars of ancient cultures have recognized how problematic the concept of religion is, we continue to talk about "ancient religions" through the use of rhetorical tropes like "embedded religion."

In a short conclusion, "After Religion?," I discuss some of the implications of this historical account of religion. It is no secret that early practitioners of comparative religion held a number of Christian presuppositions, and in the present, early-twenty-first-century atmosphere of religious pluralism, there are ongoing, commendable attempts to rid the category of religion of "Christian assumptions" in order to purify and democratize it. I propose that given the specifically Christian heritage of the category of religion, all the noble efforts to de-Christianize it are to some extent futile. Future efforts to deploy the category of religion will need to own up to its somewhat checkered past and generate creative ways of using the category while acknowledging its roots as a relic of Christian polemic.

In the writing of history, nothing is neutral or objective, not even the scheme of periodization one employs or the geographic descriptors one chooses. One of my central claims is that religion is a modern and not an ancient concept. This claim is a bit complicated because the word "modern" can have a variety of meanings. I use the designation "modern" to refer to the time after the period from roughly the middle of the fifteenth to the middle of the sixteenth century. The combined effects of events that occurred over that span (the Reformation, the invention and spread of the printing press, the discovery and colonization of the New World) had far-reaching consequences that brought about a reorganization of the material and intellectual lives of people all over the world. The especially tricky part is that this period is the very time I see religion being formed into a recognizable category. That is to say, the existence of the religious/secular division is part of what constitutes the modern world. I hope this point will emerge with some clarity during the course of this book. The traditional historiographic divide between "ancient" and "medieval" (usually located at the "fall of Rome"—whenever one chooses to date that!) is less important to me. Nevertheless, I use the conventional term "medieval" throughout this work to refer to the period roughly between the fifth century and the fifteenth century.

Geographically, I often use the term "European" (as well as its foil "non-European"). I recognize that this kind of terminology is not without its problems, especially when discussing premodern phenomena.[15] Although the term *europa* is quite ancient, the approximate region now known as Europe was, from the late Roman period through the fifteenth century, most commonly called "Christendom" (*christianitas, christianus populus,* and at the later end of that temporal spectrum *respublica christiana*). Here again, the formation of the concept of religion, of the religious/secular divide, plays a key role in allowing for the idealized severing of a geographic Europe from an ideological *respublica christiana*. When I use the adjective "European," I refer to the changing collective identity of the region now designated as Europe (though in practical terms, the authors I examine hail largely from what are now France, Germany, Italy, the Netherlands, Switzerland, and the United Kingdom). When I use the equally contestable adjective "Western," I refer to European (and later, American) identities defined against cultures perceived as foreign.

Finally, a word on people. In writing a book that covers as much ground as this one attempts to do, difficult choices about inclusion and exclusion are impossible to avoid. Some of the authors and texts I treat are quite well known and thoroughly studied; others are more obscure. In choosing authors and texts, I have availed myself of the good efforts of other scholars (the works of Peter Harrison, Tomoko Masuzawa, Wilfred Cantwell Smith, and Jonathan Z. Smith have been especially helpful in this regard). I have also made use of many specialist studies that provide context for and elucidate the primary sources that form the backbone of my account but are themselves not involved in explicitly historicizing religion. I have relied on these specialist studies especially in areas in which I lack the linguistic competence to handle original-language primary sources. When I have summarized or quoted such sources, I have tried to represent them fairly on specific points, but the overall framework of their arguments can (and often does) differ from mine since I am challenging a basic assumption of most work in the humanities, namely, the universality of religion. Registering my differences with all these authors individually on this point would be tiresome, so I do so now collectively.

I want to stress that this account is certainly not the only possible one. Different, but not incompatible, narratives could be produced. I have attempted to provide a diachronic narrative by selecting representative episodes from a two-thousand-year period to offer a nuanced historical discussion, while constantly paying attention to the specific, concrete, social and political contexts that shaped the philosophers, legal theorists, missionaries, and others whose works brought about the concept of religion. That is to say, I have tried to write a history of the idea of religion that is more than simply a history of ideas.

Is Religion "Simply There"?

In a 1964 case presented before the U.S. Supreme Court, the justices were asked to consider the legality of obscenity laws in the state of Ohio. In a short concurring opinion to the decision, Justice Potter Stewart wrote: "I have reached the conclusion . . . that under the First and Fourteenth Amendments criminal laws in this area [obscenity] are constitutionally limited to hard-core pornography. I shall not today attempt further to define the kinds of material I understand to be embraced within that shorthand description; and perhaps I could never succeed in intelligibly doing so. But I know it when I see it."[1] There is a surprising, and amusing, similarity in the way people talk about defining hard-core pornography and the way the term "religion" is used in both popular and academic contexts today. Historian of comparative religion Eric J. Sharpe has written, "To *define* religion is, then, far less important than to possess the ability to *recognise* it when we come across it."[2] When I ask my students to define religion, they generally respond with a wide range of conflicting definitions, but they usually can agree on "what counts" as religion and what does not.

The purpose of this book is to provide a history of the concept of religion. To do so, I need to talk about definitions of religion in a way that is more precise than the typical, vague "I know it when I see it" approach. The very fact that I want to write such a history suggests that I do not share the popular assumption that religion and faith are timeless mysterious things that have always been present to some degree in all human cultures throughout history. This sort of assumption runs deep. For instance, Sharpe has also declared, "Religion is simply *there* as an identifiable factor of human experience."[3] This statement accurately reflects both popular and, to a large extent, academic views about religion (although, as we have seen, some academics would no doubt want to substitute "religiousness" or "faith" for Sharpe's "religion"). What I want to do is to provide a history of this thing that people like Sharpe propose is "simply there."

Meanings of Religion: Its Use in Ordinary Speech

At several points in this book, I use the phrase "the modern notion of religion" (or one of several synonymous words and phrases—"religion," "the concept of religion," and others) as a kind of shorthand. When I say this, I am not contrasting that phrase with any "ancient notion" of religion, for religion is a modern innovation. When I refer (using any of the phrases above) to that modern concept, religion, I refer to a dominant way the term is used in the United States in the present day.

But that formulation dodges the question in some ways. Isn't the problem the fact that religion is defined in so many *different* ways in contemporary discussions? It would take an entire book (or, more likely, several books) to catalogue the myriad attempts at defining "religion."[4] In 1912, professor of psychology James H. Leuba wrote a book on the "psychological study of religion" that included an appendix with more than fifty different definitions of religion. Reflecting on this collection, historian of religions Jonathan Z. Smith concluded *not* that defining religion is a hopeless pursuit, but rather that "it can be defined, with greater or lesser success, more than fifty ways."[5] The number of proposed definitions for "religion" has only increased in the century since Leuba wrote, and the industry of proposing new, "better" definitions of religion shows no signs of flagging, despite the decreasing sense that any universal definition will ever be accepted.

Yet scholars continue to wrestle with the term. Among the more sophisticated attempts at definition is that of Bruce Lincoln, a professor of the history of religions.[6] He crafts his treatment of the idea of religion as a critique of the classic definition suggested by the anthropologist Clifford Geertz, who in 1966 defined "religion" as

"(1) a system of symbols which acts to (2) establish powerful, pervasive, and long-lasting moods and motivations in men by (3) formulating conceptions of a general order of existence and (4) clothing these conceptions with such an aura of factuality that (5) the moods and motivations seem uniquely realistic."[7] Lincoln countered that Geertz's definition of religion was grounded in a particularly Protestant mindset that located religion on the interior of people, thus effectively denying the label "religion" to groups whose self-identification is more practice-oriented.[8] Lincoln states his objection to Geertz's definition by pointing out that there are "things one intuitively wants to call 'religion'—Catholicism and Islam, for instance—that are oriented less toward 'belief' and the status of the individual believer, and more to embodied practice, discipline, and community."[9] As an alternative, Lincoln proposes a "polythetic and flexible" definition that "allow[s] for wide variations, and attend[s], at a minimum, to these four domains":

> (1) A discourse whose concerns transcend the human, temporal, and contingent and that claims for itself a similarly transcendent status, (2) a set of practices whose goal is to produce a proper world and/or proper human subjects, as defined by a religious discourse to which these practices are connected, (3) a community whose members construct their identity with reference to a religious discourse and its attendant practices, and (4) an institution that regulates religious discourse, practices, and community, reproducing them over time and modifying them as necessary, while asserting their eternal validity and transcendent value.[10]

As definitions go, this one has many commendable qualities, but what interests me is the impulse to which Lincoln refers at the outset—those "things one intuitively wants to call 'religion.'" There are certain "things" that people in the modern world are conditioned to regard as "religion," and attempts at definition are always subject to that impulse to be consistent with everyday speech.[11] In this case, Lincoln feels that Geertz's definition excludes Islam and Catholicism. This omission causes a problem because in everyday usage of modern languages, both those entities usually count as "religion." It is the desire to be consistent with this everyday usage that drives the continued production of definition upon definition of the term. For this reason, I take a less technical and more pragmatic approach to the problem of defining it. In his later work, the philosopher Ludwig Wittgenstein argued that the meaning of a word is not inherent in any proposed definition: "For a *large* class of cases—though not for all—in which we employ the word 'meaning' it can be defined thus: the meaning of a word is its use in the language."[12] Because of the pervasive use of the word "religion" in the cultures of the modern Western world (the "we" here), we already intuitively know what "religion" is before we even try to define it: religion is anything that sufficiently resembles modern Protestant Christianity. Such a definition might be seen as crass, simplistic, ethnocentric, Christianocentric, and even a bit flippant; it is all these things, but it is also highly accurate in reflecting the uses of the term in modern languages. Every attempted definition of "religion" that I have seen has implicitly had this criterion at its base. Most of the debates about whether this or that "-ism" (Confucianism, Marxism, etc.) is "really a religion" boil down to the question of whether or not they are sufficiently similar to modern Protestant Christianity. This situation should not be surprising given the history of the category of religion.[13]

Three Observations about the Use of the Word "Religion"

I need to say a bit more about definitions and current conversations about religion. For the sake of clarity, I articulate three points about the use of "religion" in contemporary popular and academic discussions. First and most important, for many modern people, religion represents an essentially private or spiritual realm that somehow transcends the mundane world of language and history. This dominant view of what religion is (or, rather, what it ideally should be) is expressed by the former nun and current best-selling author Karen Armstrong:

The external history of a religious tradition often seems divorced from the *raison d'être* of faith. The spiritual quest is an interior journey; it is a psychic rather than political drama. It is preoccupied with liturgy, doctrine, contemplative disciplines and an exploration of the heart, not with the clash of current events. Religions certainly have a life outside the soul. Their leaders have to contend with the state and affairs of the world, and often relish doing so. They fight with members of other faiths, who seem to challenge their claim to a monopoly of absolute truth; they also persecute their co-religionists for interpreting a tradition differently or for holding heterodox beliefs. Very often, priests, rabbis, imams and shamans are just as consumed by worldly ambition as regular politicians. But all this is generally seen as an abuse of a sacred ideal. These power struggles are not what religion is really about, but an unworthy distraction from the life of the spirit, which is conducted far from the maddening crowd, unseen, silent, and unobtrusive.[14]

I want to stress that I do not think of this as a good definition; I only claim that it is popular, and we can learn a great deal about widely accepted notions of religion from this short quotation. Note the dichotomy between external history and "faith." The latter is internal, "psychic," and "contemplative." Religion is not political, not concerned with current events; it is about "the heart." It is "unobtrusive." And, most important for what follows, religion is thought to be divorced from history. Thus, in this view, "religious *traditions*" have "*external* histories," but there is something timeless and ahistorical about religion.

To appreciate how pervasive and influential this kind of characterization of religion is in the United States, one need look no further than the decisions of the U.S. Supreme Court, which have characterized religion as operating in realms generally distinguished from the public sphere. For instance, in 1963, in the decision that declared formal recitation of prayers and reading of the Bible in public schools unconstitutional, the court wrote: "The place of religion in our society is an exalted one, achieved through a long tradition of reliance on the home, the church and the inviolable citadel of the individual heart and mind."[15] It is worth noting the contrast with ancient legal perspectives, in which the gods and sacrality were very much in the public sphere. A legal ruling attributed to a fifth-century Roman emperor runs as follows: "Things sacred [*res sacrae*] are then those which have been consecrated by an act of the whole people [*publicae consecratae sunt*], not by anyone in his private capacity [*non privatae*]. Therefore, if someone makes a thing sacred for himself, acting in a private capacity [*privatim*], the thing is not sacred but profane [*sacrum non est, sed profanum*]."[16]

The second point I want to make about the usage of the word "religion" (and "religions") in modern discussions is to note the habit of using the singular "religion" (largely conceived of in the way I just outlined) to refer to a genus that contains a variety of species, that is, the individual religions of the world, or World Religions. In such usage, these individual religions are generally presumed to be different "manifestations" of some sort of unitary "Ultimate Concern." For example, a recent edition of one college textbook on World Religions asserts that "all humanity, even in isolated nonliterate groups, has always been 'religious.'"[17] The authors claim that various historical circumstances, including a growing sense of individualism brought on by the rise of complex societies, created new psychological problems that ushered in the emergence of World Religions: "It is to answer the questions raised by the crises of morality, mortality, and meaning that the great world religions emerged. Once city dwellers were individuated in their identities, the old answers provided by indigenous religions no longer worked . . . That is the challenge the great world religions faced as they emerged in the three great centers of civilization in the ancient world—China, India, and the Middle East. Between 1000 BCE and 1000 CE all the great world religions developed their classical expressions, dividing much of the world among them."[18] At this point, the text refers to a map—an important part of this concept of multiple World Religions. A common feature of college textbooks on World Religions is a map of the world colorfully indicating the geographic areas to which the various religions have "spread."[19] The picture of the world as divided among major "religions" offering alternative means to "salvation" or "enlightenment" is thoroughly entrenched in the modern imagination. It is part of the common sense of twenty-first-century life. Yet, we have already seen that the assertion that people have "always been religious" is problematic, and the remainder of this book will show how the claim that the World Religions existed before the modern period is also deceptive.[20]

At this point I offer one historical caveat. From its earliest usages, the English words "religion" and "religions" (and the medieval Latin *religio* and *religiones* before them) identified a genus and its species, but the entities being classified were not what we would normally think of as "religions." So, for example, sometimes when used in this genus/species manner these terms referred to different monastic orders. At other times they referred to what modern people might call different "sects." For instance, consider the fifteenth-century English bishop Reginald Pecock, who pondered the question, "Whi ben ther so manye dyuerse religiouns in the chirche?"[21] The multiple "religiouns" were located "in the chirche" and referred to the different Christian monastic orders, a point to which I will return. For now, it is enough to note that seeing talk of multiple religions (or *religiones*) in medieval texts is not an indication of the antiquity of the modern notion of religion. That is to say, the Latin word *religio*, and even the English word "religion" (or "religioun"), existed *before* these definitions of religion as an internal, private experience arose.

My third point is more limited, having to do with how the term "religion" is used in academic discussions. In those contexts, the vocabulary of "religion" is often used in two quite distinct ways that are perhaps best called *descriptive* and *redescriptive* accounts, although an older, roughly equivalent vocabulary of "emic" and "etic" is still sometimes used.[22] From an anthropological perspective, a descriptive account is an observer's best effort at reproducing the classification systems of a group of people being studied (this is not the "native" viewpoint itself, but the observer's best effort at reproducing that viewpoint). A redescriptive account, on the other hand, freely employs classification systems foreign to those of the people being observed.

So, for example, the notion of organized political parties could be legitimately used as a descriptive concept when thinking about modern American culture, in which people routinely define themselves by "their political party" or their "political affiliation" or their rejection of the major political parties. If, however, we were giving an account of, say, ancient inhabitants of North America, the use of political parties in such an account would be redescriptive (the ancient North Americans themselves might have used other grouping strategies, such as tribal affiliation or kinship groups, which would thus be legitimate terms in a descriptive account). Unfortunately, in many academic discussions about religion, these two distinct usages can become blurred. Even quite sophisticated professionals can employ these two usages in very confusing ways. Consider the following statement from the anthropologist Benson Saler: "The testimony of various ethnographies affirms that people do not need a category and term for religion in order to 'have' a religion or be religious in ways that accord with notions of religiosity entertained by anthropologists."[23] This is a very tricky statement. The end of the sentence shows that Saler is using religion as a redescriptive concept (religion is "notions of religiosity entertained *by anthropologists*"). The quotation marks around the word "have" are thus quietly doing an impressive amount of work for Saler. It is not the case that the people who are the subject of these ethnographies describe themselves as "religious" or "secular" or talk about "their religion." Rather, they "have" religion only insofar as anthropologists are free to impose their own framework for the purpose of study. (I look again at this kind of slippery rhetoric in more detail at the end of Chapter 7.)

Do You Need the Word to Have the Thing?

I also bring up the distinction between descriptive and redescriptive usages of religion here because it relates to one final issue that I discuss as a matter of introduction. It is akin to Saler's statement that I just mentioned. The question could be put like this: Does the absence of a word or a phrase equivalent to "religion" in a given language mean that the speakers of the language also lack the *concept* of religion? Or should we allow for the possibility, to borrow a phrase from the linguist Benjamin Whorf, of covert concepts, concepts that may be present but simply unarticulated? On this question, I again defer to the later work of Wittgenstein, who argued that when one is analyzing a concept, what one is doing is analyzing "the use of a word."[24] As a historian, I study texts (even nontextual archeological artifacts must be mediated into language about artifacts in order to be part of a historical discussion). The presumption of the existence of concepts somewhere "out there" that somehow escape language is distasteful to me, not so much on philosophical grounds as on practical grounds. Such an assumption is, it seems to me, a conversation ender.[25] If a concept is defined as "beyond language," it is, then, by definition not something that can be discussed.

These sorts of issues arise frequently in conversations about religion. Even authors who argue against the universality of religion often still appear to posit the existence of some sort of universal, extralinguistic thing (call it faith, religious experience, religiosity, experience of the sacred) that transcends any language that attempts to describe it. This sort of thinking can lead to the following kinds of claims: "Even though they have no words for it, maybe the ancient Greeks were religious. Maybe they did have religious experiences. They just lacked the words to describe them." Such appeals to "experience" are problematic for a variety of reasons.[26] All experiences that enter the field of discussion are, by definition, put into words. Strictly speaking, people who claim to study religious experience are actually studying narratives of experiences. One sometimes encounters the claim that there are "raw experiences" that are universal and only *appear* distinct because the experiences are "translated" into different languages that are culturally conditioned. Those who make such assertions must presume to have direct access to the experience itself, to be able to have privileged access to "get behind" the language.

It is a bit like the fable of the blind men and the elephant. In this story, which one sometimes finds in introductory books on religion, several blind men feel different parts of an elephant and draw conclusions about what the elephant is like. The man feeling the side of the elephant thinks that the elephant is like a wall, the man touching the tusk thinks the elephant is like a spear, the man touching the trunk thinks the elephant is like a snake, and so on. The moral of the story in the textbooks? The experiences of peoples of different religions are like the experiences of the blind men: each one grasps only a part of the transcendent whole. As the cultural critic Russell T. McCutcheon has pointed out, there is a crucial problem with this parable: if everyone is blind and can grasp only a part of the whole, how can the narrator of the story in fact know what the whole elephant is "really" like?[27] The narrator, of course, cannot know. Appeals to "raw experience" falter in much the same way. What we have available to study are narratives, texts. And so, I analyze texts in the chapters that follow. Where concepts roughly equivalent to "religion" are absent, I think it would be unhelpful to impose such a concept, unless as part of a redescriptive account as outlined above.

Conclusion

An especially popular way of viewing religion is as a kind of inner disposition and concern for salvation conceived in opposition to politics and other "secular" areas of life. In this model, religion is presumed to be a universal feature of human cultures, and the individual World Religions are culturally specific examples of this general phenomenon of religion. Such a view is so common that many people in the modern world would, I think, consider it self-evident. In this book I argue that such a view of the world is foreign to ancient cultures and that we can, in rough outlines, trace how this peculiar way of viewing the world developed. These claims may seem highly counterintuitive to many readers, but I hope the material collected in the coming pages may raise a few eyebrows and leave readers at least a little less certain that religion is "simply there."

Introduction

If you pick up a translation of almost any ancient text of appreciable length, chances are you will find the term "religion" somewhere in the translation. There is also no shortage of books on the topic of this or that "ancient religion." It is no wonder, then, that many people have the impression that the modern notion of religion is present in our ancient sources. Yet the more one delves into the writings of specialist historians on the topic of "ancient religions," the more it becomes clear that the whole idea is fraught with difficulty. To begin the discussion, I offer two examples provided by experts in two different cultural complexes, the first Chinese and the second Mesoamerican:

> One indicator of the problematic nature of the category "religion" in Chinese history is the absence of any premodern word that unambiguously denotes the category. The modern Chinese word *zongjiao* was first employed to mean "religion" by late-nineteenth-century Japanese translators of European texts. *Zongjiao* (or *shūkyō* in Japanese) is a compound consisting of *zong* (*shū*), which is derived from a pictogram of an ancestral altar and most commonly denotes a "sect," and *jiao* (*kyō*), meaning "teaching." (The compound had originally been a Chinese Buddhist term meaning simply the teachings of a particular sect.) *Zongjiao/shūkyō* thus carries the connotation of "ancestral" or sectarian teachings. The primary reference of this newly coined usage for *shūkyō* in the European texts being translated was, of course, Christianity. . . . Chinese, when asked to identify what counts as *zongjiao* in their culture, are often reluctant to include phenomena that westerners would be willing to count as religion, because the word *religion*—while notoriously difficult to define—does not carry the same connotations as *zongjiao*.[1]

In spite of the fact that the highly advanced phonetic (i.e. logosyllabic) writing systems [of Mesoamerica] are capable of expressing and recognising abstract representations in the languages, extant pre-Columbian Mesoamerican inscriptions do not contain words which can be rendered as "religion." . . . [N]ative terms for "religion" [found in Spanish dictionaries of the sixteenth and eighteenth centuries] were in reality constructed by the Spanish ethnographer-missionaries in order to promote evangelisation and the conversion of the indigenous people.[2]

Conclusions such as these have led some scholars to become suspicious of the idea that religion is a category universally native to premodern cultures. Yet, as I mentioned, it is still a common practice to translate a number of words in different ancient languages as "religion." In this chapter I scrutinize ancient usages of a small group of such words: the Latin *religio*, Greek *thrēskeia*, and Arabic terms *dīn*, *milla*, and *umma*. All are routinely rendered in modern translations as "religion," but the contexts in which these terms occur often make such translations problematic. I choose these particular words because they are central to early Christian and early Muslim texts and are so frequently translated as "religion." I also would have treated a Hebrew or Aramaic term, but ancient Hebrew and Aramaic simply have no word that is routinely translated in modern languages as "religion."[3]

On the Latin Word religio

Spotlighting the history of the word *religio* demonstrates concretely that even in Latin, a language that has a term etymologically related to the modern European word "religion," the ancient meanings are quite distinct from what the modern term "religion" and its cognates cover. In fact, in the past half century, several studies have traced the fortunes of the Latin word *religio* much more thoroughly than I will here.[4] What I show here is only that the word had a variety of meanings in antiquity and that none of those corresponds to the modern notion of religion or delineates "religious" from "secular."[5]

The word *religio* occurs in some of the earliest surviving examples of extended pieces of Latin literature. The comic playwright Plautus gives us a glimpse of usage in the early second century B.C.E. In his writings, *religio* seems to be simply a sense of reserve: *"revocat me ilico, vocat me ad cenam; religio fuit, denegare nolui."* An English translation from the early twentieth century renders the passage as follows: "He calls me back directly and invites me to dinner. I had scruples, I could not decline."[6] Terence, another author of comedies, gives evidence of a slightly later period (the 160s B.C.E.), in which *religio* is synonymous with *scrupulus.* The following exchange occurs in *The Woman of Andros*:

> CHREMES: at mi unus scrupulus etiam restat qui me male habet.
> PAMPHILUS: dignus es cum tua religione, odium.

John Barsby translates in the Loeb edition:

> CHREMES: But there's one little thing which still worries me.
> PAMPHILUS: Serves you right, you and your scruples, you tiresome man![7]

As time passed, *religio* was more frequently employed in contexts that involved gods. We can see a development of this kind of usage roughly a century later in the writings of Cicero. In *On the Nature of the Gods*, the character Cotta, the representative of Academic philosophy, provides a definition of *religio*, presented here in Harris Rackham's translation in the Loeb Classical Library: "The religion of the Roman people [*omnis populi romani religio*] comprises ritual, auspices, and the third additional division consisting of all such prophetic warnings as the interpreters of the Sybil [*sic*] or the soothsayers have derived from portents and prodigies. Well, I have always thought that none of these departments of religion was to be despised."[8] At first glance, this definition appears straightforward, but as Clifford Ando has pointed out, the translation of the last sentence will not do.[9] The Latin is *harum ego religionum nullam umquam contemnendam putavi*; in Ando's translation: "I hold that none of these *religiones* should ever be neglected." The idea is that each component, each action or set of actions (*sacra, auspicia*, and the predictions of the *haruspices*), is somehow individually itself a *religio*, and the combination of all of them is also a single, Roman, *religio*.[10] Cicero offers evidence of other usages of the term as well. In one especially illuminating example, *religiones* seem to be simply rules or prohibitions instituted either by gods or by humans. In the published version of one of his speeches against Verres, Cicero attacked the actions of his opponent as being "against the law, contrary to the auspices, against all divine and human rules" (*contra fas, contra auspicia, contra omnes divinas atque humanas religiones*).[11]

A roughly contemporary but quite different use of the word *religio* occurs in Lucretius's poetic exposition of Epicurean philosophy *On the Nature of Things.*[12] For Lucretius, *religio* is a kind of force malevolent to humanity. In the opening book of the poem he writes that people are crushed beneath the weight of *religio* and that *religio* "brings forth criminal and impious deeds" (*illa religio peperit scelerosa atque impia facta*).[13] Lucretius seeks *religionum animum nodis exsolvere*, "to loose the mind from the close knots of *religiones.*"[14] Elsewhere he writes, "For if those who have been rightly taught that the gods lead a life without care, yet wonder all the while how things can go on, especially those transactions which are perceived overhead in the regions of ether, they revert back again to the old superstitions [*rursus in antiquas referuntur religiones*], and take to themselves cruel taskmasters, whom the poor wretches believe to be almighty [*omnia posse quos miseri credunt*]."[15] Thus, in the late Roman republic, *religio* seems to have ranged from meaning simply "rule" or "worship practice" to "excessive concern about the gods."

The use of *religio* to which Lucretius had attested seems to have died out for the most part.[16] In Christian writings of the third and fourth centuries, the idea of ritual practices is still present in the usage of *religio*, and the plural usage that causes modern translators of Cicero such difficulties persists in Christian writers.[17] Such usage occurs in the work of Minucius Felix, a Christian author who wrote his dialogue, *Octavius*, at some point during the third century (or perhaps the mid- to late second century).[18] In this work, the character Caecilius, providing the viewpoint of a worshipper of the traditional gods, claims that the Romans "protect their city with sacred rites, chaste virgins, and many priesthoods distinguished with dignity and titles" (*urbem muniunt sacrorum religionibus, castis virginibus, multis honoribus, ac nominibus sacerdotum*).[19] Each protective rite is a *religio*.[20] In the early third century in northern Africa, Tertullian provides evidence of a similar usage of *religio* ("worship," "rite," or "reverence").[21] He describes the sacrifice of Abel and notes that it was made pleasing by means of Abel's "reverence for the Sabbath" (*sabbati religione*).[22] Yet, in both Minucius Felix and Tertullian, *religio* also begins to have a certain boundary-marking force. Minucius Felix's dialogue opens with a contrast between "superstitious vanities" (*superstitiosis vanitatibus*, a slander against traditional Roman worship practices) and the "genuine worship" (*veram religionem*) that is veneration of the Christian god.[23] The Christian character Octavius describes Roman cultic practice as "yours" (*vestra religio*).[24] Tertullian distinguishes between the "true worship of the true god" (*veram religionem veri dei*) and the worship of other gods.[25]

Nevertheless, the more difficult plural usage continues to appear into the late third or early fourth century, when Arnobius claims that Christianity's enemies make wild accusations: " 'You practice your wicked religions,' they say, 'and rites unheard-of in the world' " (*Religiones, inquiunt, impias atque inauditos cultus terrarum in orbe tractatis*).[26] Christianity here constitutes a plural set of worship practices.[27] Arnobius himself employs similar terminology when he argues that no divine power has confirmed the non-Christian "way" and that no divine power has slandered "our ways and cultic practices" (*nostris rebus et religionibus derogavit*).[28]

In the early fourth century, Lactantius, a Christian teacher of rhetoric and tutor to the son of the emperor Constantine, provides evidence that *religio* continued to have a number of valences.[29] He maintains the use of *vera religio* to refer to the worship carried out by Christians, and he opposes *vera religio* to *falsa religio* or *falsae religiones*.[30] The idea of the plural *religiones* is clarified by another opposition that Lactantius invokes, the veneration of the one god (*religio dei*) as opposed to the veneration of many gods (*religio deorum*). He writes: "This alone is cultivation of virtue: worship and no other veneration must be kept except that of the one God" (*hic solus virtutis est cultus: nam religio et veneratio nulla alia nisi unius Dei tenenda est).*[31] Furthermore, for Lactantius, *vera religio* is a synonym for *vera sapientia;* he seeks to wed worship of the one god with philosophy.[32] These newer usages, however, stand alongside some of the older uses of *religio.* The term must mean simply "scruples" when Jupiter is said to have taken an oath *(iurare)* and then found himself forced by *religio* to fulfill the oath.[33] Elsewhere, Lactantius, actually citing Lucretius, claims to be able to do what Lucretius failed to do, namely, to free minds from *religiones* (*religionum animos nodis exsolvere*); *religiones* here seems to be synonymous with *superstitiones.*[34] The element of *religio* as simply "a rite" is still present as well. The terms *cultus* and *religio* occur in parallel. A summary of Epicurean views of the gods leads Lactantius to ask: "When he says these things does he think that any worship ought to be rendered to God, or does he overturn all *religio?*" (*quae cum dicit, utrum aliquem cultum deo putat esse tribuendum an evertit omnem religionem?*).[35] Curiously, Lactantius can also write that statues "are devoid of" or "lack" *religio* (*carent ergo religione simulacra*).[36]

To summarize, then, *religio* in these early Christian writers still has a range of meanings. While the sense of "excessive concern about the gods" is limited (appearing, as far as I can tell, only in discussions that explicitly invoke Epicureanism), the other classical meaning of simply "worship practice" or "rite" is still prevalent. The term sometimes marks out the boundaries of legitimate, or Christian, worship practice. What is most at issue for these Christian authors is the object of worship—the one, true God or the many gods.

This point comes across most clearly in the work of Augustine, the bishop of Hippo in northern Africa in the early fifth century. In the year 390, Augustine wrote a tract titled *De vera religione* (perhaps best translated as "On Genuine Worship"). On the whole, Augustine's usage of the term here is little different from that of his predecessors.[37] He summarizes the topic of *De vera religione* in *Retractationes* 1.13.1: *vera religio* is the way one worships the one true God (*disputatur unum verum deum . . . religione vera colendum*).[38] While Augustine has a sense of the plural *religiones*, the implication for him is not that there are many religions in the modern sense; rather, once again, it is the *object* of worship that is key.[39] A long string of repeated formulaic phrases at the conclusion of the work encourages such an understanding. The statements all take the form: *non sit nobis religio cultus* + genitive, "Let not our *religio* be the worship of X."[40] The series culminates with the declaration, "One God alone I worship" (*ecce unum deum colo*).[41] Elsewhere, in fact, Augustine begins to show some discomfort with using *religio* to describe Christian worship:

> Moreover, the very term *religio* too, although it would seem to indicate more precisely not any worship, but the worship of God [*dei cultum*]—and this is the reason why our translators have used it to render the Greek word *thrēskeia*—yet in Latin usage, and that not of the ignorant but of the most cultured also we say that *religio* is to be observed in dealing with human relationships, affinities and ties of every sort. Hence the term does not secure us against ambiguity when used in discussing the worship paid to God [*cultu deitatis*]. We cannot say confidently that *religio* means only the worship of God, since we should thus clearly be violating usage by abolishing one meaning of the word, namely, the observance of duties in human relationships.[42]

The phrase "our translators" refers to the Latin translation of biblical material. The Vulgate uses forms of *religio* thirteen times. Augustine would seem to be referring here especially to the New Testament, since *thrēskeia* hardly appears in the Greek translation of the Old Testament, in which *religio* most frequently appears as a translation of the Hebrew *ḥuqqah* (statute, enactment).[43] In the New Testament, on the other hand, *religio* exclusively translates the Greek *thrēskeia* (at Acts 26:5, Col. 2:18, and James 1:26 and 1:27). James 1:27 was especially influential: "*religio* that is pure and undefiled before the father is this: to care for orphans and widows in their affliction and to keep oneself from being polluted by this world."

One finds both continuity and change in the usage of *religio* as one progresses through the fifth century and into the medieval period. The classical sense of worship persists, but beginning in the fifth century, *religio* comes to be used as a designation of the monastic life.[44] Salvianus of Marseilles, a monk of the mid-fifth century, condemns men who live "under the name *religio*" but who dissent from *religio* and forsake the world only in their wardrobe (*sub religionis titulo a religione dissentiunt et habitu magis saeculum reliquere quam sensu*). Such people are not actual believers even though they simulate *religio* by their clothing and falsely imitate holiness with their cloaks (*religionem vestibus simules . . . sanctitatem pallio mentiaris*).[45] The plural *religiones* would also come to be used to describe the various monastic orders and *religio* any single one of them. Thus in a narrative of the deeds of a twelfth-century Spanish bishop, we find mention of a *monachum Cluniacensis religionis.*[46] The earliest uses of "religion" in the European vernaculars in fact seem to derive from this usage of the Latin.[47] An apt English example comes from the fourteenth-century translation (attributed to Chaucer) of *Roman de la rose:*

> Sometime I am religious,
> Now like an Anker in an hous.
> Sometime am I Prioresse,
> And now a Nonne, and now Abbesse,
> And go through all regiouns,
> Seeking all religiouns.[48]

Note that the word "religioun" refers to a genus of which the "religiouns" are species, but the entities so classified are not what modern people typically think of as religions (that is, the World Religions) but rather are different types of Christians under vows—the anchorite, the nun, the prioress, the abbess. I will note a similar phenomenon in the Greek and Arabic terms to be examined shortly.

In the thirteenth century, we find all of these meanings of *religio* side by side in the work of Thomas Aquinas. He twice uses the term *religio* in the titles of his books; in both cases, the meaning is "monastic life," *Contra impugnantes dei cultum et religionem* and *Contra retrahentes a religionis ingressu,* translated jointly under the appropriate title *An Apology for the Religious Orders.* Aquinas also offered a short discussion of *religio* in the *Summa Theologica* (at 2.2.81) that draws on both James 1:27 and Augustine's reflections on the term *religio* as well as Cicero and other older authors.[49] The fourteenth and fifteenth centuries saw a continuation of these multiple usages of *religio*.[50] Some development is visible in the writings of the fifteenth-century cardinal Nicholas of Cusa. In the aftermath of the fall of Constantinople to the Ottoman empire in 1453, Nicholas wrote *De pace fidei*, a fictitious conversation among a variety of different peoples from across the known world, "the Word of God," and the apostles Peter and Paul.[51] Nicholas referred throughout to the *religiones* of different peoples (*homines*) of the world but famously declared that there was only "one *religio* in a variety of rites" (*una religio rituum varietate*).[52] The comment is often celebrated as an early effort at "religious pluralism," but in the larger context of the work, in which the truthfulness of various Christian doctrines (the Trinity, the incarnation, the resurrection) is presumed, it appears to be more an assertion that if all the world's different peoples just exercised reason, they would recognize the truth of Christian doctrines.[53] About two decades after the completion of Nicholas's *De pace fidei*, Marsilio Ficino, a Florentine scholar (about whom I will have more to say in Chapter 5), wrote a tract titled *De christiana religione* in which *religio* is a quality found to varying degrees in all humans that directs them to seek the divine reality: "All *religio* has something good in it; provided that it is directed towards God, the creator of all things, it is sincere Christian *religio*" (*Omnis religio boni habet nonnihil, modo ad deum ipsum creatorem omnium dirigatur, Christiana syncera est*).[54] There are thus different kinds of *religio* that are in some way comparable, but *christiana religio* is the only true form.

A century later, the opening line of Ulrich Zwingli's *De vera et falsa religione commentarius* declared his intent "to write on true and false *religio* as displayed by Christians" (*scripturo de vera falsaque religione christianorum*).[55] From the outset, it is clear that what he meant was still right and wrong ways of worship and that incorrect worship could occur even within *christiana religio*. This concept of *religio* is still somewhat foreign to the modern senses of religion, but it is in the sixteenth and seventeenth centuries that *religio* (and its descendants in the European vernaculars) comes to mean what most modern people regard as "religion." I defer a detailed discussion of the reasons for this shift until Chapters 5 and 6; for now, I simply point to the highly popular work produced by the Dutch polymath Hugo Grotius in the first quarter of the seventeenth century, *De veritate religionis christianae*, "On the Truthfulness of Christian Religion."[56] For Grotius, *christiana religio* is one among many *religiones*, but it is by far the best one. What makes it superior is that "there is not, neither ever was there any other Religion [*religio*] in the whole World, that can be produced, either more *honorable* for excellency of reward [*praemio*], or more absolute and *perfect* for precepts [*praeceptis*]."[57] These bases for comparison (rewards and precepts) allow us to see that *christiana religio* had largely become a set of doctrines.[58] As such, it easily could be compared with other "doctrines" or systems of belief that European explorers had begun to encounter. These systems of belief became more concrete in the seventeenth to nineteenth centuries, as they began to be designated by attaching "-ism" to a concept previously identified as "the religion of X"; so, for example, the "religion of Buddha" becomes "Buddhism."[59] By the end of the seventeenth century, it was also becoming more and more common to confine *religio* and the *religiones* to the realm of the inner self, as when John Locke (in 1689) argued that "true and saving *religio* consists in the inward persuasion of the mind [*in interna animi fide*]" (see more in Chapter 5).[60]

It is clear that the Latin word *religio* has had a range of meanings over the centuries. Another ancient word, the Greek term *thrēskeia*, is also involved in these transformations.

On the Greek Word thrēskeia

The word that in modern Greek translates English "religion" is *thrēskeia*. This term is common in ancient Greek as well, but *thrēskeia*, like *religio*, has a long history of changing senses.[61] In its earliest appearances (in the Greek historian Herodotus, who wrote in the fifth century B.C.E.) *thrēskeia* seems to mean something along the lines of "rituals." It occurs in the plural as the direct object of verbs of completion (so the Egyptians "complete"—*epitelousi*—washings and various other *thrēskēiai*).[62] The word thus first appears in an ethnographic context. This meaning of "rite" or "ritual" persisted for centuries. In the first century C.E., the philosopher Philo of Alexandria used the term to refer to the actions that occur in a temple, namely, sacrifices (*thusiai*).[63] The word occurs four times in the New Testament, and the meaning is usually "worship," as in the phrase *thrēskeia tōn angelōn* ("worship of angels") in Colossians 2:18.[64] In the writings of Josephus, a historian of the latter part of the first century C.E., *thrēskeia* generally means either the activities that go on in a temple or "veneration" of a god more generally.[65] For example, in Josephus, the "*thrēskeia* of the Judean people" is often tied to the proper performance of sacrifices, but foreigners could also come to the temple in Jerusalem for the purpose of worship (*eis thrēskeian*).[66] It should be noted, however, that Josephus can also speak of Abraham's attempted sacrifice of Isaac as a test of Abraham's *thrēskeia* ("loyalty" or "obedience") to divine authority.[67] A similar sense of duty or obligation appears to be at work when Josephus refers to Judeans refraining from work on the Sabbath on account of *thrēskeia*.[68] Predominantly, however, he uses *thrēskeia* to refer to acts of worship, as in his descriptions of the various areas of the temple in Jerusalem specified for *thrēskeia* by different groups (non-Judeans, women, etc.).[69]

Different sorts of usages seem to have emerged during the third and fourth centuries. The older meaning persists in an intriguing passage from the Christian scholar Origen, who wrote in the first half of the third century. Origen comments on the fate of the Judean nation: "For which nation except for the Judeans has been exiled from its ancestral city [*mētropoleōs*] and from its own place for the ancestral cult [*patriōi thrēskeiai*]?"[70] The Judeans are identified as a nation (*ethnos*) that is no longer able to take part in the characteristically ethnic activity of local sacrifice (*thrēskeia*). Eusebius, the church historian under the emperor Constantine, preserves a variety of uses of the term *thrēskeia*. The older meaning of "ritual" persists. In what purports to be a letter of Constantine addressing the construction of a church in Palestine, the emperor is said to declare that the site of the church should be sanctified so that people should do nothing there except "perform fitting service" (*prepousan . . . teleisthai thrēskeian*) to the one god.[71] In the plural, the word appears in the odd phrase *sōmatikais thrēskeiais*, when Eusebius speaks of the preaching of the gospel eliminating "the whole Mosaic arrangement of images and symbols and bodily practices."[72]

At the same time, Eusebius presents evidence of a different kind of usage that seems to overlap with the developments we have examined with regard to the Latin *religio*. This is perhaps best illustrated by comparing his Greek rendering of the so-called Edict of Milan with the Latin version preserved in Lactantius.[73] The edict is often described as a foundational document for "religious freedom," and it is not difficult to see why.[74] The opening of Eusebius's version (which has no parallel in Lactantius's Latin version) declares that an earlier decree enacted "freedom of *thrēskeia*" and states that each person "should defend the *pistis* of his own *hairesis* and *thrēskeia*." The relevant passages in the body of the text state the following: "We grant both to Christians and to everyone free choice [*eleutheran hairesin/liberam potestatem*] to follow the mode of worship [*thrēskeia/religionem*] that they choose so that whatever divinity or heavenly thing exists might be enabled to be well-disposed toward us and all who live under our authority." And again, all people are to be allowed "to choose the observances of the Christians [*tēn tōn christianōn paraphulaxin ē thrēskeian/observationi christianorum*] or to that mode of worship [*thrēskeia/religioni*] which is best suited to them." What is meant here by *thrēskeia* and *religio*? Although the terms do not occur in the plural, the usage implies some sort of genus/species model. It seems clear that the edict permits adherence to and veneration of the gods of all different peoples, including the Christian god. This policy is expected to contribute to the health of the government and state: "By this reckoning, as it has been said, the divine favor [*theia spoudē/divinus favor*] toward us will continue securely for all time." Thus, the order appears to be an attempt to curry favor with all the gods. In terms of the overall goals of the legislation, then, the edict represents only a minor variation from the efforts of previous emperors to persecute Christians and the efforts of subsequent Christian emperors to persecute non-Christians. All wanted to ensure that the state as a whole maintained divine favor by making certain the populace worshipped the proper gods.[75] The only difference was the question of which god or gods were the proper object of worship. Whatever these different *thrēskeiai* or *religiones* may have been, they were not separate from a secular state government in the way that modern religions are portrayed ideally to be. This difference will become especially evident when we turn our attention to the "religious tolerance" of John Locke's *Letter Concerning Toleration* in Chapter 5.

The meaning of *thrēskeia* as "worship" seems to have persisted through the medieval period, as can be seen in the Byzantine lexicons. In the entry for *thrēskeia* in the fifth-century lexicon of Hesychius, the term is glossed as both *latreia*, the common Greek word for "service" or "worship," and *sebasma*, meaning "an object of worship."[76] The Suda, a sprawling historical dictionary and encyclopedia compiled in the tenth century, gives only *latreia*.[77] Yet, the classifying use of *thrēskeia* also comes into somewhat sharper focus in the medieval period. A good example of the kind of work that the word was able to do at that time can be found in the writings of Photius, the ninth-century patriarch of Constantinople. In his *Bibliotheca*, a collection of summaries, extracts, and reviews of hundreds of books he had read, Photius often made a brief biographical note regarding the authors whom he had read, as follows: "Read the so-called Ecclesiastical History of Philostorgius, *areianou tēn thrēskeian*"; "Read in the same [book] also the work of another John, *tēn thrēskeian nestorianou*"; "Read the *History* in three books by Candidus . . . *tēn de thrēskeian christianos ēn kai orthodoxos*"; "Read the *Histories* of Olympiodorus in twenty-two books. . . . This author was *hellēn tēn thrēskeian*";

"Read the *Histories* of Count Zosimus in six books. . . . He was *tēn thrēskeian asebēs.*"[78] The accusative *thrēskeian* marks off a discernable characteristic of these people, but the characteristics classified here—Nestorian, Arian, Orthodox, *Hellēn* (loyal to non-Christian gods), *asebēs* ("impious")—do not exactly correspond to what modern people would label as different religions. The classification combines what modern people might describe as sects, religions, and, perhaps, attitudes. Indeed, Photius levels the charge of being impious (*asebēs*) at Zosimus not so much for his conceptions about the gods, as for of his "slanders against pious emperors" (*en tais tōn eusebōn basileōn diabolais*).

In the late-tenth- or early-eleventh-century Greek translation of the tale of *Barlaam and Ioasaph* (see more in Chapter 4), the term *thrēskeia* continues to operate in multiple ways.[79] When a character is asked "Who are you?" the question is immediately clarified by the follow-up "Of what *thrēskeia* are you and what is your name?" The answer to the first part is simply *christianos.*[80] And the "*thrēskeia* of the Christians" stands in opposition to the traditional sacrifices and temple worship of the Indians in the story. Yet, to take part in the *thrēskeia* of the Christians, to "become Christian" (*christianon genesthai*) in this text is to "take up the monastic garment" (*to monachikon peribalesthai schēma*), which hearkens back to the late Latin understanding of *religio* as the monastic life.[81]

This very brief survey of the development of the term *thrēskeia* demonstrates its range of meanings. The sense of "rite" or "worship" seems to persist from the earliest appearances of the term through the medieval period. The first century saw the transformation of *thrēskeia* into a more general term (the sum total of what goes on in the temples of a particular people), and at least by the fourth century, the word could refer to all the worship practices of a given ethnic group, such that people could be identified by "their *thrēskeia.*"[82] Throughout its history, then, the term seems to have been part of an ethnographic discourse. It is clear that a simple gloss of *thrēskeia* as "religion" will not do. We find a similar situation in the case of the Arabic term *dīn.*

On the Arabic Word dīn

A look at most modern translations of the Qur'an would indeed lead one to believe that Muhammad employed a very well-defined notion of religion.[83] Consider the following example from Nessim Joseph Dawood's highly popular translation of the Qur'an in the Penguin Classics series, which was first published in 1956 and has appeared in several reprints and revised editions, most recently in 2006:[84] Sura 5:3: "This day I have perfected your religion for you, completed My favour to you. I have chosen Islām to be your faith." The terms "religion" and "faith" both translate the Arabic term *dīn*. Indeed, the word *dīn* is regularly rendered into English as "religion" or, especially in more recent translations, as "faith." There are numerous other examples of this phenomenon in Dawood's translation: "The only true faith [*dīn*] in God's sight is Islām" (Sura 3:19); "It is He who has sent forth His apostle with guidance and the True Faith [*dīn*] that he may exalt it above all religion [*dīn*], though the idolaters abhor it" (Sura 9:33); "Therefore, stand firm in your devotion to the true Faith [*dīn*], the upright Faith [*dīn*] which God created for mankind to embrace. God's Creation cannot be changed. This is surely the right faith [*dīn*], although most men may not know it. Turn to Him and fear Him. Be steadfast in prayer and serve no other god besides Him. Do not divide your religion [*dīn*] into sects, each exulting in its own doctrines" (Sura 30:30–32). Given what we have seen of the Latin and Greek traditions, this easy translation between classical Arabic *dīn* and modern English "religion" should probably arouse suspicion. And, indeed, experts in Arabic frequently point out that *dīn* does not really correspond to modern ideas of "religion." Thus, the author of the article on "Religion" in *The Encyclopaedia of the Qur'ān* opens the entry with the following statement: "Prior to the twentieth century, the English word 'religion' had no direct equivalent in Arabic nor had the Arabic word *dīn* in English. They became partially synonymous only in the course of the twentieth century as a result of increased English-Arabic encounters and the need for consistency in translation."[85] Although it may well be the case that Arabic had no word for "religion," early printed translations of the Qur'an show that modern languages did find ways to render the term *dīn*.

Let us turn to the earliest English translation of the Qur'an.[86] In 1647, André du Ryer produced the first French version, and two years later Alexander Ross (see more in Chapter 6) published an English translation of this French version.[87] Although the texts of both du Ryer and Ross were rightly scorned by contemporary academics for their omissions and additions to the Arabic text, the translations can still be useful for gaining a sense of how some of these key Arabic terms were being translated during a period when the concept of religion was still very much inchoate (see Chapters 5 and 6).[88] It is therefore instructive to compare Ross's version with the passages from Dawood's more recent translation:[89]

	N. J. Dawood (2003)	Alexander Ross (1649)
Sura 5:3	"This day I have perfected your religion [*dīn*] for you, completed My favour to you. I have chosen Islām to be your faith [*dīn*]."	"The day will come, when I shall accomplish your Law, and my Grace shall be abundantly upon you: The Law of Salvation, is the Law that I desire to give you" (p. 63).
Sura 3:19	"The only true faith [*dīn*] in God's sight is Islām."	"The Law of Salvation, is a Law pleasing to his Divine Majestie" (p. 31).
Sura 9:33	"It is He who has sent forth His apostle with guidance and the True Faith [*dīn*] that he may exalt it above all religion [*dīn*], though the idolaters abhor it."	"He hath sent his Prophet to conduct men into the right way, to preach the Law of Truth, and to make it eminent above all other Laws of the world, against the will of Idolaters" (p. 116).[90]

| Sura 30:30–32 | "Therefore, stand firm in your devotion to the true Faith [*dīn*], the upright Faith which God created for mankind to embrace. God's Creation cannot be changed. This is surely the right faith [*dīn*], although most men may not know it. Turn to Him and fear Him. Be steadfast in prayer and serve no other god besides Him. Do not divide your religion [*dīn*] into sects [*shiya'an*], each exulting in its own doctrines." | "Embrace the law of Salvation, God hath established it, that men may observe it; it admitteth no alteration, but the greatest part of the world are ignorant of it: Fear God, make your prayers at the time appointed; be not like to them that say, God hath a companion; neither like to them that are at present in the number of Heretiques, and were before as ye are; every sect is pleased in its opinions" (p. 250). |

In these excerpts from Ross's translation, the regular gloss of *dīn* (by way of the seventeenth-century French *loy*) is "law."[91] The same was true of the much earlier Latin version produced by Robert of Ketton in the twelfth century, in which *lex* was the preferred term (when his rather loose Latin translation is sufficiently literal to determine word-to-word correspondences).[92] And it turns out there is some reason to think that these earlier translations, for all their faults, capture something that more recent translations miss.

Standard scholarly discussions of the term *dīn* in early Arabic literature suggest relationships with one or more of the following: the Arabic word *dayn* (debt, money owing); the Hebrew and Aramaic term *dîn* (judgment), which is clearly the sense of a phrase that occurs often in the Qur'an, *yawm al-dīn*, the Day of Judgment; and Middle Persian *dēn* (a term to be discussed in Chapter 4).[93] Thus, the author of the entry for *dīn* in the *Encyclopaedia of Islam* proposes a wide semantic range for the word: custom, usage, judgment, direction, retribution.[94] What ties these terms together is that they refer to social transactions, a far cry from the sort of private, internal, apolitical sense of "faith" or "religion." It is thus puzzling when the author concludes that "the most general and frequent sense" of *dīn* is "religion." Yet, this statement is immediately qualified: "But the concept indicated by *dīn* does not exactly coincide with the ordinary concept of 'religion.'" And this qualification is crucial, for the author's final summation of the content of *dīn* is "the corpus of obligatory prescriptions given by God, to which one must submit." If we understand "law" as binding customs or practices that allow communities to function, du Ryer's French and Ross's English translations of *dīn* actually seem quite fitting.[95]

Although the plural of *dīn* (*adyān*) does not occur in the Qur'an, some passages do suggest a plural aspect of the concept, for example, Sura 109: "Unbelievers, I do not worship what you worship, nor do you worship what I worship. I shall never worship what you worship, nor will you ever worship what I worship. You have your own *dīn*, and I have mine."[96] A similar sense of plurality is evident in Sura 3:85: "He that chooses a *dīn* other than submission, it will not be accepted from him and in the world to come, he will surely be among the losers."[97] In her comprehensive study of the use of *dīn* in the Qur'an, Yvonne Yazbeck Haddad observes that such usage does "not imply a recognition of religious pluralism or of a plurality of 'comparable' religions, but rather refers to a distinction of quality within the one *dīn*."[98]

Nevertheless, the plural of *dīn* did become more common in later writings. A particularly good example occurs in an Arabic disputation text from the tenth century.[99] In this fictional account, a Muslim governor in Egypt oversees a disputation between a Coptic patriarch (a Christian who dissented from the conclusions of the Council of Chalcedon), a Melkite Christian (a pro-Chalcedonian), and a Jew. The governor is said to have opened the dispute with the following request: "I desire to know which *dīn* from among the *adyān* [*aya dīn min al-adyān*] is the truth." The terminology of *dīn* and *adyān* in this example is doing the work of genus/species classification (just as we saw *religio* and *thrēskeia* doing in the late antique and medieval periods), but there is another layer of complexity in that the dispute concludes with the Muslim governor exclaiming, "Truly, there is no *dīn* on this earth other than the Christian *dīn*, for it is the true *dīn*." Here again we find the plurality of the concept complicated. The extent to which all of the species are actually considered to take part in the genus is open to debate; in the polemical context in which the plural *adyān* occurs, there is only one true *dīn*. The others are merely pale imitations barely worthy of the name. (We will encounter a similar conception in Chapter 6 when discussing later developments in the usage of the Latin term *religio*.)

Also relevant to this discussion are two other Arabic terms that one often sees translated as "faith" or "religion" in contemporary translations of the Qur'an: *milla* and *umma*.[100] Several passages suggest that *milla* is roughly synonymous with the usages of *dīn* that we have been exploring. It is worthwhile to carry out a similar exercise comparing Ross's version of 1649 with that of Dawood:

	N. J. Dawood (2003)	Alexander Ross (1649)
Sura 4:125	"And who has a nobler religion [*dīn*] than he who submits to God, does what is right, and follows the faith [*milla*] of saintly Abraham, whom God chose to be His friend?"	"What better law is there, then [*sic*] to resign thy self to God, and to be an honest man? Follow the Law of *Abraham*; God chose *Abraham*, to love him" (p. 58).
Sura 6:161	"Say: 'My Lord has guided me to a straight path, to an upright religion [*dīn*], to the faith [*milla*] of saintly Abraham, who was no idolater.'"	"Say unto them, God hath guided me in the way of his Law; such as profess the Law of *Abraham*, profess the unity of God; *Abraham* was not in the number of unbelievers" (p. 90).

Just as with *dīn*, Ross's translation glosses *milla* with "Law." The term can refer to the ways of Jews, Christians, and polytheists, but it most frequently appears, as in this example, in the phrase *millat ibrāhīm*, perhaps best translated as the "law or sect of Abraham" (see more in Chapter 3).

The term *umma* is generally translated as "community" or "nation," but sometimes it is rendered in modern translations as "religion" or "faith." A good example is Sura 43:22–23, in which Arabs who are not followers of Muhammad explain (in Dawood's translation): "This was the faith [*umma*] our fathers practiced. We are merely walking in their footsteps." Compare this with Ross's translation (set in indirect speech): "they say that their fathers lived in like manner, and that they follow their steps" (p. 304). Ross's translation would seem to capture the broader sense of the term for which Islamicist Frederick Denny argues: "What 43:22, 23 means is that the Arabs were following their ancient customs, traditions, and values. Now this certainly includes religion . . . but it is not exclusively a matter of religious interests and preoccupations."[101] As was the case with *dīn*, the translation of *milla* and *umma* as "religion" or "faith" excises important resonances of the Arabic terminology.

What seems clear is that the Qur'an's demand for people to become part of the *umma*, to take up the *dīn* proclaimed by Muhammad, the *millat ibrāhīm*, was more than simply an invitation to a new kind of spirituality or private belief. To be sure, these terms imply a particular orientation to Allah, but, as we will see in Chapter 3, the Qur'an's exhortations to form a community are not best described with terms like "faith" and "religion." The summary of Islamicist Jacques Waardenburg is apt: "The calls of prophets in the course of history to make people turn or return to almighty God were not only incentives to monotheism. They also carried messages about the right way of life to be followed by each person in the community concerned and in society at large. In other words, *these calls imposed not only what we would consider a strictly "religious" belief and practice, but also rules of what we would today call social order, law, ethics or morality,* with corresponding prescriptions and prohibitions" (emphasis added).[102] This phenomenon is similar to what we have already seen with the Latin *religio* and Greek *thrēskeia*.[103] Each of these terms has a range of meanings in antiquity, but none of them corresponds well with the modern concept of religion. None of these ancient words delineates "religious" from "not-religious."

Conclusion

This exercise could continue with analysis of additional terms from other ancient cultures that one sees translated as "religion," such as *dharma, dao,* or *jiao.* But for now, I close by simply reemphasizing a key point about *religio, thrēskeia,* and *dīn* to which I have alluded multiple times: even though all these terms eventually come in the course of antiquity to be used in classification systems with the singular forms indicating a genus and the plural forms indicating various species, the entities being classified *should not* be confused with the modern religions. Those aspects of life covered by these terms (social order, law, etc.) fall outside the idealized, private, interior realm associated with the modern concept of religion. Translating these terms as "religion" or conceptualizing any particular individual ancient *religio, thrēskeia,* or *dīn* as "a religion" is thus bound to be a misleading practice.

three

**SOME (PREMATURE) BIRTHS OF RELIGION
IN ANTIQUITY**

Introduction

As we have seen, simply translating ancient words as "religion" tends to leave the impression that the concept of religion was operative before the modern era. One also finds sustained arguments from some scholars that this or that particular moment in antiquity marked the beginning of the concept of religion or the "disembedding" of religion from the politico-religio-ethnic mixture of ancient life. Four moments for which such claims have been made include the events surrounding the "Maccabean revolt" in the middle of the second century B.C.E., the Roman statesman Cicero's discussions about the gods in the middle of the first century B.C.E., the writings of the church historian Eusebius in the early fourth century C.E., and the "birth of Islam" in the seventh century.

Religion in the Revolt of the Maccabees?

Upon the death of Alexander the Great, his generals engaged in a series of wars that effectively carved the Macedonian empire into several independent kingdoms. The region of Judea sat between two of these kingdoms, the Ptolemaic kingdom to the west in Egypt and the Seleucid kingdom to the north in Syria. Judea was under the control of the Ptolemies for most of the third century B.C.E., but in 198 B.C.E., the region was taken over by the Seleucid ruler Antiochus III. After a tumultuous forty years under Seleucid control, one Judean family, the Maccabees, was able to gain control of Jerusalem and establish an independent kingdom. A number of authors, including Wilfred Cantwell Smith, have paid special attention to this episode in regard to the formation of the category of religion. It is not frequently noted that Smith presented the Maccabean phenomenon as a kind of exception to his overall thesis:

> The Greek word *Ioudaismos* occurs first in Second Maccabees (first century B.C. or later), appropriately to designate that for which loyal Jews were fighting in their struggle against Hellenism. Even here, a more faithful translation of the original meaning of the passage would be that these men were fighting for their Jewishness, rather than "for Judaism." The impact of Greek ways upon the Jewish community was a threat, they felt, to the traditional character of their living. What began, however, as designating a quality of life, eventually came to refer to the formal pattern or outward system of observances in which that quality found expression. Thus the concept "Judaism" was born. This is perhaps the first time in human history that a religion has a name.[1]

Smith is not alone in proclaiming the importance of this historical episode for the formation of the concept of religion; specialists in "ancient Judaism" have made similar claims.[2] Smith's summary of the event as an instance of "loyal Jews" fighting against something called "Hellenism" captures the popular understanding of the affair: the Seleucid king, Antiochus IV Epiphanes, attempted to force Greek ways on the unwilling Judean population and then faced a revolt from pious Jews in the countryside led by Mattathias and his son Judas along with other members of the Maccabean (or Hasmonean) family. In this understanding, the Maccabees are thought to have successfully defended "the religion of Judaism" against encroachments from outside, Hellenizing forces.

More recent studies have questioned many aspects of this traditional picture and concluded that a more complicated one exists.[3] The main sources for the activities of the Maccabees are the documents known as 1 and 2 Maccabees (included in Catholic Bibles but excluded from Protestant Bibles) and the writings of Josephus.[4] Close attention to these documents demonstrates that characterizing this period as the beginning of "Judaism as a religion" is rather misguided.

Part of the problem is that the story of the Maccabees is usually told in isolation from the broader context of Judean politics in the second century B.C.E. It is important to frame the dispute somewhat more broadly and see the conflict in the context of ongoing struggles for supremacy among certain powerful Judean families with priestly aspirations.[5] During the decades leading up to the crisis, two families were vying for power in Jerusalem, the Oniads and the Tobiads. The Oniads held the high priesthood in the third century B.C.E., and the Tobiads were a powerful family with ties to Jerusalem.[6] Various members of these two families formed alliances with the main powers in the region, the Ptolemaic rulers in Egypt and the Seleucid rulers in Syria. Squabbles within and between these two families continued for decades and, according to Josephus, left the population of Judea "divided into two camps."[7] Josephus describes a similarly tense situation during the reign of Antiochus IV: "At the time when Antiochus, who was called Epiphanes, had a quarrel with the sixth Ptolemy about his right to all of Syria, sedition fell upon the powerful men among the Judeans, and they had an ambitious rivalry over power; as each of those that were of dignity could not stand to be subject to their equals. However, Onias, one of the high priests, prevailed, and threw the sons of Tobias out of the city."[8] Shortly after this, the office of high priest fell to another Oniad, Jason, who, as his Greek name indicates, favored Greek customs. Jason is said to have set up a gymnasium in Jerusalem and encouraged the Judean people to adopt other features typical of Greek life. The author of 2 Maccabees condemned these actions as *hellēnismos* ("Hellenizing") and *allophulismos* ("foreignizing"), terms to which I will return shortly.[9] According to 2 Maccabees, Jason's tenure as high priest lasted only a few years before he was ousted by Menelaus, who also favored Greek ways. An armed dispute ensued between the two men. To quell this unrest Antiochus IV took Jerusalem by force and instituted a set of alterations to traditional Judean life, including the construction of altars in the Judean countryside and the sacrifice of pigs at the Jerusalem temple; he also forbade circumcision and observance of the Sabbath.

At this tense point in the story the sources introduce the Macca-bees. Modern scholars have tended to portray them as being re-moved from all the urban political intrigue I have just described. Typically, they are associated with the village of Modein, where they are said to have had a family burial ground, and they are represented as being part of "a bastion of country piety."[10] In fact, however, all three of our sources portray the early Maccabees as Jerusalem insid-ers. According to 1 Maccabees and Josephus, Mattathias "arose from Jerusalem" and was "a priest of the division of Joarib and a Jerusale-mite."[11] In 2 Maccabees (in which the character Mattathias does not appear), Judas the Maccabee is first introduced as fleeing from Jeru-salem.[12] This connection with Jerusalem and the fact that the Mac-cabees did in fact win a power struggle to take control of the city suggest that the Maccabees were in some ways quite similar to other powerful families in Jerusalem such as the Oniads and the Tobiads. Where the Maccabees differed from these other families was in their tactics. Whereas the Oniads and Tobiads used military force against one another, the Maccabees directed military efforts both against fellow Judeans who opposed them *and* against the ruling Seleucid forces. Also, if 1 and 2 Maccabees are to be believed, the Maccabees cast their actions as a defense of ancestral ethnic traditions and prac-tices.[13] It is in this context in 2 Maccabees that we find the earliest surviving usage of the term *ioudaismos*, generally misleadingly trans-lated as "Judaism" or "the religion of the Jews."[14] As the historian Steve Mason has pointed out, the term *ioudaismos* is part of a larger field of Greek vocabulary of ethnicity derived from verbs of the *-izō* type, such as *mēdizein*, a word Greeks used during the Persian wars to condemn those who adopted the customs of or defected to the Persians.[15] These verbs often have corresponding nouns ending in *-ismos*, such as *mēdismos*, or the activity of taking up Persian cus-toms.[16] We have already seen that 2 Maccabees condemns the taking up of Greek customs using the term *hellēnismos*, an action elsewhere equated with "the destruction of the ancestral *politeia*."[17] It comes as little surprise that the alternative to this *hellēnismos* is *ioudaismos*, or the defense of Judean ethnic customs and civic life (equated in 2 Macc. 2:21 with the activity of "pushing out the barbarian hordes").

Thus, the introduction of the term *ioudaismos* is not, as Smith would have it, "perhaps the first time in human history that a religion has a name."[18] The term was coined in the midst of a dispute among some Judeans over how much "foreign" practice ought to be adopted. In that context *ioudaismos*, or "Judaizing," was an aggressive promotion of a Judean way of life formed in dialogue with the actions of some Judeans who were perceived as engaging in *hellēnismos* or *allophulismos*, or practicing foreign customs. As we will see briefly, later Christian authors would come to use the term *ioudaismos* in rather different ways, but the point I stress here is that these early occurrences of the word in 2 Maccabees refer to an activity associated with ethnic and civic customs; they do not, as Smith would have it, "name a religion."

Religion in Cicero?

I move now from Judea to Rome and from a fairly simplistic claim that a *name* (*ioudaismos*) establishes an ancient religion to a more interesting and sophisticated claim that an ancient *discourse* marks the emergence of religion. In 1986, the classicist Mary Beard offered a radical rereading of Marcus Tullius Cicero's tract *On Divination*. She made the case that this tract, along with *On the Nature of the Gods*, marks the beginning of a Roman discourse on religion.[19] In her words, this age was "the period when 'religion,' as an activity and a subject, became clearly defined out of the traditional, non-differentiated, politico-religious amalgam of Roman public life."[20] In the standard reading of the two books that comprise *On Divination*, the first book is a weak defense (put in the mouth of Cicero's brother, Quintus) of the utility of divination by means of a litany of examples of accurate predictions from the distant and recent past. The second book is a devastatingly convincing response in the voice of Marcus Cicero himself that argues against divination through a series of counterexamples from history and a mockery of some of Quintus's examples.

The usual understanding of the dialogue is that the second book gives Cicero's "real" opinion of the matter; Cicero is revealed to be not just an Academic skeptic, but a rationalist, enlightened skeptic when it comes to the gods. On this reading, Cicero, himself an augur, cynically encourages elite Romans to play along with the traditional practices of divination for the benefit of the uneducated masses. It is the view expressed by Marcus (the character) throughout the second book:

> For we Roman augurs are not the sort who foretell the future by observing the flights of birds and other signs. And yet, I admit that Romulus, who founded the city by the direction of auspices, believed that augury was an art useful in seeing things to come—for the ancient had erroneous views on many subjects. But we see that the art has undergone a change, due to experience, education, or the long lapse of time. However, out of respect for the opinion of the masses and because of the great service to the State we maintain the augural practices, discipline, rites and laws, as well as the authority of the augural college [*retinetur autem et ad opinionem vulgi et ad magnas utilitates rei publicae mos, religio, disciplina, ius augurium, collegi auctoritas*].[21]

Beard points out that attributing such a view to Cicero (the author) shows no respect for the dialogue as a literary form nor for Cicero's allegiance to the Academy. She notes that the real conclusion of the work (the actual final words) is exactly what one might expect in a dialogue written by an Academic skeptic—the withholding of judgment:

> "Moreover, it is characteristic of the Academy to put forward no conclusions of its own, but to approve those which seem to approach nearest to the truth; to compare arguments; to draw forth all that may be said in behalf of any opinion; and, without asserting any authority of its own, to leave the judgement of the inquirer wholly free. That same method, which by the way we inherited from Socrates, I shall, if agreeable to you, my dear Quintus, follow as often as possible in our future discussions." "Nothing could please me better," Quintus replied. When this was said, we arose.[22]

What is important for Beard is not the mystery of Cicero's personal opinions and beliefs, but rather the fact that a discussion on these topics exists at all. Other Romans of this period shared Cicero's interests. While Beard focuses on Cicero, she acknowledges that he was not alone, noting in her discussion, "It may be that 'Cicero' should stand as shorthand for his whole generation."[23] It was during the age of Cicero that Marcus Terrentius Varro compiled encyclopedic collections of priestly rites and rituals in *Antiquitates divinarum*. Lesser known figures, such as Cicero's friend Publius Nigidius Figulus, also were writing works about the gods and their interaction with humans, taking part in the "differentiation" of this new "activity and subject."[24]

We may then ask: What constituted this new activity and subject that exercised the interest of these late republican authors? Cicero gives us a clue of his own conception in the opening of the second of the two books of *On Divination*. Cicero (here the author of the dialogue and not the character Marcus Cicero) provides some context for the composition of *On Divination*: "After publishing the works mentioned I finished three volumes *On the Nature of the Gods*, which contain a discussion of every question under that head. With a view of simplifying and extending the latter treatise I started to write the present volume *On Divination*, to which I plan to add a work *On Fate;* when that is done, every phase of this particular branch of philosophy will be sufficiently discussed" (*erit abunde satis factum toti huic quaestioni*).[25] The discourse Cicero outlines thus consists of philosophical theology (the main topic of *On the Nature of the Gods*), various means of predicting the future (*On Divination*), and the philosophical problems associated with fate (*On Fate*).[26] We should likely add at least one other element to this list: Roman civic and ethnic identity.[27] The importance of this identity permeates the preamble to the second book of *On Divination*. The quotation above is bracketed by notices of Cicero's "concern for the state" (*consulere rei publicae*) and his desire to make philosophy accessible to speakers of Latin.[28] Indeed, before moving on to recount the second speech in the dialogue, Cicero explains that "it would be to the fame and glory of the Roman people to be made independent of Greek writers in the study of philosophy, and this result I shall certainly bring about if my present plans are accomplished."[29] Thus, along with philosophical theology, prediction of the future, and fate, civic and ethnic identity is also intimately involved even in Cicero's "enlightened" approach to the gods.

Here we encounter a major difficulty in how we talk about the ancient world. For Beard is certainly correct to point out that something new is going on here with Cicero and his contemporaries, with the beliefs and practices that they bundle together in these treatises. What I question is the helpfulness of describing this discourse as "Roman religion." How well do Cicero's concerns correspond to what modern people mean when we speak of "religion"? Beard is far too sophisticated to suggest that the "activity and subject" of "religion" that she finds in Cicero's works entails the privatized, apolitical interiority of the modern notion of religion, but her choice to use the terminology invites confusion. In what sense is Cicero distilling "religion" out of "the politico-religious amalgam of Roman life" if his discourse is still overtly concerned with Roman civic and ethnic identity?[30] There is no simple solution, but I think it is clear that the terminology of religion has some severe drawbacks when applied to ancient Roman evidence. Students of the ancient world need to work on generating a better vocabulary for talking about the various ways that ancient peoples conceptually carved out their worlds, a better means of describing the clusters of practices and beliefs outlined by ancient authors (see the conclusion to this book).

Religion in the Works of Eusebius?

The problem is all the more pressing when we turn our attention to Christian materials. Unlike Judeans and Romans, ancient Christians had no immediately obvious geographic locale to act as an anchor for their cultic practices. It is thus not surprising that various Christian texts have been identified as marking the beginning of the concept of religion. An especially interesting discussion in this regard has arisen recently, centered on the writings of the church historian Eusebius. The Talmudic scholar Daniel Boyarin claims to have refuted the contention of the anthropologist Talal Asad and others that the category of religion was a product of a uniquely modern set of circumstances.[31] Boyarin argues that authors in the fourth century employed the concept of religion as distinct from ethnicity "contra the commonplace that such definitions are an early modern product."[32] Thus, Boyarin asserts that Eusebius presents "a clear articulation of Judaism, Hellenism, and Christianity as religions."[33] Although I think Boyarin misreads both Asad and the ancient literature, a closer look at the passages from Eusebius to which Boyarin refers to substantiate this claim is still worthwhile for the light it sheds on how Eusebius, without the concept of religion, classified the peoples he recognized as "others."[34]

Boyarin appeals to passages from the *Demonstratio evangelica*, a complementary volume to an earlier work, the *Praeparatio evangelica*. Both were likely written in the second decade of the fourth century. While the *Praeparatio* defends Christians' preference for Hebrew traditions over against those of Greeks, the *Demonstratio* seeks to ground Christian claims about Jesus in the Hebrew scriptures.[35] Boyarin, however, argues that in *Demonstratio* 1.2, Eusebius portrays Christianity as "a third form of religion" along with "Judaism" and "Hellenism."[36] In fact, Eusebius's terminology here concerns *tropoi theosebeias* ("methods of worship") that are very explicitly associated with *ethnicities*. Eusebius claims that Jesus "instituted the union of a new nation [*neou ethnous*] to be called by his own name."[37] Far from isolating "religion" as a separate entity from nationality, Eusebius defines Christianity quite specifically as an *ethnos*.[38] Similar ethnic and civic overtones permeate Eusebius's discussions of *ioudaismos* and *hellēnismos*. In a departure from the earlier usages that we have seen, Eusebius defines *ioudaismos* as a civic body, a *politeia* arranged by the law of Moses.[39] He contrasts this definition with *hellēnismos*, which he defines in a parallel clause as *deisidaimonia* toward many gods in accordance with the ancestral customs (*ta patria*) of all the nations (*tōn ethnōn hapantōn*). The connection of *hellēnismos* with "the customs of all the nations" reflects Eusebius's project of redrawing traditional Greek ethnic mappings in order to create a place for Christians.[40] One of Eusebius's main goals in both the *Praeparatio* and *Demonstratio* is to show that the Christians are Greeks—thus his inclusive use of the first-person plural when discussing Greeks—who have changed races and become Christians.[41]

In *Demonstratio* 1.2.10, Eusebius defines *christianismos* not as a kind of *ioudaismos* or *hellēnismos*, but rather as a citizenry of piety (*politeuma eusebeias*) and a kind of philosophy (*tis philosophia*).[42] For Eusebius, both civic terminology and the rhetoric of "philosophies" have ethnic overtones.[43] Eusebius and other Christian authors definitely altered the typical ethnic mapping of the classical world, but what they produced was *not* a nonethnic, religious map of the world; it was a *new ethnic map*.[44] Eusebius's model did transgress old ethnic boundaries, but it also created new ones—the Christians were a race both old and new.[45] Among the early criticisms of Christians, one of the most frequently occurring is the charge that they constituted a strange, new race of people. Christians claimed to worship the ancestral god of the Judeans, but they also emphatically did not take on other Judean customs and even denied being Judean. One of Eusebius's main goals in the *Praeparatio* and *Demonstratio* is to show that the Christians are indeed heirs to an ancient heritage—the most ancient heritage, in fact. According to Eusebius, the oldest race (*genos*) or nation (*ethnos*) of humans is that of the Hebrews. All other cultures ultimately derive from the Hebrews, in that, at some point in hoary antiquity, other nations fell away from the worship of the one Hebrew god and became idolaters of various sorts. The Greeks, the Hellenes, for example, went astray from the ancient Hebrew ways, following the teachings of Plato rather than those of Moses. Eusebius asserts that Christians, however, are actually part of that most ancient race, the Hebrews.

Now, tracing ancestry back to Abraham and the patriarchs was part of the repertoire of even the earliest followers of Jesus. The apostle Paul had claimed that his non-Judean converts were in fact sons of Abraham.[46] What is innovative in Eusebius is the bold claim that not only are Christians descendants of the oldest race, the Hebrews, but also, according to Eusebius, the ancient Hebrews were themselves Christians. It is worth pausing to watch this remarkable argument unfold in these excerpts from the opening of Eusebius's *Demonstratio evangelica:* "The law and life of our Savior Jesus Christ . . . , reestablished the most ancient and pre-Mosaic piety [*tēn palaitatēn kai presbuteran Mōseōs eusebeian*], according to which Abraham, the friend of God, and his forefathers are shown to have lived as citizens [*pepoliteumenoi*]. And if you wanted to compare the life of Christians and the worship [*theosebeian*] introduced among all nations by Christ with the lives of the men who with Abraham are witnessed to by Scripture as pious and righteous, you would find them one and the same [*hena kai ton auton heurēseis*]."[47]

Eusebius claimed to find support for this contention in a number of biblical passages, in which he surmised that pre-Mosaic figures who were said to have encountered the Hebrew god had instead actually met Christ. Eusebius clinched the argument with some intriguing exegesis of the Septuagint, the Greek translation of the Hebrew scriptures:

> The things concerning Christ have been given in common both to us [Christians] and to them [the patriarchs]. Therefore you can find pre-Mosaic god-fearing men being called "Christs" [*christous*] just as we are called "Christians" [*christianous*]. Hear what the oracle in the Psalms says about them:
>
> > "When they were few in numbers,
> > very few, and strangers in the land,
> > and they went from nation to nation,
> > from one kingdom to another people:
> > He allowed no man to wrong them,
> > and he reproved kings for their sakes,
> > saying: Touch not my anointed [*tōn christōn mou*],
> > and do no evil to my prophets."

The whole context shows that this must refer to Abraham, Isaac, and Jacob: they therefore shared the name of "Christ" in common with us.[48]

The payoff for this exegetical move is substantial. By making the Hebrews, the most ancient race of humans, into Christians, Eusebius creates an ethnic map in which any non-Christian group can be seen as a deviation from a pure, ancient Christian past. This helps to explain why groups such as *ioudaioi* (that is, Judeans or Jews), Platonists, and Scythians so frequently appear in lists of Christian heresies. In the model of history presented by Eusebius, any non-Christian group, no matter how old or how (apparently) distant from contemporary Christians, can ultimately be classified as a Christian heresy. As we will see, this heresiological mode of classification had a long afterlife among Christian writers. And in fact, it was only the breakdown of this heresiological framework in the sixteenth and seventeenth centuries that allowed the modern framework of World Religions to come into being.

The Case of Muhammad and His Early Followers

In the seventh century, a movement grew up in the Arabian peninsula around the figure of Muhammad. In both popular and scholarly discussions of the beginnings of this movement, Muhammad is often portrayed as founding a completely new religion distinct from others. Thus, Bernard Lewis has characterized "early Islam" and the Qur'an in the following way: "Unlike most earlier religious documents, [the Qur'an] shows awareness of religion as a category of phenomena, and not merely as a single phenomenon. There is not just one religion; there are religions. The word used in Arabic is *dīn*. . . . The notion of religion as a class or category, in which Islam is one and in which besides Islam there are others, seems to have been present from the advent of the Islamic dispensation. The Qur'ān contains a number of passages in which the new religion defines itself against others."[49] Setting aside the problems of agency (how can "a religion" define itself?) and the problems of terminology (we have already examined the difficulty of translating *dīn* simply as "religion"), I focus on the claim that the composition of the Qur'an somehow ushered in the new religion of Islam fully formed; the assertion is as common as it is misleading.

First, however, a brief overview is needed of the traditional Muslim account of "early Islam" (an account that was, until quite recently, largely accepted by most scholars). The Qur'an itself tells us surprisingly little about Muhammad and the formation of the movement. Historians have thus relied on later sources to construct a picture of the man and his early followers. The earliest of these sources go back to the middle of the eighth century, that is, about a century after the death of Muhammad.[50] According to these accounts, Muhammad was a merchant in the town of Mecca in Arabia. Around the year 610, he is said to have begun to receive revelations from the angel Gabriel. These revelations, which encouraged him to take up a strict monotheism and to preach to others this message of monotheism and submission to Allah, continued over the next two decades and, according to tradition, would eventually be recorded as the Qur'an. As Muhammad began to spread his message, he found some supporters but faced growing hostility from other Meccan tribes. In 622, he and several Meccan families left Mecca for Yathrib (modern Medina) in an act that is called the *hijrah*, or emigration. At Medina, the emigrants (*muhajirun*) were received by residents of the city sympathetic to Muhammad's message, the so-called helpers (*ansar*). Muhammad is said to have consolidated his authority at Medina by fighting and defeating troublesome tribes, especially tribes of Jews, smoothing over difficulties that arose between the *muhajirun* and the *ansar*, and eventually marching to and occupying his former hometown, Mecca, in the year 630. By the time of his death in 632, Muhammad and his supporters, now known as Muslims, are said to have controlled much of western Arabia. Muhammad's successors, so the story goes, carried this new religion, Islam, across the Mediterranean as they won military battles from Mesopotamia to Spain. Scholars have described this process as the birth and spread of the religion of Islam.

It is true that passages in the Qur'an contain the terms *islām* and *muslim*, but these terms need not be understood as "the religion of Islam" and "an adherent of Islam." In fact, there is good reason to interpret them differently in these early contexts. The word *islām* in the Qur'an is best understood not as the name of a religion, but rather as a verbal noun (submission, surrender, obedience). The verbal form *aslama* occurs more than twenty times in the Qur'an. The nominal form *islām* occurs only eight times, and its verbal aspect is often underplayed. Consider Dawood's translation of Sura 49:17: "They think they have conferred on you a favour by embracing Islām. Say: 'In accepting Islām you have conferred on me no favour. It was God who bestowed a favour on you.'" His parallel formation "accepting Islām . . . embracing Islām" is not really representative of the syntax of the Arabic. The first phrase is actually a verbal form, *aslmau*, "they have surrendered"; and although the second phrase is in fact the nominal form *islām*, it is accompanied by a personal pronoun (*islamukum*), which, for Dawood, would yield the somewhat awkward translation "your Islam."[51] A better translation would let the verb in the first phrase govern the noun in the second phrase. Arthur J. Arberry takes this approach in his translation of the passage: "They count it as a favour to thee that they have surrendered! Say: 'Do not count your surrendering as a favour to me.'"[52] Paramount in this and other instances of the noun *islām* is the activity of submission.

Much more frequent than the noun *islām* in the Qur'an is the related participle *muslim* ("one who submits to authority, surrenders, obeys"). This term occurs more than forty times, and again, the translations vary. A good illustration of the difficulty of the term is Sura 3:52, which relates a short conversation between Jesus and his disciples (Dawood's translation): "When Jesus observed that they had no faith, he said: 'Who will help me in the cause of God?' The disciples replied: 'We are God's helpers. We believe in God. Bear witness that we submit to him.'" The words "we submit to him" translate the Arabic *bi-annā mus'limūna* and have been rendered by other modern translators as "we are Muslims."[53] On either translation, this is an intriguing statement about the status of Jesus's followers in Muhammad's movement.

These lexical complexities demonstrate that the simple existence in the Qur'an of the terms *muslim* and *islām* does not mean that those words conveyed in the seventh century what the terms "Islam" and "Muslim" convey in modern languages. Furthermore, the lack of clarity about what exactly constitutes a *muslim* in the Qur'an raises the possibility that the beginnings of Muhammad's movement are perhaps not as clear-cut as later Islamic interpretation and much Western scholarly interpretation might lead one to believe. In fact, recent years have seen a spate of studies of Muhammad and his early followers that diverge from this traditional narrative.[54] Of these accounts, one of the most compelling is that of Fred Donner, who has emphasized that the movement that centered around Muhammad included both Jews and Christians.[55] Donner notes that most of the Qur'an's exhortations are directed to "Believers" (*mu'minun*), a term that is not, as later commentators would claim, simply synonymous with *muslim*.[56] Rather, *muslimun* were a subset of the Believers, what Donner calls "Quranic monotheists," or members of the community of Believers who were neither Jews nor Christians.

The content of the Qur'an's messages to Believers is relatively straightforward. They are to worship only one god. Thus, there is a great deal of polemic against those who worship anything besides the one god. Such people are *mushrikūn*; they are guilty of the sin of *shirk*, "associating" something with God. The label primarily applies to worshippers of traditional Arabian gods, but it may also be directed against those Christians who insisted on the divinity of Jesus.[57] The Believers are also exhorted to hold an intense expectation of an upcoming Day of Judgment (*yawm al-dīn*), in which Allah will dispense justice, rewarding those who act righteously and punishing those who do not. Believers are also expected to perform regular prayer, fasting, pilgrimage, and charity to the socially oppressed and to pay the *zakat* ("a fine or payment made by someone who was guilty of some kind of sin, in exchange for which Muhammad would pray in order that they might be purified of their sin and that their other affairs might prosper").[58] Thus, the Believers depicted in the Qur'an were at base rigorously demanding monotheists with a strong interest in eschatology, evinced by their concern for the Day of Judgment. But such beliefs and practices do not constitute a "new religion." As Donner writes:

> Indeed, some passages make it clear that Muhammad's message was the same as that brought by the earlier apostles: "Say: I am no innovator among the apostles; and I do not know what will become of me or of you. I merely follow what is revealed to me; I am only a clear warner" (Q. 46:9). At this early stage in the history of the Believers' movement, then, it seems that Jews or Christians who were sufficiently pious could, if they wished, have participated in it because they recognized God's oneness already. Or, to put it the other way around, some of the early Believers were Christians or Jews—although surely not all were.[59]

The Qur'an itself provides support for the argument, as shown in Sura 3:113–15 (Dawood's translation): "Yet they are not all alike. There are among the People of the Book [that is, Jews and Christians] some upright men who all night long recite the revelations of God and worship Him; who believe [*yu'minūna*] in God and the Last Day; who enjoin justice and forbid evil and vie with each other in good works. These are righteous men: whatever good they do, its reward shall not be denied them. God well knows the righteous." Donner is thus able to establish that, on principle, Jews and non-Trinitarian Christians *could* be members of the community of Believers. But is there evidence that any Jews and/or Christians actually were among Muhammad's followers? At this point, Donner turns to the so-called Constitution of Medina, a document, or perhaps a set of documents, purported to be agreements from the time of Muhammad's arrival in Medina. It is preserved only in the work of later writers, but there is wide scholarly consensus that the constitution has been faithfully preserved, and in the words of one expert, "from the historical viewpoint it is not less in importance than the Qur'ān itself."[60] These documents contain a series of rules and pacts between Muhammad and various tribes of Medina, including Jewish tribes. Donner translates a portion of one of these documents as follows: "The Jews of the tribe of 'Awf are a people [*umma*] with the Believers; the Jews have their *din* [law?] and the *muslimun* have their *din*. [This applies to] their clients [*mawali*] and to themselves, excepting anyone who acts wrongly and acts treacherously."[61] It thus seems clear that at this stage, Muhammad's movement, his community (*umma*), did include some Jews. Sura 3:52 (discussed above), which describes Jesus's followers as *muslimun*, suggests that some Christians were part of the community of Believers as well. Now we are in a position to consider how helpful is it to talk about this phenomenon as "the religion of Islam." If the movement included Christians and Jews, could the movement properly be said to constitute "their religion"? If the *muslimun* have their own *dīn* and the Jews have their own *dīn* but both are part of the *umma*, what would their common "religion" be? There is no good answer to these questions, I think, because the vocabulary of "religions" is not the most helpful means for approaching premodern evidence.

Before leaving this body of evidence, I briefly note one other phenomenon of interest to the present study. In Chapter 2, I touched upon the term *milla*, which is sometimes translated as "religion." This term is part of a phrase, *millat ibrāhīm* (the law or sect of Abraham), that occurs several times in the Qur'an. The expression provides Muhammad's message with a connection to antiquity. Consider Sura 22:77–78 (I have slightly adjusted Dawood's translation): "You who are true Believers, kneel and prostrate yourselves. Worship your Lord and do good works . . . He has chosen you, and laid no burdens in the observance of your *dīn*, the *milla* of Abraham your father." The genealogical connection, Believers as descendants of Abraham, is intriguing in light of what we have observed of Eusebius's treatment of the patriarchs. Indeed, this connection between Abraham and the Believers also allows for the classification of those Jews and Christians who were not among the Believers as deviants. The point is made most clearly in Sura 3:67–68: "Abraham was neither Jew nor

Christian, rather he was a *hanifan musliman* (a committed monotheist) and not one of the *mushrikūn*. Surely the men who are nearest to Abraham are those who follow him, this Prophet, and the true Believers."[62] Jews and Christians who are not believers are depicted as people who have fallen away from the pure revelations they had received. Only the Believers can claim Abraham as their father. It would seem that, like Eusebius, the followers of Muhammad also developed a heresiological mode of conceptualizing "others."

Conclusion

The four examples reviewed in this chapter suggest that the various moments that have been proclaimed as "the emergence of religion" in the premodern period are considerably more complicated than that label implies. In each of these cases, the episodes that modern authors have identified as ancient "religion" have turned out to involve discourses that ancient authors themselves seem to have understood primarily in ethnic or civic terms. I close by glancing back for a moment to the fifth century B.C.E. At the conclusion of Book 8 of his *Histories*, Herodotus presents the Athenians' own explanation of why they will make no compacts with the Persians (*barbaroi*): to do so would be an insult to "Greekness" (*to hellēnikon*), which consists of shared blood, speech, and shrines and common sacrifices and customs.[63] These qualities together make a people.

Much had changed by the time of Eusebius. As we have seen, "Greekness" (*hellēnismos*) had become for Eusebius "the ancestral customs of all the nations." Animal sacrifices were on the decline in the fourth century. Christians spoke not one but many languages. But some things remained the same. To worship a god or gods was still part of an integrated complex of ideas involving ancestral traditions, even if that complex of ancestral traditions now appeared more mutable. Even for Eusebius in the fourth century, worshipping the Christian god meant having a genealogical connection to ancient ancestors. "Greekness," for Eusebius, stood in opposition to Christianity, the ancestral customs of the ancient Hebrews. While sacrifice, the activity most closely associated with temples, died out, *thrēskeia* continued to be carried out at new locations under Constantine's rule. We even see the persistence of this complex in the case of "early Islam" with the suggestion that Believers are marked by a familial connection to Abraham (and the contention that the Ka'ba, the cubic shrine in Mecca that is a focal point for prayer and pilgrimage, was built by Abraham and Ishmael).[64] Introducing "religion" into these discussions would seem to cause more problems than it solves, as ancient peoples had different ways of conceptualizing themselves and others.

four CHRISTIANS AND "OTHERS" IN THE PREMODERN ERA

Introduction

The arguments in the preceding two chapters have been largely negative: first, modern translators do a disservice when they use "religion" to render words in ancient texts, and second, ancient events or discourses that modern scholars describe as the "birth of religion" in the modern sense are much more usefully described in other terms. Nevertheless, in the course of my arguments about what sorts of ideas and concepts were *not* around in antiquity, we encountered some more positive suggestions about how ancient peoples *did* conceptualize some of their differences. One of these is Eusebius's model of history, in which Christians are the oldest race and anyone with views or practices diverging from Christian orthodoxy (however that may be defined) can be understood as wayward Christians of a sort. This "heretical" model proved extremely useful for Christian thinkers in late antiquity and beyond, and I use it as a starting point for answering the following question: If ancient peoples did not have the category of religion, how did adherents of the groups that modern scholars often designate as "different ancient religions" conceptualize one another (or, at a more basic level, to what degree does the modern practice of naming "different religions" actually establish boundaries between different ancient groups)? This chapter examines three instances of Christian interaction with what modern scholarship has labeled "other religions."

The first two case studies involve Eusebius's heresiological take on history. I direct attention first to the self-styled prophet Mani, who lived in the third century. The movement he began established communities across the known world from Egypt to China, and although modern scholars have had a fondness for describing this movement as the first World Religion, ancient authors (those both inside and outside the group) seem to have regarded Manichaeans as Christians, although more orthodox Christians like Eusebius identified them as a heretical sect. The second case is a related but somewhat more jarring instance of the heretical framework. In the eighth century, the Christian monk John of Damascus set a lasting precedent by classifying followers of Muhammad not as members of a separate religion but as Christian heretics. Although it may seem odd from a modern standpoint to classify Muslims as Christians, this mode of classification persisted among Christian writers for centuries. The final example is of a rather different sort but nonetheless draws together some of the complications highlighted by the first two case studies. The moralizing text that tells the tale of the Christian saints Barlaam and Ioasaph was long (incorrectly) thought to have been written by John of Damascus. Manuscript discoveries over the past two centuries have shown instead that the story is a reworked version of the life of Buddha. Thus, this text is an example of what modern scholars would designate as the foundational narrative of "another religion" (Buddhism) simply being transformed wholesale into a Christian narrative. All three of these examples emphasize the point that the adherents of the ancient groups that modern scholars discuss as distinct religions had rather different vocabularies and different means for conceptualizing one another, if they even chose to differentiate themselves from one another at all.

Mani, the Apostle of Jesus Christ and the Buddha of Light

We begin with the phenomenon that modern scholars have come to call "Manichaeism."[1] I might have included it in the previous chapter because Manichaeism is often held out as a great exception to the claim that the concept of religion did not emerge until the modern period. Mani is thought to have self-consciously gone about forming his own World Religion. Wilfred Cantwell Smith, for example, credited him with "deliberately establishing a religion."[2] In recent years, however, experts have become more circumspect. In an anthology of Manichaean texts produced in 2004, the editors, Iain Gardner and

Samuel Lieu, open with a statement that echoes Smith's declaration from forty years earlier: "We might say that Manichaeism is the first real 'religion' in the modern sense, because Mani established it directly and deliberately, with its scriptures and its rituals and its organisation all in place."[3] Yet Gardner and Lieu are too sophisticated to share Smith's conception; they later raise a note of concern, warning that "we should be cautious in our use of the term 'religion,' and not impose anachronistic conceptions derived from the modern discipline of the history of religions."[4]

For centuries, Mani was known to ecclesiastically minded Europeans as a Christian heretic condemned in the writings of many different patristic writers. Augustine of Hippo provides especially useful information, since he was himself an enthusiastic follower of Mani's teachings from the time he was about twenty years old until he was nearly thirty.[5] The life and teachings of Mani were thus known almost exclusively through hostile outside sources. This situation changed drastically in the twentieth century, which saw a series of manuscript discoveries that set the study of Mani and his followers on new ground. From 1902 to 1914 expeditions in the Silk Road oasis of Turfan and surrounding areas in Chinese Turkestan (the northwestern region of the modern People's Republic of China) brought to light documents written in a variety of Persian, Turkish, and Chinese languages and scripts. Included in these finds were many fragmentary Manichaean texts and examples of Manichaean artwork that shed light on Manichaean life in central Asia during the late medieval period. At about the same time, another discovery of a hoard of manuscripts in the Temple of the Thousand Buddhas in Tun-huang yielded important Manichaean manuscripts in Chinese and Uighur.[6]

Then in the late 1920s, a group of seven Manichaean papyrus codices appeared on the antiquities market in Egypt. They were most likely discovered in the town of Medinet Madi, about 120 kilometers southwest of Cairo. Written in Coptic, these manuscripts were translations from Syriac and probably date to the fourth or fifth century C.E. The original find included letters of Mani, Manichaean psalms and homilies, and the so-called *kephalaia*, or assorted teachings of Mani. The decipherment and publication of these texts was hampered by World War II, during which some portions of this find were lost or destroyed.[7] Publication of the Medinet Madi materials continues to this day. In 1970, a miniature vellum codex (3.8 by 4.5 centimeters, with letters about 1 millimeter tall!) from the papyrus collection of the University of Cologne was published. Now known as the Cologne Mani Codex, this Greek book was probably copied in the fifth century and appears to be a translation from Syriac. It no doubt came from Egypt, but its exact provenance is unknown. The book contains a collection of the writings of Mani's followers that provide biographical details and quotations from Mani himself.[8] As recently as the early 1990s, new collections of Manichaean documents have come to light. Excavations of a house in the area of the Dakhleh Oasis at the Egyptian town of Kellis have uncovered a cache of papyri including Manichaean literary works and documentary papyri that provide a window into the daily life of a Manichaean cell.[9] Thanks to these new materials, we have a much richer picture of Mani, his followers, and the history of their movement than we did just a century ago.

Mani was born in Mesopotamia in the early third century (probably 216 C.E.). He grew up as part of a community of baptists said to be associated with the early-second-century teacher Elchasaios. At the age of twelve, Mani is reported to have begun to receive visions revealed to him by a figure he regarded as his heavenly twin (the Greek term is *syzygos*). When he was in his mid-twenties Mani broke with the baptist group and began his own prophetic mission. He came to regard himself as the Paraclete (the heavenly "comforter" or "advocate" that the Gospel of John claimed would be sent from heaven to teach Jesus's disciples). He traveled as far as India, teaching and gaining a reputation as a miracle worker before returning to the more central areas of the Sassanian empire when Shapur I became the sole ruler (242 C.E.). He enjoyed imperial favor for nearly thirty years until Vahram I came to power in 274. Mani was then imprisoned and died in the year 276 or 277. By the time of his death he had already accumulated many followers and left behind many writings. His teachings proved both popular and adaptable to new contexts. Thus even after the death of the teacher, the movement spread rapidly both to the west and to the east.

It is not so much the content of Mani's teachings but the way in which he is understood to have presented his teachings that has led many scholars to speak of Mani "founding a religion."[10] Here is an example drawn from the surviving fragments of a Manichaean text called the *Šābuhragān*. This passage is frequently invoked as an example of Mani's self-conscious creation of a religion:

> The religion which was chosen by me is in ten things above and better than the other religions of the ancients. Firstly: The older religions were in one country and one language; but my religion is of the kind that it will be manifest in every country and in all languages, and it will be taught in far away countries. Secondly: The older religions (remained in order) as long as there were holy leaders in it; but when the leaders had been led upwards, then their religions became confused and they became slack in commandments and pious works, and by greed and fire (of lust) and desire were deceived. However, my religion will remain firm.[11]

Mani contrasts his own teaching with that of previous movements, which were geographically and ethnically limited. The term translated as "religion" here, the Middle Persian *dēn*, is one we have already met in Chapter 2, so it should not be surprising to learn that *dēn* has a rather broader semantic range than simply "religion." Indeed, a look at the reference works presents a dizzying variety of definitions. Proposed meanings in addition to the standard offering of "religion" include community, church, omniscience, wisdom, goodness, vision, revelation, religious rites, the sum of man's spiritual attributes and individuality, inner self, and conscience.[12] The *Dēnkard*, a tenth-century compendium written in Middle Persian, although it is generally called in English "the acts of the religion," in fact treats a range of topics, including (but by no means limited to) law, apologetics, cosmogony, kingship, medicine, the story of Zoroaster, music, time, fate, and meteorology.[13] We are clearly dealing with a complex and multifaceted term.

A clue to how the word might best be understood in the above passage from the *Šābuhragān* is provided by a recently published version of a closely related passage preserved in Coptic. There, we read, "The church [*ekklēsia*] I have chosen is superior in ten aspects over the first churches [*ekklēsia*]."[14] Here, the key term in Coptic is *ekklēsia*, a loan word from Greek, which gives the passage a rather different feel; what is under discussion are social groups, not disembodied "religious" systems. An additional possible reading of the passage is suggested by another fragment of the same text preserved in Arabic by the late-tenth- or early-eleventh-century writer Al-Biruni: "In the beginning of his book called Shâbûrkân, which he composed for Shâpûr b. Ardashîr, he [Mani] says: 'Wisdom and deeds have always from time to time been brought to mankind by the messengers of God. So in one age they have been brought by the messenger, called Buddha, to India, in another by Zarâdusht [Zarathustra] to Persia, in another by Jesus to the West. Thereupon this revelation [*waḥy*] has come down, this prophecy in this last age through me, Mânî, the messenger of the God of truth to Babylonia.'"[15] Mani is said to have placed himself in a series of figures who revealed divine teaching to humans. All these movements are fit into a model of a linear series of revelations, of which Mani's is the latest and greatest. Mani's movement thus stands in continuity with its predecessors and represents a perfected form of what has come before.

I have already mentioned that for ecclesiastical writers, Mani and his followers were regarded as Christian heretics.[16] This dominant viewpoint emerged quite early, and the Manichaeans became regulars on orthodox Christians' lists of heresies. The initial reaction of Roman government, however, seems to have been to portray Manichaeans as dangerous Persian foreigners. At the turn of the fourth century, the Roman emperors issued a rescript punishing Manichaeans as Persian infiltrators. Manichaeans represented a threat to "ancient modes of worship" (expressed as both a singular, *vetus religio*, and a plural, *veterioribus religionibus*) by injecting "the accursed customs and perverse laws of the Persians" into the lives of the "modest and tranquil Roman people."[17] The depiction of Manichaeans as Persian outsiders determined to upset the stability of the Roman empire is also present in the writings of the church historian Eusebius, but he combined this charge of foreignness with the accusation of diabolical heresy: "At that time the madman [*maneis*], named after his demonic heresy [*daimonōsēs haireseōs*] . . . pretended that he himself was Christ, announcing that he was the Paraclete and the Holy Spirit himself. . . . He stitched together false and godless doctrines that he had collected from the countless, long-extinct, godless heresies, and infected our empire [*tēn kath' hēmas oikoumenēn*] with, as it were, a deadly poison that came from the land of the Persians; and from him the impious name of the Manichaeans is still today commonly spoken."[18] It was the charge of heresy that became the chief label of the Manichaeans. If, therefore, "orthodox" Christians viewed these followers of Mani simply as a different (and bad) kind of Christian, the question before us is: How did Mani and his followers portray themselves? The answer is surprising, given those frequent claims of modern scholars that Mani "deliberately founded a religion," for Mani and those whom modern scholars call "Manichaeans" believed that they were Christians. In fact, in some ways, they were the mirror image of the orthodox Christians who persecuted them. That is to say, Manichaeans viewed themselves as Christians, and they saw "orthodox" Christians as inferior, or we might even say "heretical."

In Mani's "Fundamental Epistle" preserved in part by Augustine and another contemporary north-African bishop, Evodius, Mani refers to himself as "Apostle of Jesus Christ through the providence of god the father" (*Manichaeus apostolus Iesu Christi providentia dei patris*), and Manichaeans as a group are "the holy church and the elect" (*sanctam ecclesiam atque electos*).[19] In the early-fourth-century text the *Acts of Archelaus*, Mani is presented as claiming to be "a disciple of Christ" and "an apostle of Jesus," who believes that he instructs others in the proper Christian lifestyle.[20] Mani's self-understanding as operating within the sphere of Christian activity has found further support in the more recently discovered Manichaean literature as well. In what appears to be the first fragment of an important Manichaean text called *The Living Gospel*, Mani is reported to have declared his identity right from the outset, "I, Mani, apostle of Jesus Christ, through the will of God, father of truth."[21] This impression is confirmed by the recent finds from Kellis, in which the Manichaeans refer to themselves in their letters as "the holy church."[22] As Samuel Lieu notes, the owners of the Manichaean materials found at Kellis "saw themselves as a chosen élite in the Christian sense. They promoted themselves as the Church of the Paraclete and as such were the Christians in the Dakhleh Oasis."[23] The flip side of this self-identification is the denigration of "orthodox" Christians. Augustine reports that the Manichaean teacher Faustus referred to the "orthodox" as only "half-Christian" (*semichristianos*).[24]

But the story of Mani and his followers is not confined just to the ancient Mediterranean world. By the seventh century, followers of Mani had migrated into China, largely via the trade routes of the Silk Road.[25] By the twelfth century, Manichaean groups were a well-established feature of the southeastern coastlands of China. These eastern Manichaean groups adopted many ideas from the Buddhists and Taoists with whom they interacted. A regular title for Mani in the Chinese literature is "Mani the Buddha of Light" (*Moni guangfo*), and other sources identify him as a reincarnation of Laozi, the reputed author of the *Dao de jing*.[26] Nevertheless, Jesus remained a key figure even for these Manichaeans, who at times seem to fully identify Jesus with the Buddha as Jesus-Buddha (*Yishu fo*).[27] Indeed, as late as the thirteenth century, there is some evidence of a Manichaean group self-identifying to Mongol rulers (at the behest of none other than Marco Polo!) as Christians along with local Nestorian Christians.[28] Thus, groups of Manichaeans were different entities in different contexts to different observers. They constituted a Christian heresy at Rome, they were *the* Christianity in Kellis, and in Chinese settings they appeared in a range of manifestations, from simply another type of Christian alongside the Nestorians of China to something like a Buddhist heresy.

Even though many modern scholars discuss Manichaeism as a religion, my own presentation of the Manichaean evidence using the ancient conceptual scheme of heresies should not be too discomfiting for modern readers. A similar but more striking set of problems arise when the heresiological model is applied to another phenomenon not so frequently thought of as Christian—namely, Islam.

John of Damascus and the Heresy of the Ishmaelites

When Khalid ibn al-Walid, an opponent-turned-companion of Muhammad, captured Damascus in 635 C.E., one of the civic administrators who negotiated the surrender of the city was Mansur ibn Sarjun. He retained his position as a civil servant under the new Arab rulers, and his posterity followed in his footsteps. His grandson, also called Mansur, is now better known in the Christian world by the monastic name he would later adopt, John.[29] John of Damascus was one of the first Christian authors to offer a substantial account of Muhammad and his followers, and the context and content of this account are informative for our discussion.[30]

John of Damascus was born at some point in the middle of the seventh century. He was well educated and, like his father and grandfather, worked for many years in the Arab bureaucracy of Damascus. Probably in the first quarter of the eighth century, he retired from public life to become a monk, perhaps to the Mar Saba monastery outside Jerusalem. While there, he wrote, and among the works attributed to him is the tripartite *Pēgē gnōseōs*, the *Fount of Knowledge*. The exact date when the work was composed is unknown, though most scholars attribute it to the monastic phase of John's life. It begins with a discussion of philosophical logic and ends with an exposition of orthodox faith. Between these two sections is a tract with the heading *Peri haireseōn*, or a list of heresies. The list contains many of the usual suspects for Christian heresiologists—Gnostics, Carpocratians, and many others (including the Manichaean heresy). Lists of heresies had been a common feature of Christian literature for centuries. In fact, the first eighty entries on John's list appear to be almost entirely based on a summary of the *Panarion*, the list of heresies par excellence written three centuries earlier by Epiphanius of Salamis (in Cyprus). The last twenty heresies seem to be the work of John himself, but as one recent commentator has noted, "It looks as if a certain amount of ingenuity, as well as genuine historical information, went into the compilation of John's century of heresies."[31]

For our purposes, that distinction between "genuine historical information" and "ingenuity" is not crucial. I am interested in how Christians *perceived* early followers of Muhammad, and for this purpose, John's *Peri haireseōn* is ideal. Its one hundredth and final entry treats Muhammad and his followers:[32]

> Number 100: There is also current the powerful, deceptive worship [*thrēskeia*] of the Ishmaelites, the fore-runner of the Antichrist. It originates from Ishmael, who was born to Abraham from Hagar, and on this account they are called Hagarenes and Ishmaelites. . . . Until the time of Heraclius, they were clearly idolaters; from that time on, a false prophet appeared among them named Mamed, who, having stumbled upon the Old and the New Testament and having, it seems, encountered an Arian monk, established a heresy [*hairesin*] of his own. And then, by deception, he became accepted by the nation as a pious man, and he spread rumors that a piece of writing was brought down to him by god from heaven. Thus, having marked down some laughable ordinances in his book, he handed it down to them as an object of reverence.[33]

The entry then outlines the practices and tenets that "Mamed" propagated. It becomes quite clear that "the laughable ordinances" are the Qur'an.[34] For our discussion, the key points are these: First, John provides a biblical framework for understanding these people.[35] Ethnically, they are the descendants of Abraham through Ishmael (as opposed to Abraham's other son, Isaac, whom both Jews and Christians claimed as an ancestor). Second, like other heresies, this one has a founder and leader, Muhammad, who is said himself to have been the student of an Arian monk (the Christian Arius was branded a heretic in the fourth century because he denied that Jesus was fully divine). The notion that Muhammad had a heretical Christian teacher would persist for centuries among Christians.[36]

In this passage, two different terms describe the followers of Muhammad. The second of these, *hairesis*, or heresy, is to be expected in this context. The first term is *thrēskeia*, the word that in *modern* Greek is often best translated by the English "religion."[37] There is a temptation, then, to suppose that occurrences of the term in ancient Greek should be translated in the same way. As we saw in Chapter 2, however, *thrēskeia*, like the Latin *religio*, has a long history of changing senses, and the language of *thrēskeia* during this period does not imply the modern notion of religion. I am emphasizing the point because this understanding of the followers of Muhammad as a deviant Christian sect, although it is well known among scholars and has been for some time, is often brushed aside as a category error on the part of ancient authors, or the ancient language is said to "mean" something other than what it "says." In the words of one recent critic discussing this passage in John of Damascus, "Surprise has sometimes been registered at Islam being described as a Christian heresy, but that is clearly not what is meant here."[38] But, seeing as this assessment occurs in a list of Christian heresies and explicitly describes Muhammad and his followers as a *hairesis*, such an assertion is difficult to defend. Rather than assuming a misunderstanding on the part of our ancient author or attributing a sloppy use of language to him, I suggest we take seriously John's classification. In doing so, we afford ourselves a glimpse at how ancient and medieval Christian thinkers went about organizing their worlds.

Indeed, John is far from alone among Christian authors in claiming that Muslims constitute simply one of many erroneous Christian sects; the view is actually quite common.[39] For example, the same kind of perspective is espoused in the middle of the ninth century at the western extremity of Muslim expansion. The setting is Córdoba in Spain about 140 years after Muslims conquered the area.[40] After a series of monks invited their own executions by presenting themselves to local Muslim officials and blaspheming the name of Muhammad, the Christian populace of Córdoba disavowed the monks' actions, which had upset what had been a relatively stable living situation established under Muslim rule. Near the end of the 850s, Eulogius of Córdoba, a Christian priest who would himself become a voluntary martyr, composed the *Liber apologeticus martyrum*, which defended the Christian extremists. Eulogius presents Muhammad in this work not as an external threat to Christians, but rather, as Kenneth Wolf has noted, as a heresiarch: "Of all the authors of heresy [*haeresum auctores*] since the Ascension, this unfortunate one, forming a sect of novel superstition [*novae superstitionis sectam*] at the instigation of the devil, diverged most widely from the assembly of the holy church, defaming the authority of the ancient law, spurning the visions of the prophets, trampling the truth of the holy gospel, and detesting the teachings of the apostles."[41] Even for Eulogius in the ninth century, Muhammad and his followers were part of a heresy that had diverged far from the gospel. To consider yet another example of this mode of thought, we can turn to Peter the Venerable, abbot of the monastery at Cluny during the second quarter of the twelfth century. After a visit to Spain in 1142, he commissioned a Latin translation of the Qur'an.[42] Though this act is sometimes portrayed as an early effort at "interreligious dialogue," it is clear that Peter's goal in having the Qur'an translated was to improve his ability to fight what he regarded as deviant Christian doctrine—thus the Latin title of the translated text, *Lex Mahumet pseudoprophete* ("The Law of Muhammad the False Prophet") and the titles of Peter's writings about Muslims: *Summa totius haeresis Saracenorum* ("A Summary of the Entire Heresy of the Saracens") and *Contra sectam sive haeresin Saracenorum* ("Against the Sect or Heresy of the Saracens").[43]

In pointing out this Christian understanding of Muslims as heretics, I do not mean to imply that this model was the *only* way that Christians conceptualized Muslims. Some Christian writings from the Crusades, for example, depict Muslims as idolaters rather than wayward Christians.[44] Peter the Venerable, in fact, reflected on this very issue: "I cannot sufficiently discern whether the Mahumetan error should be called a 'heresy' and its adherents 'heretics,' or if they should be called 'pagans.'"[45] Thus, the heresiological model was not the only way through which Christians interacted with groups that modern scholars identify as "other religions." I turn now to another rather different mode of interaction (which again is problematic for the idea of independent, unified "religions" in antiquity) illustrated in the tale of the Indian prince Ioasaph and his teacher Barlaam.

Saint Siddhārtha: Making the Buddha a Christian

In the year 1580, amid the growing proliferation of the practice of local congregations independently declaring people to be saints, Pope Gregory XIII assigned a commission headed by Cardinal Caesar Baronius the task of producing an official list of Christian saints to try to reassert the Vatican's authority in the matter of canonizing saints.[46] The result of Baronius's labors was the *Sacrum Martyrologium Romanum*, an extended calendar listing the officially sanctioned saints in the order of their feast days. Included in the catalogue for 27 November is the following notice: *Apud Indos Persis finitimos Sanctorum Barlaam & Iosaphat, quoru[m] actus mirandos sanctus Ioanes Damascenus conscripsit* ("In India at the borders of Persia, the Saints Barlaam and Ioasaph, whose wonderful deeds were recorded by Saint John of Damascus").[47]

Although the names Barlaam and Ioasaph (sometimes Latinized to Josaphat) may not be familiar to modern audiences, their story was extremely popular all across the late medieval Christian world, which explains its preservation in manuscripts of a wide variety of versions and languages, including Greek, Latin, Arabic, Georgian (a language spoken in regions on the east coast of the Black Sea), Slavonic, Ethiopic, and Armenian, as well as many of the early modern European vernaculars.[48] Echoes of episodes from *Barlaam and Ioasaph* can be found in many early European literary productions, such as the tale of the caskets in Shakespeare's *Merchant of Venice*. Given this widespread popularity of the story, it is no great wonder that the protagonists were regarded as saints, not only by the Western church but by the Eastern as well.[49]

In brief, the story of Barlaam and Ioasaph is as follows (I omit the various edifying tales and parables):[50] At the same time as the rise of Christian monasticism in Egypt, many monks began to populate India, which had been exposed to Christianity through the work of the apostle Thomas. At this time, a king called Abenner rose to power. He was a non-Christian who was a successful military leader and enjoyed great wealth and a life of luxury. The one thing he deeply desired was a son, and eventually, he did father a son, Ioasaph. After offering the gods appropriate sacrifice as thanks, he consulted astrologers about the boy's future. They said he would be mighty and great, but the most learned astrologer predicted that the boy's greatness would be in a higher kingdom and that he would become a Christian. Abenner had felt threatened by the growing number of Christian monks and had been persecuting them; thus, he was intensely worried by this prophecy and wanted his son never to be exposed to Christians and their teachings. He therefore built a beautiful palace in a secluded city where the boy would be placed in order to avoid ever being exposed to death, disease, old age, poverty, or anything that might upset his happiness. In this atmosphere, Ioasaph grew up into a fine young man of great intelligence.

His learning, however, made him curious about the outside world, and he eventually asked the king to let him leave his sheltered palace. The king reluctantly allowed it. When Ioasaph ventured out, he was shocked upon seeing a blind man, a maimed man, and an old man who was near death. Ioasaph became deeply troubled. At that time, an especially devout Christian monk received a revelation about Ioasaph's state and came in disguise to visit the prince. In a long dialogue, Barlaam imparted to Ioasaph the Christian message and informed him of his father's persecution of the monks in India. Moved by Barlaam's speech, Ioasaph requested to be baptized and to join Barlaam in the monastic life. Barlaam baptized Ioasaph but dissuaded him from leaving because his presence among the monks would put them at risk. Barlaam then departed, and the king learned that Ioasaph had become a Christian. After attempting to persuade Ioasaph to abandon his new Christian convictions, Abenner tried to use beautiful women to tempt the prince back to a life of worldly pleasures. Ioasaph survived this temptation, and his father finally relented and divided his kingdom with Ioasaph. Ioasaph Christianized his portion of the kingdom and was hailed as an ideal ruler. When many people began abandoning Abenner's kingdom for that of his son, Abenner was overcome with grief. He repented and was baptized. The two ruled together, preaching the Christian message and destroying non-Christian temples for four years before Abenner died. At that time, Ioasaph gave up the kingship to his friend Barachias and fled into the wilderness to find Barlaam. After two years of seeking, Ioasaph found Barlaam, and the two lived together as ascetics for many years before first Barlaam and then Ioasaph died. King Barachias learned of their deaths in a vision and had their miraculously undecayed bodies brought back to the city, where the presence of their bodies caused many miracles to occur.

Today, anyone with a basic education in World Religions will recognize this story's many close similarities to the legendary biography of Siddhārtha Gautama, the Buddha. This connection between the stories of Buddha and Ioasaph, however, was not always so obvious. While the story of Barlaam and Josaphat was well known throughout Europe and the Mediterranean world in the late medieval and early modern era, the story of the Buddha was not so widely known in those regions. Clement, a Christian philosopher active in Alexandria during the late second century C.E., mentions that "some among the Indians follow the commands of *Boutta*, who, on account of his extraordinary holiness, they honor as a god."[51] The Buddha appears sporadically in some later Christian authors, but there seems to have been little cognizance of the Buddha among Christians in the West.[52] We have already seen that writings attributed to Mani mention the Buddha as one in a line of prophets, but this knowledge was not prominent among groups of Mani's followers in the West, where Clement's hazy notion of the Buddha as an Indian god prevailed. Indeed, well into the nineteenth century in Europe it was common to speak of the Buddha not as an historical figure, like Jesus or Muhammad, but rather as a god.[53]

It was not until the middle of the nineteenth century, with the acquisition and decipherment of Buddhist manuscripts, that European scholars were able to demonstrate that *Barlaam and Ioasaph* was derived from Buddhist stories.[54] Although *Barlaam and Ioasaph* does not appear to be drawn from any single surviving Indian account of the life of Buddha, it does overlap significantly with some of the episodes and themes of different early Indian versions of the Buddha's life. For example, in the *Buddhacarita*, a poetic work of the first or second century C.E., the main character is a young prince who had grown up insulated from suffering in a palace. When he encounters a decrepit old person, a diseased person, and a corpse, he reacts with horror and sadness, just as in the story of Ioasaph.[55] The similarities even reach the verbal level. In the *Buddhacarita*, the disturbed young prince questions his attendants about the unfortunate individuals he has seen: "Is this law of being peculiar to this man, or is such the end of all creatures?"[56] Ioasaph's questions to his own attendants are a clear echo: "Is this fate common to all men? . . . And does this fate befall all human beings?"[57] In addition to these points of similarity with the details and shape of the plots of the lives of the Buddha, *Barlaam and Ioasaph* also shares recurring themes with these works. Ioasaph is described as follows: "He made a parade of his detestation and hate for the transitory world, exclaiming: 'Abominable in my sight are the pleasures of this earth!' And he spurned all the ways of the world and its devotees, until his reputation was spread in all places."[58] The sentiment mirrors the typically Buddhist declaration in the *Buddhacarita*: "By teaching everything to be impermanent and without self and by denying the slightest happiness in the spheres of existence, He raised aloft the banner of His fame and overturned the lofty pillars of pride."[59] Other such similarities with *Barlaam and Ioasaph* can be found in the fourth-century C.E. *Lalitavistara* and the *Mahavastu*, two other legendary lives of the Buddha.[60]

As these sorts of texts were published and translated, it became clear that the Christian tale of Ioasaph was a reworked version of the life of the Buddha.[61] This recognition, and its perceived implications in the nineteenth century, is nowhere more eloquently expressed than in the words of a lecture given in 1870 by Max Müller, a figure many regard as a founder of the modern academic field of religious studies:

St. Josaphat is the Buddha of the Buddhist canon. It follows that Buddha has become a Saint in the Roman Church; it follows that, though under a different name, . . . the founder of a religion which, whatever we may think of its dogma, is, in the purity of its morals, nearer to Christianity than any other religion, and which counts even now, after an existence of 2400 years, 455,000,000 of believers, has received the highest honours that the Christian Church can bestow. And whatever we may think of the sanctity of its saints, let those who doubt the right of Buddha to a place among them read the story of his life as it is told in the Buddhist canon. If he lived the life which is there described, few saints have better claim to the title than Buddha; and no one either in the Greek or Roman Church need be ashamed of having paid to Buddha's memory the honour that was intended for St. Josaphat, the prince, the hermit, and the saint. History, here as elsewhere, is stranger than fiction; and a kind of fairy, whom men call Chance, has here, as elsewhere, remedied the ingratitude and injustice of the world.[62]

For Müller, and indeed for many scholars of religion after him, the lesson of the Buddha's status as a Christian saint is a confirmation of the commensurability of all religions—that is, all religions of a specific type.[63] The appeal of the Buddha for many Europeans of Müller's generation was in a perceived closeness to Protestantism; indeed, Buddhism was *the* Indian Protestantism. (Müller himself wrote that the Buddha "is the offspring of India in mind and soul. His doctrine, by the very antagonism in which it stands to the old system of Brahmanism, shows that it could not have sprung up in any country except India. The ancient history of Brahmanism leads on to Buddhism, with the same necessity with which mediaeval Romanism led to Protestantism."[64] In any event, I wish to take away a rather different lesson from the story of this complex of texts: they illustrate another instance of premodern people handling what modern people would designate as "another religion" in a way that does not at all invoke the idea of religion. A brief discussion of what we can know of the transmission history of the text will clarify this point.

The combined work of specialists of many languages has established many of the key relationships among the different manuscript versions of *Barlaam and Ioasaph*.[65] Until the twentieth century, the preface to the Greek version seemed to provide a satisfactory account of the genesis of the tale: "An edifying story from . . . the land of the Indians, thence brought to the Holy City, by John the Monk (an honourable man and a virtuous, of the monastery of Saint Sabas); wherein are the lives of the famous and blessed Barlaam and Ioasaph." The "John" of the monastery at Mar Saba was assumed to be none other than John of Damascus. More recently, however, study of the manuscripts in other languages has undermined confidence in the accuracy of the Greek preface and the extrapolation that its "John" is John of Damascus.

It is clear that the manuscripts in the European vernaculars derive from the Latin version. A manuscript of the Latin version carries both a prologue and an epilogue from which we learn that the Latin text was translated in 1048 or 1049 from a Greek version, which was itself translated from a Georgian version by Euthymius the Georgian in the late tenth or early eleventh century. This point would appear to be confirmed by two Greek manuscripts of *Barlaam and Ioasaph* that also describe Euthymius as the translator. Syntactical features of the Georgian version demonstrate that it was derived from an Arabic version that circulated under the title *Kitab Bilawhar wa-Yudasaf*.[66] This Arabic version, first translated perhaps in the early ninth century, is presumed to be derived from one of the Sanskrit accounts of the life of the Buddha, perhaps by way of a Middle Persian translation. Such a course of transmission helps to explain little philological details, such as the origins of the name Ioasaph. In Sanskrit, the "pre-Enlightenment" Buddha is called Bodhisattva. This name becomes in Arabic *Bodhasaf*, but when the Arabic letters ﻱ (*y*) and ﺏ (*b*) occur at the beginnings of words, they differ only by one sublinear dot. So, a misreading of the Arabic most likely led to the Georgian *Iodasaph*, and thus *Ioasaph* in the Greek and *Josaphat* in the Latin.

While this sequence seems reasonably clear, the exact point (or points) at which the story of the Buddha transformed into the story of the "Christian" saint Ioasaph remains something of a puzzle. It is generally observed that the Georgian versions (a long recension and a short recension) are the earliest clearly Christian incarnations of the story. The Arabic *Kitab Bilawhar wa-Yudasaf*, upon which the Georgian versions are based, lacks definitively Christian characteristics.[67] The discovery among the Turfan finds of what appear to be fragments of a copy of *Barlaam and Ioasaph* along with both identifiably Manichaean literature and fragments of Aśvaghoṣa's *Buddhacarita* suggested to many scholars that Manichaeans were responsible for transplanting the story from India to the Western world.[68] On this proposal, Manichaeans would have transformed the Indian story at an early stage in central Asia, and then it would have passed through a Middle Persian phase en route to the Arabic version, which, according to one prominent scholar, was still essentially Manichaean despite "superficial islamicisation."[69] The Georgian version would then be a reworking of the story from a more orthodox Christian standpoint. The facts that Mani's followers, and perhaps even Mani himself, interacted with Buddhists and that the asceticism advocated in *Barlaam and Ioasaph* has affinities with Manichaean practices make this hypothesis quite attractive. Recently, however, another scholar has argued that the key to the transformation of the story is to be found not with the Manichaeans, but in the Arabic versions of the story, at least one of which shows the work of a Muslim redactor.[70] According to this theory, the alleged Manichaean features of the *Kitab Bilawhar wa-Yudasaf* are more closely related to Sufi asceticism and piety, and thus "when the Buddha became a Christian saint, it was only after he had first been reborn as a Muslim mystic."[71]

Absent new evidence (such as the discovery of the hypothesized Middle Persian version of the story, which could perhaps confirm or disconfirm the hypothesis of an early Manichaean role in transmission), this disagreement will likely remain unsettled. Fortunately, for my purposes, this dispute need not be resolved. On either reckoning, we have here a scenario in which the story of the Buddha was not seen as part of a story of a separate religion (or *religio*, or *dēn*, or *dīn*); rather, a late medieval Christian, and an earlier Manichaean Christian or a Muslim, simply absorbed the story of the Buddha and made it their own. This method of appropriation is clearly quite different from the heresiological approach to managing difference that I discussed earlier in this chapter, but it represents another way that premodern peoples operated outside the modern framework of religions.

Conclusion

Groups that modern scholars discuss as different "ancient religions" did not discuss one another in that way. Instead, premodern people used other strategies for articulating difference. For some Manichaeans, "orthodox" Christians were simply ill-informed Manichaeans in need of better teaching. For many (indeed most) Catholic writers in the medieval period, the followers of Muhammad were heretical Christians, but in some circumstances, they could be classified as idolatrous pagans. Unless one resorted to singling out individual manuscripts, one would be hard-pressed to assign a particular "religion" to the story of Ioasaph. Discussing materials like these in terms of different "religions" creates boundaries that are alien to the boundaries that ancient authors constructed. It is true that by the late medieval period, many Catholic Christian authors did classify the populations of the world using a four-part division: proper Christians, Jews, Mohammedans, and pagans. In this framework, the latter three were not people of different religions, but rather were deeply flawed Christians. What I explore in the following chapter is how and why it has become so easy and natural for us to think of those groups as religions.

five

RENAISSANCE, REFORMATION, AND RELIGION IN THE SIXTEENTH AND SEVENTEENTH CENTURIES

Introduction

We have seen that religion was not a concept native to the ancient world and that the things that modern people group under the heading of "religion" were not so grouped by premodern peoples. The ancient world was not divided into different "religions," conceived of as voluntary associations of people with similar "religious experiences." I now provide an account of the development of this popular notion of religion. If religion has not simply "just been there" since antiquity, how did this particular way of conceiving of the world, the manner of carving the world into "religious" and "not-religious," come to be so dominant?

In this chapter and the next, I present the results of some disparate strands of scholarship that have been converging toward what I view as a useful understanding of the emergence of the religious/secular divide. I begin by observing that several broad developments took place simultaneously in early modern Europe. One was the fragmentation of Christendom resulting from the various reform movements in the wake of Martin Luther. Although Christians had never been a wholly united group, the Christian factions breaking away from the Catholic Church in the centuries following Luther had material support that allowed them to have a much greater effect on the intellectual landscape than had the dissidents who preceded them. Indeed, the volatile political scene in Europe during the sixteenth and seventeenth centuries created a space for new ways of thinking about "different" groups. Another major development was Europeans' struggle to grapple with increasing amounts of information, primarily from the "New World" but also from the "rediscovery" of antiquity, that called into question many biblical frameworks for understanding the world. The combined effect of these two phenomena helped to set the stage for conceiving of the world's population as being divided into different religions, that is, different systems of privately held beliefs about how individuals attain salvation.[1] Interpreting the newly discovered peoples around the world in light of Christian sectarian strife in Europe led to what Peter Harrison has aptly described as "the projection of Christian disunity onto the world." The idea that the different religions stand in tension, offering competing ways to salvation, "can be attributed to the grammar of the term 'religions'" that developed in the eighteenth and nineteenth centuries.[2]

I begin by looking at how the idea of *vera religio* among certain Italian Neo-Platonists and so-called English deists developed, more or less by accident, into the "science" of comparative religion. I then turn to the so-called Wars of Religion in the sixteenth and seventeenth centuries as a context for discussing works of authors usually regarded as political theorists (Jean Bodin and John Locke), whose writings during and after the birth of the modern nation-state are representative of a decisive change that took place in the conceptualization of religion. My treatment of material in this chapter is again highly selective, and once again I acknowledge that sources other than the ones I explore could produce a different, although not incompatible, narrative.[3]

Christiana religio *from the Italian Neo-Platonists to the English Deists*

In the *Retractationes*, written nearly forty years after *De vera religione*, Augustine attempted to clarify a sentence he had written in the earlier work. He had made a reference to *christiana religio* "in our times" (*nostris temporibus*), and he felt that he needed to clear up a possible misunderstanding: "I was speaking of the name, here, and not of the thing so named. For what is now called the *christiana religio* existed of old and was never absent from the beginning of the human race until Christ came in the flesh. Then *vera religio* which already existed began to be called *christiana*. . . . When I said, 'This is the *christiana religio* in our times,' I did not mean that it had not existed in former times, but that it received that name later."[4] This formulation can be read in light of the argument of Eusebius that was treated in Chapter 3. Since Christian worship, genuine and proper worship of the one God, had always existed, all other worship practices, both ancient and contemporary, were divergences from this original *vera religio*, or genuine worship.

A corollary of this view is the observation that non-Christian thought, even if vastly deficient, might be expected to show at least some qualities of this *vera religio*. It is not so surprising, then, to find that educated Christians like Lactantius discovered elements of Christian doctrine and prophecies about Christ even in "pagan" authors, such as Hermes Trismegistus, who were thought to be exceedingly ancient.[5] For Lactantius, such testimonies served an apologetic purpose; even these ancient "pagan" authors testified to the revelation of Christ and the Trinity, an argument for the truth of Christian teaching from universal agreement (*consensus gentium*). In the ninth century, Photius described (not without some disapproval) a massive work written by an anonymous author in Constantinople in the seventh or eighth century who compiled Greek, Persian, Thracian, Egyptian, Babylonian, Chaldean, and Roman texts and attempted to show that they "agree with [*sumpheromenas*] the immaculate, excellent, and divine *thrēskeia* of the Christians."[6] This practice of finding harmony between Christianity and "pagan" wisdom (particularly Platonic thought) hit its apex among the group of Italians who revived the study of Plato during the fifteenth and sixteenth centuries.[7] They called this notion of Christian wisdom in ancient "pagan" authors the Ancient Theology (*prisca theologia*) or the Ancient Philosophy.[8] The employment of the Ancient Theology by these Renaissance Neo-Platonists and their intellectual heirs provides an important background for the subsequent development of religion into the generic category familiar to us today.

The first figure I examine in this regard is the scholar Marsilio Ficino, who, among other notable achievements, provided the modern world with its first full Latin translation of Plato's dialogues. He also produced a multivolume *Theologia Platonica* that sought to harmonize

Christian and Platonic thought.[9] In 1463, Ficino's patron, Cosimo de' Medici, interrupted Ficino's project of translating Plato and set Ficino at the task of immediately translating a manuscript that he had recently acquired containing fourteen of the documents now known as the *Corpus Hermeticum*.[10] Ficino obliged and completed the translation quickly, although it was not published until 1471.[11] The work was immensely popular; sixteen editions appeared before the close of the sixteenth century.[12] In his preface to the translation, Ficino outlined how these texts preserved knowledge of ancient truths parallel to the revelation given to Moses and the prophets. Hermes Trismegistus was a link in a chain that extended Plato's wisdom backwards in time. Hermes "is named the first author of theology" (*primus igitur theologiae appellatus est auctor*), and Ficino asserted that "there is one Ancient Theology, in all respects consistent . . . taking up its origin in Mercury and being absolutely perfected in divine Plato" (*itaque una priscae theologie undique sibi consona secta . . . exordia sumens a Mercurio a Divo Platone penitus absoluta*).[13] Ficino's mature view would trace this heritage from Plato, back through Pythagoras, Aglaophemus, Orpheus, Hermes Trismegistus, and ultimately to Zoroaster.[14] This Ancient Theology suggested that genuine worship had a unified beginning and found many imperfect expressions through the ages until the more perfect revelation of Christianity appeared on the scene.

Ficino became a priest in 1473, and in 1476 he published *De christiana religione*, which reflected on the plurality and unity of *religio*. There, Ficino wrote that although "divine Providence does not permit any region of the world at any time to be entirely without religion [*prorsus religionis expertem*]," it always allows "different rites of worship to be observed [*ritus adorationis varios observari*]."[15] At first glance, Ficino's model appears quite close to the modern framework of religion as a genus with the individual religions as species. Yet, Ficino's method of classification possesses some features that place considerable distance between it and the modern framework. In addition to the all-encompassing nature of *religio* (there is no "secular" for Ficino), Ficino's most celebrated modern interpreter, Paul Oskar Kristeller, has emphasized the importance of recognizing that for Ficino, "every genus possesses a supreme element on which the quality of all the other elements depends."[16] Therefore, just because members of a class share some common characteristics, this does not mean that all members of a class are of equal value. Kristeller continues, "For Ficino, on the contrary, the members of a genus, like all existing things, for that matter, constitute a continuous and well-defined hierarchy."[17] It is in this context that we should understand the quotation from Ficino mentioned in Chapter 2 ("All *religio* has something good in it; provided that it is directed towards God, the creator of all things, it is sincere, Christian *religio*").[18] In this schema, Christianity is not simply one item in a class, on par with the other examples of *religio*. Rather, it is the pinnacle of what *religio* can and should be. Nevertheless, in Ficino's scheme, every form of worship, "however primitive, is related, though unconsciously, to the one, true God."[19] This notion of Christian worship differs significantly from Augustine's dichotomy of *vera religio* as opposed to *religio deorum*.

Ficino died quietly at the villa at Careggi outside Florence in 1499. A century later, another Neo-Platonist Christian would meet a less pleasant end—Giordano Bruno was burned at the stake as a heretic in the Campo dei Fiori in Rome in 1600. Probably born in 1548 in the Italian town of Nola, Bruno entered a Dominican monastery in Naples in 1565. Over a period of eleven years he seems to have become extremely well read, absorbing a great deal of classical and contemporary literature that was available to him in Naples. In 1576, he was forced to flee the monastery because of accusations of heterodoxy. For the next sixteen years, he lived an extraordinary life, traveling widely across Europe and moving in the intellectual circles of Geneva, Paris, Oxford, London, Wittenberg, and Prague before finally being imprisoned and executed.[20] The *prisca theologia* played a very important role in Bruno's thought, but he made significant departures from the ways Ficino and his other predecessors used that notion.[21] For Bruno, the ancient Hermetic (or, perhaps more properly in Bruno's case, Pythagorean) wisdom was *the* true *religio*, from which even Christianity was derivative.[22] In *The Ash*

Wednesday Supper, a set of dialogues written in 1583 during Bruno's stay in London, the character Theophilo sets forth the views of "the Nolan," understood by most interpreters as a mouthpiece for Bruno's own views. Near the end of the first dialogue, Theophilo states in no uncertain terms the superiority in all aspects of life of those who adhere to the ancient ways:

> And, in conclusion, are we, who make a beginning of the renewal of the ancient philosophy, in the morning which makes an end to the night, or are we rather in the evening which ends the day? And certainly this is not difficult to decide, even if we judge hastily by the fruits of the two different kinds of contemplation. Now let us see the difference between the former [the advocates of the Ancient Theology] and the latter [Aristotelian Christians]. The former are moderate in life, expert in medicine, judicious in contemplation, unique in divination, miraculous in magic, wary of superstition, law-abiding, irreproachable in morality, godlike in theology, and heroic in every way. All this is shown by the length of their lives, their healthier bodies, their most lofty inventions, the fulfillment of their prophecies, the substances transformed by their works, the peaceful deportment of their people, their inviolable sacraments, the great justice of their actions, the familiarity of good and protecting spirits, and the vestiges, which still remain, of their amazing prowess. I leave to the judgment of anyone with good sense the consideration of the fruits of the latter.[23]

Bruno is like Ficino in seeing *religio* as a class with many members, but Bruno becomes especially interesting because he was able, while working from within Christian tradition, to create an intellectual space where Christianity is simply one of many *religiones*, and not even necessarily the best one.[24]

What was troubling about Christianity, especially Protestant groups, was their multiplicity and mutual bickering. In another of Bruno's dialogues written during his time in London, one of the characters expresses this sentiment: "For among ten thousand of such Teachers, there is not to be found one, who has not form'd to himself a Catechism, ready to be publish'd to the World, if not publish'd already; approving no other Institution but his own, finding in all others something to be condemn'd, disapprov'd, or doubted of: besides that the greater part of them disagree with themselves, blotting out to day what they had wrote yesterday."[25] This complaint would echo through the seventeenth century. Rival claims to the "true religion" caused a number of difficulties. Peter Harrison writes: "Following the Reformation, the fragmentation of Christendom led to a change from an institutionally based understanding of exclusive salvation to a propositionally based understanding. Formerly it had been 'no salvation outside the Church.' Now, it had become 'no salvation without the profession of the "true religion."' But which religion was the true religion? The proliferation of Protestant sects . . . had made the question exceedingly complex, for there were not simply two opposing Churches, but many."[26] This variety of true religions and the disagreement it created is evinced in the proliferation of polemical literature. As Bruno was well aware, the number of short tracts being published exploded, all of them written by different Christians and all of them spelling out how their own particular set of propositions led to salvation. These maps to Christian salvation often took on a question-and-answer format, such as the anonymous pamphlet *A Booke of Christian Questions and Answeres. Wherein are set foorthe the chiefe pointes of Christian Religion. A woorke right necessarie and profitable, for all such as shall have to deale with the captious quarellinges of the wrangling adversaries of Gods truth* (1578). Quite similar is Thomas Gouge's frequently reprinted *The Principles of Christian Religion, Explained to the Capacity of the Meanest* (1668).[27] These works begin with questions like "Who is the maker of all things?" and "How many persons are in the god-head?" The proper answers to these questions are necessary components to the answers of the later, more pressing question of "How is one saved?" Thus Christianity was distilled to a set of ideas, and salvation was achieved by internal, private, mental assent to this (single, correct, true) set of ideas.[28]

Since salvation was at stake, it is not surprising that strong polemic was a part of these exchanges. An especially important type of polemic was "Pagano-papism." The practice of drawing parallels between pagan and Catholic practices goes back at least to Luther, but the concept is perhaps best summarized in this (abbreviated!) title of a book by Oliver Omerod originally published in 1606: *The Picture of a Papist: Or, A relation of the damnable heresies, detestable qualities, and diabolicall practises of sundry hereticks in former ages, and of the papists in this age: Where in is plainly shewed, that there is scarse any heresie which the auncient Church knew, and withal condemned to the pit of hell, which the Romish Church hath not raked up againe, and propounded to the world with new varnish and fresh colours . . . Whereunto is annexed a certain treatise, intituled Pagano-papismus: wherein is prooved by irrefragable demonstrations, that papisme is flat paganisme: and that the papists doe resemble the very pagans, in above sevenscore severall things.*[29] The book contains exactly what one might expect: a series of supposed parallels between Catholic and ancient pagan practices. In a set of dialogues, such activities as prayer before a cross, the veneration of the saints, and reliance upon papal authority and priests are compared not only to pagan practices, but also to various Christian heresies and the practices of "Rabbinicall Jewes" and "Turkes." This method of polemic was not simply a tool for Protestants to use against Catholics; such charges also appeared in disputes among different groups of Protestants.[30] John Edwards, author of a book titled *The Doctrines Controverted Between Papists and Protestants Particularly and Distinctly Consider'd: And Those which are held by the Former Confuted* (1724), also attacked Protestant groups. In another book about the theology of the Socinians (a group of Christians who denied the divinity of Jesus), Edwards had the following to say: "It is patch'd up of several different Opinions fetch'd from sundry quarters, it is a Fardle of mix'd and disagreeing Notions, it is a Nest of Heterodoxies, a Galimafrey of Old and New Errors, a Medley of Heresies taken from *Ebion* and *Cerinthus*, the *Sabellians, Samosatenians, Arians, Photinians, Macedonians*, who corrupted the doctrine of the *Holy Trinity*. They joyn with *Jews, Pagans* and *Mahometans* in disowning and denying this Great Mystery of Religion."[31] This kind of polemic itself contributed to the formation of distinct religions. By associating these different groups with one another, this type of attack had a double effect; it not only painted the Socinians as not-quite-Christian heretics, it simultaneously constructed "Jews" and "Mahometans" as false, perverted Christians.

Such prolific argumentation led some English thinkers to deal with these disputes about Christian truth by trying to determine the lowest common denominator of all the creeds, the things about the divine upon which everyone agreed. To explore this point, I return to the Neo-Platonic milieu but this time in an English setting, with Edward Lord Herbert of Cherbury.[32] Herbert is perhaps best known as "the Father of Deism," but he did not receive this reputation until well after his death.[33] During his lifetime, he had a respectable military and diplomatic career (even if he did frequently "indulge his favourite pastime of issuing challenges to duels").[34] His philosophical works were read with approval by such notable contemporaries as René Descartes and Hugo Grotius.[35] While it is Herbert's later work on "pagan religion" that is most relevant here, this piece is best understood in light of the opinions on religion he expressed in *De Veritate, prout distinguitur a Revelatione, a Verisimili, a Possibili, et a Falso*, which was published in 1624.[36] *De Veritate* gained Herbert a degree of notoriety in intellectual circles and set the stage for his later work. In *De Veritate*, Herbert sets out his theory of truth and knowledge. He argues that all normal people naturally have "Common Notions" (a concept drawn from the Stoic notion of *koinai ennoiai*), which form the basis for determining Truth. What determined Truth was the *consensus gentium*, the presence of a notion in all sane people.[37] The Common Notions are not always (or even usually) immediately visible to people; rather, they often have to be uncovered because the accretion of traditions has obscured these natural, universal features of humanity. He claims that religion, since it is universal, is such a Common Notion.[38] At the conclusion of the work, he dedicates a section to "Common Notions Concerning Religion."[39] He prefaced his list of five Common Notions of religion with the claim that "the system of Notions, so far at least as it concerns theology, has been clearly accepted at all times by every normal person, and does not require any further justification."[40] Yet, as Herbert realized, the religions of the heathen could at times appear to bear little resemblance to "normal" religion. Thus his claim did indeed require further proof, and this proof formed the centerpiece for *De religione gentilium*, which examined the diversity and origins of ancient "pagan" religions in order to substantiate the universality of his Common Notions of religion. These five Common Notions, described as "five undeniable Propositions" in *De religione gentilium*, are:

1. That there is one Supreme God.
2. That he ought to be worshipped.
3. That Vertue and Piety are the chief Parts of Divine Worship.
4. That we ought to be sorry for our Sins, and repent of them.
5. That Divine Goodness doth dispense Rewards and Punishments both in this Life, and after it.[41]

Herbert arrived at these principles by ignoring any offensive rites and rituals of "pagans" because such things were merely "the Invention of the Priests," who had corrupted an older, purer form of the religions.[42] For example, Herbert searched through ancient Greek and Roman texts about worshippers of the sun (as well as some literature about the pagans of the New World) and determined that the more intelligent of them worshipped not the sun itself, but what it represented: "The Sun was only a kind of sensible Representation of the Supreme God under which consideration only the most Wise among the Heathens worshipped him, knowing very well that GOD himself could not be discerned in any one thing."[43] Herbert made similarly generous assumptions about worshippers of the planets, stars, and elements, showing along the way that there is universal agreement on his five Common Notions. The pagans appear foolish only because of their reliance upon priests:

> I must lay this down for an *Establisht Truth*, That the *Religion* of the Antient *Heathens* was not so absurd and stupid as is generally imagin'd. . . . When the *Heathens* had receiv'd the Notion of the Attributes of the *Supream GOD* mention'd before, there sprung up a Race of *Crafty Priests*, who not thinking it sufficient that there should be just one GOD in all this *Universe*, judg'd it would conduce much

more to their *Interest*, to join and associate some others to this *Supream Deity.* . . . Their *Design* of Introducing other *Gods*, drove farther . . . They also expected to reap more Profit, and have larger Stipends from the various *Rites, Ceremonies,* and Sacred *Mysteries* which they contriv'd and divulg'd.[44]

Surveys of the beliefs of various peoples were nothing new. What is interesting is that Herbert provided such a sympathetic account of the religions. Both his list of Common Notions and his argumentation are noteworthy. What stands out about the list (and what earned Herbert the posthumous title Father of Deism) is that none of his Common Notions is specifically Christian.[45] For Herbert, Christianity is, in theory but certainly not in practice, no longer the measuring stick by which all other members of the genus "religion" are measured. Christianity is just another form of the original religion. Some Protestant Christian biases, however, are inherent in Herbert's comparative methodology. He was interested in showing that all religions are at a basic level good religions, but his criteria for what constitutes "good" and what constitutes "religion" are very much indebted to the Christianity of his day. To take but one example, his disdain for priesthood seems to owe a large debt to the kind of Protestant anti-Catholic polemics outlined above. Nevertheless, Herbert's explanation of the variety of distasteful worship practices by reference to priestly interference can be viewed as paving the way for the eighteenth-century "natural histories of religion," such as that of David Hume.[46] As a means of defending the universality of the five Common Notions of religion, Herbert sets the stage for later reductive discussions of the origins of religion, projects of which he would almost certainly not have approved. It is for this reason that I describe this shift as an "accidental" transformation of the *prisca theologia* into comparative religion.[47]

Before leaving Herbert, I call attention to his strict focus on ideas (the Common Notions are just that—notions). By shearing away all the practices of ancient people in his discussions of what was essential and original in these religions, Herbert contributed to the growing sense that religion was a matter of beliefs *apart from* "various

Rites, Ceremonies, and Sacred Mysteries." Religion was for Herbert a mental phenomenon.[48] This view of religion as a set of beliefs that could be either true or false would become standard in the next century.

Later writers more firmly identified with the label "deist" were even bolder in their placements of "other" religions on an equal standing with Christianity. The prolific Irish author and noted heretic John Toland is a case in point.[49] He wrote a tract in favor of Jewish integration and also defended followers of Muhammad.[50] Driven by an interest in the formation of the Christian canon, he studied Christian apocryphal writings, and while in Amsterdam in 1709, he discovered a manuscript of the Gospel of Barnabas, which he believed to be an ancient composition. This lengthy gospel, purporting to be the story of Jesus told by the apostle Barnabas, contains a heavy element of Islamic ideas, such as predictions of the coming of Muhammad. Toland later published a description of the manuscript as a part of a defense of the Nazarenes, "the Primitive Christians most properly so call'd."[51] Partially on the basis of analogy of the relationship of Jews to the true Christianity and partially on the basis of what he believed to be the ancient harmony between the teachings of Jesus and those of Muhammad he had uncovered in the Gospel of Barnabas, Toland asserted that Muslims were indeed "a sort of Christians, and not the worst sort neither, tho farr from being the best."[52] Toland's views did not find a large following, but the incipient pluralism that characterized his work makes him interesting.

With these deist authors, we find the concept of religion being used in a way that is beginning to approach its current use. Yet, differences are still apparent. The idea of a Muslim Christian, for example, would seem to be a contradiction in terms in the current World Religion paradigm.[53] And there is still another crucial dimension to this story that involves the sharp differentiation of religion from the public sphere in the context of the development of the nation-state. To flesh out more fully these developing characteristics of religion and the religions, it is necessary to examine some of the political aspects of the Reformation.

The Formation of the State and the Formation of Religion

My discussion thus far may have given the impression that the development of the notion of religion is one of disembodied ideas taking shape in the serene venue of intellectual discussions. The sixteenth and seventeenth centuries in Europe, however, were anything but stable and serene. It is during this period that we witness the Wars of Religion and the tumultuous beginnings of the modern system of nation-states.[54] Rather than offering a detailed examination of this complex phenomenon, I instead focus on the writings of two figures, Jean Bodin and John Locke, who can be understood as heirs to the debates about *vera religio* that I have just sketched. Selections from their works shed light upon another crucial dimension of the modern notion of religion that developed during this era—the idea that the focus of a religion is the salvation of an individual soul. Religion becomes a much more private affair. In Locke and Bodin, we can begin to see how the development of the nation-state gave rise to religious pluralism as a means of subduing citizens.

First, however, a brief word of clarification on the Reformation will be helpful. It is not simply the case that the Reformation produced variety where there had been unity. Christendom of the late medieval and early modern periods included an extremely diverse set of phenomena.[55] What makes the reformers of the early sixteenth century different is that they were able to garner enough material support so that when doctrinal conflicts (or economic conflicts or legal conflicts) arose, they could resist repression by Catholic authorities.[56] The effects of the reformers' protests thus went beyond the realm of what we might call "religious ideas." When Luther began calling for local rulers to resist papal authority, they listened to him; Frederick the Wise of Saxony provided Luther sanctuary from ecclesiastical authorities when he was excommunicated, and within fifteen years the list of princes and cities supporting Luther and his reforms was substantial.[57] The changes that figures such as Luther, John Calvin, and Ulrich Zwingli brought about in various church policies are important, but what interests me here are the changes

97

wrought in European governance. M. J. Tooley has nicely summed up this shift:

> The break-up of the medieval Church destroyed the framework of the older forms of political thinking. So long as there was a universally recognized Church, having authority, it was possible to conceive of a realizable order in Christendom in terms of obligation to the Church. To require princes to act as the sword of the Church, or subjects to renounce their allegiance to an excommunicate ruler, might be unpalatable, but were not impracticable commands. But when princes and subjects alike had first to make a decision as to what was the Church they recognized, such commandments could only, and did, lead to confusion.[58]

"Confusion" is an appropriate term. Although the ensuing Wars of Religion are generally narrated as a tale of Protestants versus Catholics, the disputes and alliances were considerably more complex. Catholic princes actively resisted papal authority, and Protestant leaders did not hesitate to form alliances with Catholics.[59] Many nobles switched confessional allegiances during the course of the wars.[60] It thus seems that confessional loyalties often were of secondary importance. These observations have led William T. Cavanaugh to conclude that calling "these conflicts 'Wars of Religion' is an anachronism, for what was at issue in these wars was the very creation of religion as a set of privately held beliefs without direct political relevance."[61]

Jean Bodin's Ideal and Pragmatic States

This point is illustrated most clearly in the writings of Jean Bodin, who emerged from the intellectual tradition of the Renaissance Neo-Platonists and lived in the midst of the French wars of the sixteenth century.[62] His political affiliations shifted over the years, but he was most associated with the *politiques*, a group that claimed that the role of a government was the maintenance of peace rather than the enforcement of a particular creed.[63] In his *Six Books of the Commonwealth*, Bodin provided practical instructions for the ideal, successful government.[64] He warned about the threats of divisiveness, especially when such daungerous seditions and factions be not grounded upon matters directly touching [one's] estate, but otherwise, as it hath happened almost in all Europe within this fifty yeares, in the warres made for matters of religion: for we have seen the kingdome of Sweden, of Scotland, of Denmarke, of England, the Cantons of the Swissers, yea and the Germaine empire also, to have changed their religion, the estate of every of these monarchies and commonweales yet standing entire and whole: howbeit that the truth is, that it was not done, but with great violence, and much bloodshed in many places.[65]

When disputes arise regarding the church, the result is violence. And yet, Bodin asserted, religion could be useful to the magistrate, given the proper circumstances:

Seeing that not onely all wise law-givers and Philosophers, but even the very Atheists themselves also . . . are of accord, That there is nothing which doth more uphold and maintaine the estates and Commonweals than religion: and that it is the principall foundation of the power and strength of monarchies and Seignories: as also for the execution of justice, for the obedience of the subjects, the reverence of the magistrates, for the feare of doing evill, and for the mutual love and amitie of every one towards other, it is by most strait and severe lawes to be provided, that so sacred a thing as is religion be not by childish and sophisticall disputations (and especially by such as are publickely had) made contemptible.[66]

Religion, if it is not a bone of contention, can work to stabilize a state. Total agreement about religion would be ideal, and discourse about religion is thus to be closely regulated to avoid disputations. If such disputes should occur, they certainly should not be in public, in order to prevent any larger disturbance from happening. Bodin's picture, however, is not as draconian as it might first appear. In fact, in the real world, where complete agreement about religion is not possible, the ruler who most embodies the model stance toward religion is "the great emperour of the Turkes," who, "with as great devotion as any prince in the world honor[s] and observe[s] the religion by him received from his ancestours, and yet destesteth hee not the straunge religions of others; but to the contrarie permitteth every man to live according to his conscience: yea and that more is, neere unto his pallace at Pera, suffereth four divers religions, *viz.* That of the Jewes, that of the Christians, that of the Grecians, and that of the Mahometanes."[67]

When uniformity of religion is impossible to achieve, the best means for subjugating a people and maintaining a stable state is to allow distinct groups to live according to their own beliefs. This point is also the conclusion of another of Bodin's works, the *Colloquium of the Seven about Secrets of the Sublime.*[68] Set in Venice, the work recounts a discussion among seven characters—a Catholic (the host), a Calvinist, a Lutheran, a Muslim, a Jew, a philosophic naturalist, and a skeptic. Their dialogue, which touches on various philosophical and practical matters, concludes when they turn to the question of *vera religio.* The Jewish speaker argues that the schisms among Muslims, Christians, and Jews could be avoided if everyone were "to embrace that most simple and most ancient and at the same time the most true religion of nature, instilled by immortal God in the minds of each man from which there was no division."[69] The discussion that follows leaves the impression that such a return to the *vera religio* is not possible in the modern day. Their talk comes to a close with the Lutheran stating that "we are unable to command religion because no one can be forced to believe against his will."[70] The narrator notes that "everyone approved of these things," but "afterwards, they held no other conversation about religions."[71] Discussion about different creeds was to be a matter of the private sphere. In such a situation, multiple different creedal affiliations could exist peacefully under a single, dominating state government.

This notion of pluralism and tolerance was novel.[72] As Ingrid Creppell notes in her recent study of the emergence of tolerance in Europe, for "toleration to be the prudent policy, people have to be able to imagine themselves as functioning in a political sphere in which they refrain from asserting religious cohesion. The creation of this prudential world required strategies of the self that were new."[73] One of these new strategies was a highly personalized notion of religion that focused on the salvation of the individual soul. It is here that the theoretical differentiation of something called "religion" from the civic arena becomes quite clear.

Restraining Religion in John Locke's Letter Concerning Toleration

A century after Bodin, the writings of John Locke illustrate the full emergence of this individualized religious self.[74] Trained in medicine at Oxford, Locke became a prominent voice in the domestic and international affairs of British government during the second half of the seventeenth century. His chief patron from the 1660s through the early 1680s was Lord Ashley, First Earl of Shaftesbury, a highly influential politician who had been granted joint proprietorship of the American province of Carolina. Locke himself held the office of secretary of the Board of Trade and Plantations from 1673 to 1675 and the office of commissioner of the Board of Trade from 1696 to 1700.[75] Like Bodin, Locke was not a stranger to Neo-Platonic speculation about "religion" (Locke had very likely read the early work of John Toland and in fact had met him in 1693).[76] While in exile in Holland in the late 1680s, Locke composed his *Letter Concerning Toleration*, which attempted to provide reasonable arguments for allowing a variety of worship practices in a single state.[77] To do so, he made a crucial distinction: "I esteem it above all things necessary to distinguish exactly the Business of Civil Government from that of Religion, and to settle the just Bounds that lie between the one and the other."[78] In Locke's scheme, religion would ideally not be a part of the political world. He claimed that "the care of Souls cannot belong to the Civil Magistrate, because his Power consists only in outward force; but true and saving Religion consists in the inward perswasion of the Mind."[79] For Locke, religion ought to be purely a matter of the salvation of the individual. It is not surprising then that he radically redefined the idea of "church." Whereas the medieval church had been conceived of largely "as an inviolably holy body, possessed of unchallengeable, because divine, authority,"[80] Locke presented the church, or rather churches, as much more circumscribed entities:

> *Let us now consider what a Church is.* A Church then I take to be a voluntary [*libera*] Society of Men, joining themselves together of their own accord, in order to the publick worshipping of God, in such a manner as they judge acceptable to him, and effectual to the Salvation of their Souls. I say it is a free and voluntary Society [*societatem liberam et voluntariam*]. No body is born a member of any Church. . . . No man by nature is bound unto any particular Church or Sect, but everyone joins himself voluntarily to that Society in which he believes he has found that Profession and Worship which is truly acceptable to God. The hopes of Salvation, as it was the only cause of his entrance into that Communion, so it can be the only reason of his stay there.[81]

To be sure, Locke envisioned a worship that was "publick," but the impetus to the formation of the church in the first place was to be an entirely private affair. The church was now a voluntary assembly of individuals who gather together for the sole purpose of obtaining salvation. Any gathering for this purpose ought to be tolerated by the civil authorities, provided that the participants played by the rules of the game, the most important of which was, do not disturb the functions of the state (which Locke had earlier delineated as "Civil Interests": "Life, Liberty, Health, and Indolency of the Body; and the Possession of outward things, such as Money, Lands, Houses, Furniture, and the like").[82] All "Ecclesiastical Laws," wrote Locke, should be confined to matters concerning "the acquisition of Eternal Life. . . . Nothing ought, nor can be transacted in [a 'Religious Society'], relating to the Possession of Civil and Worldly Goods. No Force is here to be made use of, upon any occasion whatsoever: For Force belongs wholly to the Civil Magistrate, and the Possession of all outward Goods is subject to his Jurisdiction."[83] As long as beliefs about God did not interfere with those interests, said Locke, they should be tolerated; thus the only groups that he explicitly excluded from toleration were atheists (though Catholics and Muslims would also seem implicitly to be excluded).[84] This new proposed legal "protection" for religions raised the question of what exactly constituted "a religion." In fact, after the conclusion of the *Letter*, Locke added an appendix that posed a closely related question:

> We are to enquire, therefore, what men are of the same Religion. Concerning which, it is manifest that those who have one and the same Rule of Faith and Worship, are of the same Religion: and those who have not the same Rule of Faith and Worship are of different Religions. For since all things that belong unto that Religion are contained in that Rule, it follows necessarily that those who agree in one Rule are of one and the same Religion: and *vice versâ*. Thus Turks and Christians are of different Religions: because these take the *Holy Scriptures* to be the Rule of their Religion, and those the *Alcoran*. And for the same reason, there may be different Religions also even amongst Christians. The *Papists* and the *Lutherans*, tho' both of them profess faith in Christ, and are therefore called Christians, yet are not both of the same Religion: because These acknowledge nothing but the Holy Scriptures to be the Rule and Foundation of their Religion; Those take in also Traditions and the Decrees of Popes, and of these together make the Rule of their Religion.[85]

We can thus include adherence to a certain set of scriptures as another defining feature of a religion for Locke.[86] This assemblage of ideas—religions as groups of individuals who freely choose to associate with each other and adhere to a particular set of writings for the purpose of salvation, and who ideally operate in ways that do not interfere or overlap with the concerns of the state—now begins to look quite similar to modern conceptions of religion.

Yet there are still some differences. Locke's schema still allowed for Christianity to be subdivided into different "religions," which is not usually the case in modern scholarship (although one does sometimes see "Catholicism" and "Protestantism" discussed as separate religions). Locke's model also presupposed that citizens would be socialized and educated by churches and thus that in some sense, "church" would still have a role to play, at least indirectly, in "state."[87] Nevertheless, Locke's *Letter Concerning Toleration* can be viewed as a turning point. From the late seventeenth century, the isolation of religion as a distinct sphere of life ideally separated from other areas of life allowed for a new kind of mental mapping of Europe and the world.

Conclusion

I close this chapter by emphasizing the context in which these intellectual developments occurred. I have accentuated European domestic strife, but the wider global context is also important. Locke may not have agreed with his patron on everything, but his passion for toleration was a characteristic he shared with Lord Ashley. It is worth considering the circumstances in which Ashley's opinions developed. In his biography of Locke, Maurice Cranston writes:

> Ashley's very zeal for toleration was indeed but an aspect of his interest in trade. It was not simply a case of his desiring toleration of dissenters because of his own Presbyterian views, still less a case of his having achieved a Christ-like forbearance beyond the spiritual range of the average sensual man. Ashley opposed religious persecution because religious persecution divided a nation, drove many of its most industrious citizens to emigrate, and generally impeded commercial development. He saw more clearly than most Englishmen of his time how colonial expansion and international trade could be made to bring enormous fortunes to investors like himself and at the same time increase the wealth and power of the country as a whole. The example of Holland had taught him how trade and toleration could flourish splendidly together. He was the complete progressive capitalist in politics; he might almost have been invented by Marx.[88]

As we will see, trade and colonization had a role to play not only in the formation of the category of religion, but also in the formation of the entities we have come to call "religions." The fragmentation of Christendom and the proposed response of toleration and confinement of religion for the benefit of the stability of the state allowed for the perception of Europe as a group of independent nations superimposed over a nonoverlapping map of different, antagonistic religions in coexistence. This model would prove to be an important tool for Europeans as they began to produce knowledge about the foreign peoples they had been increasingly encountering abroad since the late fifteenth century.

Introduction

In the preceding chapter, I tried to show how a world that had previously not been differentiated into "religious" and "secular" spheres became one in which religion was conceived of as an ideally private and nonpolitical realm.[1] Along with a number of other scholars, I have come to see this period and locale as central to the production of the modern concept of religion. Yet it would be a mistake to ignore the effect of the foreign exploration and colonization in which Europeans engaged during this same period of time. After all, it was in 1492, just seven years before Ficino's death, that Columbus sailed the ocean blue. More to the point, it was in October 1493 that a vernacular Italian ballad recounting Columbus's discoveries was printed in Ficino's hometown of Florence.[2] With the growth of the printing industry, news of far-flung peoples hovered over the internal Christian disputes racking Europe. At the same time that the genus of religion was coming to be thought of as ideally an internal, private, depoliticized entity, interactions with previously unknown peoples were beginning to create new species of individual religions.

Of course, even before the age of exploration and colonization, Europeans had been confronted with previously unknown peoples, most notably the Mongols in the thirteenth century. European reactions to the Mongols' capture of Poland and Hungary early in 1241 both resembled and differed from the colonial setting of later centuries. A crucial distinction is that in the thirteenth century, Europeans were facing invasion from a superior fighting force, a difference that helps to explain why the understanding of the Mongols that came to dominate was an apocalyptic one: the Mongol invaders were Gog and Magog of Revelation 20:8.[3] Yet alternative understandings that saw the Mongols as the ten lost tribes of Israel are precursors to some of the interpretive strategies for handling new peoples that became more common during the colonial era.

Without underplaying the trauma of these early encounters, it is safe to say that it was the sixteenth century that saw the question of *difference* among human populations emerge with new urgency. There was an increasing knowledge of southern Africans, thanks to the Portuguese and later the Dutch. The English and Dutch presence in India brought about more awareness of the Indian subcontinent. French Jesuit missionaries of the seventeenth century took Catholic teachings to the Chinese and brought back knowledge of ancient Chinese scripts and gods. The most surprising new people, though, were certainly the Americans. J. H. Elliott writes of the discovery and interpretation of America:

> Here was a totally new phenomenon, quite outside the range of Europe's accumulated experience and of its normal expectation. Europeans knew something, however vaguely and inaccurately, about Africa and Asia. But about America and its inhabitants they knew nothing. It was this which differentiated the response of sixteenth-century Europeans to America from that of fifteenth-century Portuguese to Africa. . . . The very fact of America's existence, and of its gradual revelation as an entity in its own right, rather than as an extension of Asia, constituted a challenge to a whole body of traditional assumptions, beliefs and attitudes.[4]

As exploration and interactions with the peoples of the Americas, Africa, and Asia increased, a flood of new information was created about these new peoples. The organization and systematization of this information provides another part of the context in which the modern notion of religion took shape.[5] I will have more to say about the role of reports about "religion" in the Americas in Chapter 7, but for now, I carry my account of the development of the concept of religion from the sixteenth century into the twentieth by focusing on different ways that colonial interactions helped to generate what are now known as religions in India, Africa, and Japan. I choose these three examples because they each illustrate different aspects of the complex sets of interactions between European academics and the indigenous peoples of these areas that were decisive in the formation of the religions and in the sharpening of the generic concept of religion.

Before proceeding, I emphasize that it was not only academics and indigenous peoples who participated in this creation of religions. Recall that in Chapter 2, one of the authors whose works represented a shift into the more modern way of using the term *religio* was Hugo Grotius in the early seventeenth century. The context in which Grotius was writing sheds an interesting light on his new usage of the term. He began his treatise *De veritate religionis christianae* ("On the Truth of Christian Religion") by explaining that the work was written for those in the Dutch shipping industry who would no doubt be meeting the other three of the world's four kinds of peoples, "Pagans, Jews, and Mahometans," on their voyages.[6] Such sailors would need a way to maintain their Christian identity and propagate the gospel. Grotius elaborated on his reasoning in the preface to the work:

> For my design was, to compose something that might be serviceable indeed to my fellow citizens in general, but especially to the seafaring part of our community; that so they might employ usefully, rather than beguile idly, as too many of them do, the number of leisure hours they must necessarily have upon their hands at sea. And therefore prefacing the work with some encomiums on the Dutch nation, representing them as easily capable of excelling others in the art of navigation, I urged them to employ that art, as a blessing peculiarly given from above, not only for the service of their private ends and temporal advantage, but also for the propagation of the *true*, or in other words the *Christian* religion. Sufficient opportunities, I observed, would constantly present themselves, in the course of long and distant voyages; continually meeting, as they must be, every where, either with Pagans, as in China or Guinea; with Mahometans, as in the Turkish, the Persian, and the African dominions; or indeed, lastly, with Jews, (these also being now become professed enemies of Christianity) dispersed and scattered, as they are, into almost every country of the known world.[7]

This newly developed sense of the word *religio* arose in this context of Dutch nationalism and economic expansion. In Grotius's ideal world, part of the mission of the Dutch shipping industry would be the spread of the true, Christian religion, which must be articulated by *whoever* happened to be confronting and interacting with foreign peoples. As we will see, all manner of people were involved in these colonial interactions.

"Religion" in India

In April 1853 a former employee of the British East India Company, one Malcolm Lewin, testified before the House of Commons. At issue was a dispatch that described "the body of Pagan natives of India" as "heathen." Under questioning from the members of Parliament, Lewin protested the use of that word. We pick up in the midst of the exchange:

Lewin: ". . . All I know is, that the word 'heathen' conveys an insult."

"What word would you have used?"

Lewin: "Hindoos."

"A Hindoo may be a Christian?"

Lewin: "He may."

"[If the] question was between a converted Hindoo, and a Hindoo adhering still to the religion of his ancestors; would you say between a Christian and a Hindoo, when in fact both were Hindoos?"

After Lewin made further protests against the use of the word "heathen," the questioning resumed:

"What word would you have proposed to use[?]"

Lewin: "The word which hitherto had been in use was that of Hindoos. A Hindoo Christian is a Christian convert from Hindooism; a Hindoo is a person of the Hindoo faith."

"But supposing the Christian was also a Hindoo, how could you say that a Christian was on one side and a Hindoo was on the other?"[8]

This almost humorous failure of communication helps to illustrate a change that had been occurring slowly for decades. The term *hindu*, which is itself ancient, was derived from the local name of the Indus river and was a geographic identifier, referring to people or things from India.[9] By the eighteenth century, *hindu* (or "Hindoo") was already well on its way to becoming used primarily as a "religious" identifier (note the use in the excerpt of both "Hindooism" and "Hindoo faith"). Lewin, in fact, uses the term both ways in this example from the nineteenth century. In the phrase "Hindoo Christian," the word "Hindoo" must be a geographic or ethnic label, while in the phrase "Hindoo faith," the term clearly describes a religion. Thus the miscommunication.

The term "Hindooism" seems to have first appeared in the late eighteenth century (at this stage in our study, it should not be surprising to find that there is no word in an ancient Indian language that approximates "Hinduism").[10] It seems to have gradually replaced such older phrases as "the religion of the Hindoos" and "the religion of the Banians," which were in use as early as the sixteenth century.[11] We can get a sense of what such phrases were thought to convey by dissecting the title of one of the earliest English published accounts of India. It is a tract printed in 1630 by Henry Lord, an Anglican chaplain stationed with the British East India Company in the northwestern port city of Surat: *A Discoverie of the Sect of the Banians Containing their History, Law, Liturgie, Casts, Customes, and Ceremonies. Gathered from their Bramanes, Teachers of that Sect: As the Particulars were comprized in the Booke of their Law, called the Shaster.*[12] Much is instructive in this title. We see here the easy interchange of the vocabulary of "sects" and "religions." In fact, the title line in the header of the actual pages of the book reads "A Discoverie of the Banian Religion." The vocabulary is further blurred when the topic under discussion is described as a "heresy."[13] What constitutes this sect/religion/heresy is "history, law, liturgie, casts, customes, and ceremonies." The information is gathered from the "Booke of their Law" and was mediated to the author through the aid of Brahmins, "whose eminence of place, was an attractive to draw on this discovery and manifestation."[14] Lord claimed that in researching the book, he, "with the helpe of Interpreters, made collections out of a booke of theirs called the SHASTER, which is to them as their Bible, containing the grounds of their Religion in a written word."[15]

The actual contents of Lord's book in some ways reflect the contents of the Old Testament: a creation story; followed by the "Morall Law," a series of commandments in the "Thou shalt . . ." format; followed by a critique of parts of the commandments that Lord found objectionable. This portion of the work is characterized by not only a number of biblical citations, but also a series of comparisons with ancient cultures (Greeks, Romans, Egyptians, Carthaginians) and citations of ancient Greek and Latin literature. The last two sections of the book offer an account of "Ceremoniall Law" of the Banians and a description of the caste system (notable here is Lord's observation that, contrary to the opinion of some, the "Bramanes" are not in fact descended from Abraham and were never called "Abrahmanes").[16] The work then concludes with an additional short refutation of some of the precepts outlined in the book (that the refutation is a key part of this account is intimated by the presence on the title page of a quotation of Isa. 9:16: "The Leaders of this people cause them to erre: and they that are led of them are destroyed").[17]

The knowledge produced in Lord's book, the generation of "the religion of the Banians," is a complex product and a forerunner of European scholarship of the eighteenth and nineteenth centuries. Lord's interests as a Christian chaplain abroad in India are merged with the interests of his native Brahmin interpreters (not to mention the interests of the Company officials who introduced Lord to the Brahmins). Also important is the centrality of text in Lord's account. He sought out what he regarded as "their Bible" and built his account around it. As such, his work stands near the beginning of a European scholarly interest that centered on "sacred texts" as representing the essence of "religions." Thus, even though it is now generally agreed that in premodern India no single text played a role analogous to that of the Bible in European cultures, it would be wrong to call Lord's book and works like it "distortions" of some sort of more "authentic" native "religion." Rather, the legacy of Lord's book and other similar works is the creation of an Indian religion in which texts have become central. Indeed, the massive amount of energy directed during the eighteenth and nineteenth centuries by scholars toward the production of critical editions and translations of what were regarded as "sacred texts" not only of India but of "the Orient" more generally owes a great deal to the work of decidedly nonscholarly writers such as Lord. The most spectacular product of these later efforts was undoubtedly the fifty volumes of *Sacred Books of the East* produced under the editorial oversight of Max Müller, which appeared from 1879 to 1910.[18]

The *Sacred Books of the East* and other translations produced during this era had a wide readership. That these scholarly efforts were central to the formation of what many regard as the establishment of "authentic" Hinduism is demonstrated by the fact that none other than Mahatma Gandhi, considered by many as a standard bearer of "Hinduism" and a celebrated Hindu interpreter of the *Bhagavad Gita*, recalled in his autobiography that he first encountered the *Gita* in the English translation of Edwin Arnold introduced to him by Theosophists during a stay in England in the late nineteenth century.[19]

It is also worth emphasizing that these texts being edited, translated, and designated as "sacred" in the nineteenth century were *ancient*. As scholars wrote about the religious systems they detected in these ancient texts, they generated pure, textual religions that provided a standard by which Europeans could judge (and often condemn) the practices of modern peoples as not being true to these ancient "authentic" religions. This opinion held not only for Hinduism, but for all of the "Oriental religions." Thus, in the course of a discussion on modern Parsis (devotees of the ancient Persian prophet Zoroaster) in India, Müller writes that the Parsi priests

> would have to admit that they cannot understand one word of the sacred writings in which they profess to believe. . . . A Parsi, in fact, hardly knows what his faith is. The Zend-Avesta is to him a sealed book; and though there is a Guzerati [the language spoken in Gujarat in western India] translation of it, that translation is not made from the original, but from a Pehlevi paraphrase, nor is it recognized by the priests as an authorized version. Till about five-and-twenty years

ago [that is, about 1837], there was no book from which a Parsi of an inquiring mind could gather the principles of his religion. At that time, and, as it would seem, chiefly in order to counteract the influence of Christian missionaries, a small Dialogue was written in Guzerati—a kind of Catechism, giving, in the form of questions and answers, the most important tenets of Parsiism.[20]

Müller's evident disdain for the inability of Parsis to understand their own "sacred writings" was not uncommon among European scholars, and it is perhaps not the most interesting feature of this quotation.[21] What instead merits special attention is the production *by native peoples*, apparently *in response to* Christian missionary work, of texts that distilled and produced "Parsi religion" in opposition to Christianity. It is exactly this sort of give-and-take between Europeans and Indians that was fundamental in the creation of "Indian religions."

I will not dwell on this topic as a number of scholars have recently produced much more in-depth studies of how the "religions of India" took shape during the colonial era.[22] These studies have met with considerable resistance from other scholars interested in defending the notion of a kind of precolonial "authentic ancient Indian religion."[23] For example, the introduction to a recent reference work refers to "Hinduism" as "an ancient religion that still flourishes."[24] I hope that by now I have shown just how problematic that kind of claim is. "Religion" is a modern concept, and "the religions" are the products of modern interactions. In the example above, one portion of the life of a community of Parsi people is parceled out into a "Catechism" (apparently in response to the work of local Christians) representing the essence of something called "Parsiism." Clearly, ideas of "continuous existence" and authenticity are extremely complicated in such situations.

"Religion" in Southern Africa

David Chidester has produced a fine study on the colonial interactions of Dutch and British colonists and native peoples in southern Africa from the sixteenth century through the nineteenth century.[25]

Here I examine just one of the many examples Chidester presents of the creation of religion in the frontiers of southern Africa: the case of the German writer Peter Kolb. Well educated in mathematics and astronomy (he was a lecturer at the University of Halle), Kolb set out for the Cape of Good Hope late in 1704 in order to make astronomical observations, having secured passage on a ship belonging to the Dutch East India Company.[26] Unfortunately, "he proved incompetent" and "according to his critics, Kolb spent his time smoking and drinking, having to resign his post and return to Germany in 1713 because he had gone blind."[27] Kolb did, however, capitalize on his eight years in the Cape. He made many observations about the physical characteristics of the area and the habits and customs of the natives. The end result of these efforts was the production of a detailed and highly influential study of the Cape of Good Hope that paid special attention to the religion of the "Hottentot" (now generally called Khoikhoi) natives of the area. It was first published in 1719 after his return to Europe.[28] Kolb presented his account as a vast improvement of previous publications on the Cape, stressing his firsthand knowledge: "But I had not been at the *Cape* a long Time, before I saw the Folly of trusting almost to any Report there. Upon which I threw away the Historical Rubbish I had gather'd upon Information, and made it a Rule, not to believe any Thing I did not see, of which a Sight could be had."[29] In the absence of native written texts, Kolb's observations, along with his interviews of natives (often, it seems, induced with bribes), provided the raw materials for his production of Hottentot religion.[30]

The natives of southern Africa had been known to Europeans through regular interaction since the Dutch East India Company set up a way station at the Cape in 1652. At the time Kolb wrote, the received wisdom was that the Hottentots were without religion. Kolb opened his chapter "Of the RELIGION of the Hottentots" by noting that "it is doubted by many whether the Hottentots have any Notion of a Deity."[31] He was quick to prove such claims wrong by comparing Hottentot behaviors to those of Jews and Catholics. Early on in his work, Kolb wrote:

In their Customs and Institutions they cannot be said to resemble any People besides the *Jews* and the Old *Troglodytes*. They resemble the *Jews* in their Offerings, the Regulation of their Chief Festivals by the New and Full Moon, and in their Withdrawing at certain Times from their Wives. They agree with that People in abstaining from certain Sorts of Food; in particular, Swine's Flesh, which hardly any of 'em will taste. At a certain Age, they undergo a Sort of Circumcision. And Women are excluded the Secret and Management of certain Affairs, much as they are among the *Jews*. And in several other Customs do the *Hottentots* agree with that People.[32]

Yet the connection with the Jews was not, in Kolb's opinion, direct:

But as they have no Memory of the Children of *Israel*, of *Moses*, or the *Law*, Things of which, had they derived their Origin or these Customs from any of the *Tribes*, some Traces, in highest Probability, had remain'd, it cannot be thought, on any good Grounds, that they deduce either their Origin or these Customs from them. A far greater Probability lies on the side of the *Troglodytes*, the Descendants of *Abraham* by his Wife *Chetura*, who not only observed all or most of the Customs in which the *Hottentots* agree with the *Jews*, but likewise several others, observed by the *Hottentots* at this Day.[33]

After describing Hottentot worship of the moon, which involves "Shouting, Screaming, Singing, Jumping, Stamping, Dancing, Prostration on the Ground, and an unintelligible Jargon," Kolb writes, "I shall observe, by the Way, that this Dancing-Ceremony gives a new light into the Origin of the *Hottentots;* since 'tis pretty certain, Dancing enter'd into the Divine Worship in Times as early as the Flood. And the *Jews* retain it, on certain Festivals, to this Day."[34] Again, after describing the Hottentot veneration of a certain insect, Kolb carries on: "The Hottentots likewise pay a Religious Veneration to their Saints and Men of Renown departed. They honour 'em not with Tombs, Statues or Inscriptions; but consecrate Woods, Mountains, Fields and Rivers to their Memory."[35] He also notes that the Hottentots call the person upon whom this insect lands "a Saint" and "a Holy Man."[36] He concludes his discussion of Hottentot religion by claiming that they are even worse than the Jews when it comes to hindering the (true, Protestant) Christian mission: "Never certainly were there, in Matters of Religion, so obstinate and so infatuated a People. Stiff as are the *Jews*, many of 'em embrace the Faith of *Christ* and die in it. But I never heard of a *Hottentot* that died a Christian."[37]

Whereas earlier interpreters had found no religion among the Hottentots, thanks to these comparative efforts of Kolb, the Hottentots now had a religion. As Chidester writes: "They might have had a 'false' religion that was similar, in Kolb's terms, to Judaism or Roman Catholicism, which stood as an obstacle to Protestant Christianity. But at least they had a recognizable religious system."[38] The "discovery" of Hottentot religion came about through the rich combination of a number of factors, which included among other elements Dutch economic aspirations, the peculiar interests of Peter Kolb, and the active participation of native informants. Chidester has noted that Kolb's attribution of religion to the Hottentots occurred at a time when they posed no threat to the colonists. In the later eighteenth century, when greater European encroachments led to renewed hostilities, European writers would again deny that the Hottentots had a religion.[39] The southern African situation raises a key point to which I will return in the concluding chapter: the energy spent on trying to produce a "good definition" of religion or trying to decide whether or not something "really is" a religion might better be directed to individual acts of naming some phenomena as religion and others as not religion. Who gets to make these decisions and what are their reasons?

"Religion" in Japan

The invention of religion in Japan involves many of the kinds of power relationships and colonial encounters we have been examining, but this story is a particularly good example of the role that government can play in the creation of a religion, even an ancient religion.[40] In the late nineteenth century, "Shinto" began to be portrayed by the imperial Meiji government as the ancient, indigenous religion of Japan, and this Meiji view continues to be reproduced even in some academic circles. The view is enshrined in the opening statement of the entry for "Shinto" in a standard reference tool of the late twentieth century: "Shintō is the name given to the traditional religion of Japan, a religion that has existed continuously from before the founding of the Japanese nation until the present."[41] The idea of Shinto "continuously existing" implies a stability and an essentialism that would be problematic as a description of any social formation, but in the case of Shinto, it is an especially misleading statement. The term *shintō* does indeed date back at least as far as the *Nihon shoki*, a historical chronicle produced in the eighth century C.E. It entered the Japanese vocabulary from Chinese as a combination of the Chinese character *shin*, meaning *kami*, or divinities associated with weather and natural calamities, and the character *tō*, meaning "way." The term *shintō* is thus frequently translated as the "way of the *kami*," but it can refer to the activities of or worship of the *kami* or simply the state of being a *kami*.[42] Furthermore, in ancient Japan, the rites for these divinities were not clearly distinct from Buddhist rituals and institutions.[43] Thus, as Sarah Thal has noted, Shinto "was neither a fully independent set of institutions nor a distinct philosophical tradition during most of the millennium before 1868."[44] That particular year marked the beginning of the "Meiji Restoration," which displaced the rule of the shogun, or military governors, and installed in their place the emperor Meiji Tenno in the role of head of state. The early days of his rule were marked by a nativist movement to purge supposedly foreign elements from "indigenous" Japanese worship. Early in 1868, the government issued edicts that denigrated the status of Buddhist priests and ordered objects identifiable as Buddhist to be removed from shrines.[45] In 1870, the Meiji government implemented the Great Teaching Campaign (*taikyō*), which melded *kami* worship and nationalist interests into a kind of state religion that purported to be the revived ancient religion of Japan.[46] The questionable "authenticity" of this enterprise was not lost on some contemporaries. In 1872, Mori Arinori, a Japanese diplomat educated in the United Kingdom and assigned to work in the United States, published a pamphlet (in the form of an open letter to a top government official) that highlighted the artificiality of "Shinto" as it was being promoted by the state. He criticized the government's "attempt to impose upon our people a religion of its creation," protesting that the "notion of making a new religion or precept by the authority of the State, which now prevails in our country, has a strange appearance."[47] Whether through the effect of criticisms such as these or through other forces, by 1887, the government was proclaiming that Shinto was in fact not a religion at all: "There can be no question of the evil deed of viewing our Way of the Gods (*Shintō*)—the public way of Heaven and Earth, the spirit of the world—as identical with religion in general . . . this Way cannot be included in 'religion' any more than can ice in ashes."[48] In fact, it took a military directive from the Allied powers in 1945 to officially (re?-)establish Shinto as a religion distinct from the state apparatus. The directive prohibited all state-related Shinto rituals in order "to separate religion from the state, to prevent the misuse of religion for political ends, and to put all religions, faiths, and creeds upon exactly the same legal basis, entitled to precisely the same opportunities and protection."[49]

With Shinto, then, we have a clear example of the creation of a religion specifically to fit the model of World Religions. Shinto "is neither ancient, unchanging, nor peculiarly indigenous."[50] Various parties used the designation "Shinto" to represent *the* indigenous religion of Japan, something distinctly *not* religion, and eventually simply *a* religion among other religions.

Classifying All These "Religions"

Given the complicated histories associated with the entities we have come to call "religions," it is not surprising that different means of organizing these new religions proliferated from the seventeenth century on. European Christians were beginning to recognize themselves as a fractured, diverse group, and the "heathen" were beginning to be seen as divisible into distinct groups. A great deal of intellectual energy was expended in attempts to produce comprehensive catalogues of the religions, and the acknowledgement of these multiple religions in turn focused attention on the singular, generic "religion."[51]

These points are nicely illustrated in the seventeenth-century writings of such authors as Samuel Purchas and Alexander Ross. Purchas, an ordained minister educated at Cambridge, published in 1613 a large tome that bore the informative title *Purchas his Pilgrimage: Or Relations of the World and the Religions Observed in all Ages and Places discovered, from Creation unto this Present*.[52] The organizational structure of the book is a mix of new and old. It is divided into nine parts: Asia covered in five chapters, and Africa and America covered in two chapters each. But within this framework based on the geography of the "New World," Purchas narrated a very old biblical story, beginning (under the heading of "Asia") with the Genesis account of creation and reflections on the Trinity. By the second edition of the work in 1614, however, this creation account was dotted with references to the studies of Copernicus and Galileo.

When it came to the actual discussion of the "Religions Observed in All Ages," Purchas offered an eclectic collection using a variety of formulations, including "Religion of the world before the flood," "Syria, and the ancient Religions there," "the Theologie, and Religion of the Phoenicians," "the Hebrew Nation and Religion," "the Arabians, Saracens, Turkes, and of the ancient Inhabitants of Asia Minor: and of their Religions," "Arabia, and the ancient Religions, Rites, and Customes there," "the Successors of Mahomet, their different Sects, and of the dispersing of that Religion through the World," "the Opinions holden by the Turkes in their Religion," "the Regions and Religions of Asia Minor," "the Armenians, Medes, Persians, Parthians, Scythians, Tartarians, Chinois, and of their Religions," "the Religions and Rites of the Virginians," and "Cumana, Guiana, Brasill, Chica, Chili, Peru, and other Regions of America Peruviana, and of their Religions." The descriptions of each vary in the level of detail provided (presumably based on the level of detail in the travel narratives that constituted his sources), but Purchas managed to convey a sizable amount of information on the customs of a wide range of peoples. Despite the interest in diversity, Purchas emphasized unity when he came to reflect on the phenomenon of religion more generally. He stood in the tradition that regarded Christianity as "the first (and therefore best) Religion." He asserted that "the true Religion can be but one, and that which God himselfe teacheth, as the onely true way to himselfe; all other religions being but strayings from him, whereby men wander in the dark."[53] Even as he set out to describe the outward behaviors of numerous peoples from the far ends of the world, Purchas claimed that religion was an internal affair: "Religion it selfe is in the heart, and produceth those outward cerimoniall effects thereof."[54] Early on in the work, he offered an etymological discussion: "Religion in it selfe is naturall, written in the hearts of all men, which wil (as here we shew) rather be of a false then no Religion: but the name whereby it is so called, is by birth a forreiner, by common use made a free-denizen among us, descended from the Romans, which by their swords made way for their words, the Authors both of the thing it selfe and of the appellation, to a great part of this Westerne world."[55] After citing and discussing several Latin authorities, Purchas settled on a definition, not of "religion," but of "true Religion": "The true Religion is the true rule and right way of serving God. Or to speake as the case now standeth with us, *True religion is the right way of reconciling and reuniting man to God, that he may be saved.*"[56] We have seen this sort of language in the sixteenth century. Religion is a "rule" that leads to salvation, and there is only one "true" rule, that of (Protestant) Christians like Purchas. The other "Religions," despite their variety, can be classed as the subtitle of Purchas's book indicates into "*Heathnish, Jewish, and Saracenicall.*"

Alexander Ross, whom we have already encountered in his capacity as producer of the earliest English translation of the Qur'an in 1649, provides another example of this interest in the religions of the world.[57] In 1653, one year before his death, Ross published a 578-page work with a title that suggests something like the World Religions model: *Pansebeia: Or, A View of All Religions in the World, with the Several Church-Governments, from the Creation, to These Times. Together with a Discovery of All Known Heresies, in All Ages and Places,*

Throughout Asia, Africa, America, and Europe.[58] Yet, it becomes clear that Ross's understanding of religion and the religions is somewhat foreign to typical modern discourses. First, his vocabulary, like that of Henry Lord in *A Discoverie of the Sect of the Banians,* appears to blend older sectarian terminology with the newer vocabulary of different religions. He complained that "the world is pestered with too many Sects and Heresies" but expressed the same idea with the lament that "the world is pestered with too many Religions."[59] For Ross, religion was a human universal: "all Societies of men in all Ages, and in all parts of the Universe, have united and strengthened themselves with the Cement of Religion."[60] Yet, his treatment of the topic of "all the Religions in the World" includes a total of three sections on the ancient and modern religions of Asia, Africa, and the Americas and no fewer than eleven sections devoted to "the Religions of Europe" (ten for varieties of Christians and one for "Mahumetanism"). Roughly a sixth of the book consists of a rambling concluding chapter of general questions about religion and the consequences of a plurality of religions. Ross here brings together a number of the topics I covered in Chapter 5. After first establishing that "Religion is the pillar on which every Common-wealth is built," he moves on to the issue of multiple religions: *"Are pluralities of Religions tolerable in a State?* Publickly one Religion onely is to be allowed, because there is but one God . . . Religion (as is said) is the Foundation of all States and Kingdomes; therefore in one State and Kingdome there ought to be but one Religion, because there can be but one foundation."[61] A second question follows:

> *May a State tolerate different Religions in private?* 1. If they be such Religions as doe not overthrow the fundamentals of truth. 2. Nor such as impugn or disturb the government established in that State or Kingdom. 3. If the professors thereof be such as are not factius, ambitious, or percinacious; but honest, simple, tractable, obedient to Superiors, having no other end in holding their opinions of Religion, but Gods glory, and satisfaction of their own conscience . . . diversity of Religions, with the limitations aforesaid, may be connived at; especially when it cannot be avoided without the danger and ruin of the State.[62]

Ross thus treats "All the Religions of the World" from a standpoint not unlike that of Jean Bodin examined in the previous chapter. The ideal state would have one religion, but when necessary, a multiplicity of religions within a state is permissible, provided that the religions "do not disturb the government" and are "private." On the question of classifying the religions of the world, Ross offered a theory of mixtures: *"What else may we observe in view of all these Religions?* That some of them are meerly *Heathenish;* some *Jewish;* some meerly *Christian;* some mixed, either of all, or some of these; *Mahumetanism* is mixed of *Judaisme, Gentilisme,* and *Arianisme,* the *Moscovit* Religion is, partly *Christian,* partly *Heathenish:* In the East are many Sects, partly *Christian,* partly *Jewish.*"[63] Such theories of religions being the result of "mixing" stood in some tension with the "Pagano-papist" theories of the priestly corruption of an original, pristine monotheism. The eighteenth century, however, would produce theories of the origins of religion that displaced both of these hypotheses.[64]

The goal of comprehensive accumulation seems to have persisted into the eighteenth century, as indicated by the titles of the various compilations that continued to appear. The most celebrated of the eighteenth-century works of this genre, *Cérémonies et coutumes religieuses de tous les peuples du monde,* was published by Jean-Frédéric Bernard and featured fine engravings by Bernard Picart; it appeared in seven volumes from 1723 to 1737.[65] It was translated into English as *The Ceremonies and Religious Customs of the Various Nations of the Known World Together with Historical Annotations and several Curious Discourses Equally Informative and Entertaining* and was reprinted, excerpted, and plagiarized numerous times over the next one hundred years.[66] The work was more detailed than its predecessors (the first English translation ran to almost three thousand pages), but its organizational structure was still roughly the fourfold division. The major sections are "Ceremonies of the Jews," "Customs and Religious Ceremonies of the Roman Catholics," "Ceremonies and Religious Customs of the Idolatrous Nations," "Ceremonies and Religious Customs of the Greeks and Protestants," "the Doctrine and Discipline of the Church of England, Presbyterians, Independents,

Anabaptists, Quakers, &c.," and "Various Sects of Mahometans."
Curiously, in addition to the seventh volume dedicated to the "History
of Mahometism" and its sects, the Mahometans were also treated
under the heading of "the Greek Religion" (that is, Greek Orthodox
Christian religion): "As the Religion of the *Mahometans* is a Compound only of the Doctrine of the *Jews* and the *Christians,* we have
thought proper to give the Reader an Abstract thereof."[67] Thus,
Picart also appears to have simultaneously held a theory of "mixing"
of religions and a theory of priestly corruption, a theme outlined in
the opening chapter of the first volume: "[R]eligious Worship being
once confined to Temples, the Appointment of Ministers for the
Deities became necessary . . . From hence sprang up a numerous
Crowd of worthless Creatures, who pretend a Right to serve at those
Altars which maintain them. True Religion by Degrees became less
Spiritual."[68]

Just after Picart's volumes appeared in English, Thomas Broughton, a well-educated Anglican clergyman, authored the two-volume
work *An Historical Dictionary of All Religions from the Creation of the
World to this Present Time.*[69] It provides a good example of the complex
overlap of different classification systems. In the preface, Broughton
outlined his classification scheme: "The first general division of *Religion* is into *True* and *False. True Religion* must ever be the same and
invariable, and therefore there can be but ONE TRUE RELIGION. That
infinite variety, therefore, in the doctrines and modes of worship,
which have prevailed in the world (only one scheme excepted) are
but so many deviations from the truth, so many FALSE RELIGIONS."[70]
Thus, there is a single "True Religion" and many "False Religions."
Yet, Broughton adhered to the fourfold model as an alternative
means of organizing the religions: "But religion may be still more
particularly distinguished into *Pagan, Jewish, Christian,* and *Mohammedan.* These are the four grand Religions of the world, and include
those of every particular country and people."[71] While multiple, seemingly independent "religions" could be recognized and described,
ultimately they all could be classed as one of "the four grand Religions
of the world."

Even toward the close of the eighteenth century, the fourfold division remained in effect. A good example is the compendium of William Hurd, which seems largely derivative of Picart's *Ceremonies and Religious Customs*. In fewer than 950 pages, Hurd produced *A New Universal History of the Religious Rites, Ceremonies and Customs of the Whole World; Or, A Complete and Impartial View of All the Religions in the Various Nations of the Universe; Both Ancient and Modern, From the Creation Down to the Present Time*, which seems to have been published first in 1788 and subsequently reprinted in 1799, 1811, and 1814.[72] Like the others, it offered a large catalogue of "religions." After beginning with a history of the "ancient Jews," Hurd moved geographically through the cultures of the ancient world, then the modern. The "Heathen" religions are enumerated into more separate groups, and the accounts are generally more detailed, thanks to the continuing accumulation of travel reports and other sources of knowledge. Hurd made use of, for example, Peter Kolb's work on southern African peoples from earlier in the century, though he rejected many of Kolb's conclusions.[73] Hurd also noted more divisions among Christians. His work maintained the basic hostility toward Catholics characteristic of earlier Protestant works. He compared "the Rites and Ceremonies of the *Church of Rome*" to "genuine *Christianity*," which is "The Protestant Religion," but he outlined an array of newly formed groups, including such lesser known groups as the Muggletonians and the Hutchinsonians.[74] All of this detailed discussion, however, still took place basically within the framework of the fourfold division of Christians, Jews, Mahometans, and heathens (for instance, each of his many accounts of "the religions" of foreign lands is classified as "pagan": "THE RELIGIONS OF CEYOLON. The inhabitants of Ceylon are all Pagans").[75]

It was the nineteenth century that saw the final demise of this fourfold division of humanity and the establishment of the modern framework of World Religions.[76] The complex processes involved in this shift are the subject of a penetrating study by Tomoko Masuzawa.[77] She has compellingly argued that it was *not* the case that "the change from the old four-part classification to today's world religions list

[was] simply a revision and refinement, that is, a matter of subdivision of the fourth category of the old system (the pagans/heathens/idolators) into more specific, individual religions, hence a matter of more precise differentiation supposedly made possible by the increasingly more exact and accurate state of empirical knowledge."[78] Instead, the change ought to be read in the context of a number of nineteenth-century discourses—that of comparative theology, that of the newly emerging science of languages, and that of race and the formation of European identity. Viewed from those angles, the emerging World Religions paradigm should be given more credit for giving substance to the objects it is supposed to describe: "The collapse of the old taxonomy was not . . . simply a matter of one framework losing ground and eventually being replaced by another. What changed was not so much the method of how to count and categorize religions, but the very manner in which—in an important sense, for the first time—a 'religion' was to be recognized, to be identified as such, so that it might be *compared* with another."[79] Examples like the three case studies in this chapter suggest to me that this change was already under way in the seventeenth century and continued even into the twentieth century, but Masuzawa's point is well taken.

I close this chapter by briefly surveying three proposals for the classification of "religions" that emerged in the nineteenth century. The terminology of World Religions seems to have appeared at least as early as 1864.[80] In a book on Zoroastrian religion, the Dutch scholar and theologian Cornelis P. Tiele had declared that "the highest class [of religions] includes only three, namely the familiar triad, to which one could give the name universalist or world-religions [*wereld-godsdiensten*], Buddhism, Christianity, and Mohammedanism."[81] According to Tiele, these religions were able to break free from a particular nation and spread geographically. This particular mode of classification and defining criterion were not, however, instantly successful. Other writers proposed other distinguishing criteria.

Professor of Sanskrit William D. Whitney provides our first example. In 1881, he described his topic as "the comparative study of the non-Christian religions," and his stated purpose was "to see what are the fundamental views held, rightly or wrongly, by those who are dedicating themselves to the science [of religion]."[82] Yet, in the bulk of the essay, he elaborated his own views about the origins and classifications of religions. The question of origins was no question at all. That "polytheism" preceded "monotheism" was "so clear as to call for no labored argument to sustain it" (Hume's arguments had by this time become highly influential).[83] His scheme of classification called for a two-part division:

> There is no more marked distinction among religions than the one we are called upon to make between a race-religion, which, like a language, is the collective product of the wisdom of a community, the unconscious growth of generations, and a religion proceeding from an individual founder, who, as a leading representative of the better insight and feeling of his time (for otherwise he would meet with no success), makes head against formality and superstition, and recalls his fellow men to sincere and intelligent faith in a new body of doctrines, of specially moral aspect, to which he himself gives shape and coherence. Of this origin are Zoroastrianism, Mohammedanism, Buddhism; and, from the point of view of the general historian of religions, whatever difference of character and authority he may recognize in its founder, Christianity belongs in the same class with them, as being an individual and universal religion, growing out of one that was limited to a race.[84]

Charismatic founding figures were thus the central feature that set apart for Whitney a group of distinctive religions from the rest of the "race-religions." Whitney did not see a need to delineate these "race-religions" individually, but presumably they would include at least Hinduism, Judaism, and the "primitive" religions. In any event, their influence on history is negligible: "The old race-religions could not but become effete . . . they have had to submit to complete overthrow, and the substitution of faiths of a different origin."[85] As we will see, estimations of the political effect of various "religions" was a regular feature in the development of the World Religions paradigm.

My second example comes from the Dutch scholar of the Old Testament Abraham Kuenen, who employed different designations but basically the same division of religions when he gave the Hibbert Lectures in 1882.[86] Kuenen had a clear two-part division: "The *universal religions* are, with fair unanimity, placed in one group, and opposed to the *national religions*. Nothing is more natural."[87] Given the "naturalness" of this distinction, disagreement on classification is puzzling: "Some will only admit Buddhism and Christianity to the title [of universal religion], while others add Islam as a third. How is any difference of opinion on such a matter possible?"[88] Kuenen's answer hinged on the meaning of the word "universal." He argued that this descriptor did not signify a fact (the spread of a religion over a large area containing many nations) but rather a quality (the "character" of the religion). On those grounds, Kuenen excluded Islam from the universal category ("True universalism is to Islam . . . unattainable").[89] Thus, for Kuenen, only Christianity and Buddhism were universal religions in terms of "character," and "we can have no hesitation in pronouncing Christianity the most universal of religions; and that because it is the best qualified for its moral task—to inspire and consecrate the personal and the national life."[90]

For my final example, I return to the work of Cornelis P. Tiele, which operates with a similar binary division of the religions. A little more than a decade after his book on Zoroastrian religion, Tiele produced a more systematic treatment of religion in general, *Outlines of the History of Religion to the Spread of the Universal Religions*, which was quite widely read.[91] Tiele summarized his *Outlines* in his entry on "Religions" in the popular ninth edition of the *Encyclopaedia Britannica*, which both surveyed previous scholarship and presented Tiele's own views.[92] Tiele discussed various religions in a list organized by a combination of linguistic and geographic divisions (the marginal subheadings are Aryan, Semitic, African, Mongolian, Chinese, Japanese, Finnic, Eskimo, Other American religions, and Malayo-Polynesian). When it came to *classifying* religions, however, he distinguished between "nature religions" and "ethical religions." Most of what would become the usual members of the World Religions list were included among the ethical religions: Taoism, Confucianism, Brahmanism, Jainism, Buddhism, Mazdaism (Zarathustrianism), Mosaism, Judaism, Islam, and Christianity. These ethical religions were subdivided into those "founded on a law or Holy Scripture" and those "universal or world religions" that "start from principles and maxims." The latter elite group contains only three members: Buddhism, Christianity, and Mohammedanism.[93] In general, Tiele wanted to dismiss the term "world religions," but he would allow it to designate these three religions, "which have found their way to different races and peoples and all of which profess the intention to conquer the world." Though these three religions stand together above the rest, Tiele assures the reader that

> we are far from placing them on the same level. Islâm, *e.g.*, is not original, not a ripe fruit, but rather a wild offshoot of Judaism and Christianity. Buddhism, though the most widely spread, has never been victorious except where it had to contend with religions standing on no very high degree of development . . . Both Islâm and Buddhism, if not national, are only relatively universalistic, and show the one-sidedness, the one of the Semitic, the other of the Aryan race. . . . If religion really is the synthesis of dependence and liberty, we might say that Islâm represents the former, Buddhism the latter element only, while Christianity does full justice to both of them.[94]

By now we should not be surprised or distracted by the overt Christian triumphalism of Tiele's account. What is far more interesting is his attempt to deal with the tensions in the criteria for the various subdivisions of the religions in these schemes. The phenomenon of Mohammedanism/Islam stymied the nineteenth-century classification systems because its geographic spread was large and it won many converts, but it was Semitic, and hence, by the logic of the time, necessarily particularistic and national.[95] A similar problem arose in the classification of Judaism (was it a "race" or "national" religion, or did it belong with the other two "Abrahamic religions," Christianity and Islam?).[96] Problems like these led to the gradual abandonment of the binary divisions (race religion versus founder religion, national versus universal, natural versus ethical). What was left was the list of distinct, named religions (the "religions of the world," or World Religions), along with a catch-all category of "savage," or "primitive" or "primal" religions (more recent treatments often use the less offensive designation "native religions" or "indigenous religions," but the logic that groups these systems together remains intact even though the names have changed). In fact, Tiele's list of the ten "ethical religions" is basically the same list that one finds in modern textbooks on World Religions. The widely used textbook of Huston Smith treats Hinduism, Buddhism, Confucianism, Taoism, Islam, Judaism, Christianity, and "Primal Religions."[97] The third edition of *World Religions Today* contains chapters on "Indigenous Religions," Judaism, Christianity, Islam, Hinduism, Buddhism, and "East Asian Religions," along with a final chapter titled "Globalization: From New to New Age Religions."[98] Other texts provide nearly identical lists.[99] The usual changes from the nineteenth-century lists are minimal: Brahmanism is replaced by Hinduism; Mohammedanism and its variants are replaced by Islam; Zoroastrianism is dropped because it cannot claim enough adherents; and Mosaism is either reclassified as "the religions(s) of ancient Israel" or dropped altogether since it is no longer "living."[100]

Conclusion

Textbooks, departmental websites of universities, and the media tend to present the model of World Religions as a self-evident fact: these religions are "simply there," and classifying them in this way is a natural and neutral activity. I have shown, however, that there is nothing natural or neutral about either the concept of religion or the framework of World Religions. Jonathan Z. Smith has argued that the various groups that populate the World Religion model are largely the result of political factors:

> It is impossible to escape the suspicion that a world religion is simply a religion like ours, and that it is, above all, a tradition that has achieved sufficient power and numbers to enter our history and form it, interact with it, or thwart it. We recognize both the unity within

and the diversity among the world religions because they correspond to important geopolitical entities with which we must deal. All "primitives," by way of contrast, may be lumped together, as may the "minor religions," because they do not confront our history in any direct fashion. From the point of view of power, they are invisible.[101]

Even though, as we have seen, the crystallization of religion as a category was enmeshed in various power struggles between emerging nation-states in Europe and at colonial frontiers, the kinds of political concerns to which Smith refers have been largely absent from the discussion of World Religions until very recently.[102] Today, religious practitioners and many academicians in the field of religious studies prefer to discuss religions in terms not unlike those outlined in the quotation from Karen Armstrong in Chapter 1. Religion is defined in experiential terms. In the early twentieth century, this position was articulated especially clearly by the Harvard professor of philosophy and psychology William James as well as by Rudolf Otto, who held a chair in theology at Marburg. In 1902, James defined religion in the following way: "Religion . . . shall mean for us *the feelings, acts, and experiences of individual men in their solitude, so far as they apprehend themselves to stand in relation to whatever they may consider the divine.*"[103] For James, religion was largely an individual affair. So also for Otto, who characterized religion as an experience of "the *numinous,*" which elicited "a feeling" of "*mysterium*" that could be characterized as "*tremendum*" ("the daunting and repelling moment of the numinous") and "*fascinans*" ("the attracting and alluring moment of the numinous").[104]

In the early twenty-first century, the view of religion as a kind of pure unconditioned experience (and the World Religions as different, culturally conditioned responses to or manifestations of this experience) is still prevalent. In the typical World Religions textbook, each individual religion is celebrated for its uniqueness, and all are thought to be legitimate paths to individual "salvation," or "liberation" or "self-realization." The viewpoint of the influential theologian John Hick represents this dominant outlook: humans are "religious beings"; they are subject to "religious experiences"; all religions are "authentic contexts of salvation/liberation"; all religions are "authentic contexts of salvific human transformation" and "part of a universal soteriological process."[105] With this portrayal of "the religions" as convictions, privately held by individuals, that constitute multiple valid paths to salvation, we have arrived at something like the modern, liberal concept of religion and the religions.

Introduction

In broad strokes, the preceding two chapters have outlined how the category of religion came into being and how we have come to think of the world as being carved up into different World Religions. What remains to be discussed is exactly how this recent innovation has come to seem so universal, natural, and necessary. Many factors are at play, but the one I emphasize is the role of specialists in ancient history in producing and maintaining the category of religion. In Chapters 2 and 3, I critiqued translators of ancient texts for rendering ancient terms as "religion," and I argued that descriptions of various ancient events as "the birth of religion" were problematic. Since religion is such a recent development, how and why we have come to speak so easily of ancient religions requires some explanation.

I shed light on these questions by undertaking three tasks in this chapter. First, I outline how, during the age of European colonial encounters with modern "pagans" and "idolaters," the entities we now designate as Greek and Roman gods went from being demons in a biblical Christian system to being the central figures of what we now call "ancient Greek and Roman religions." I then quickly trace the intertwined stories of Greek religion and Roman religion through the twentieth century to provide some background for the current state of affairs, in which most classicists, despite recognizing that the concept of religion is ill-suited to the materials they study, persist in speaking of ancient Greek and Roman religions. Second, I look at how a "new" ancient religion is constructed. That is to say, if the gods and cults of ancient Greeks and Romans had been known (at least in the guise of demons and satanic ritual) to Europeans continuously and were transformed into actors in these new entities, Greek and Roman religions, then what of the heretofore unknown gods and rituals revealed by the discovery and deciphering of ancient texts from previously unstudied cultures? I explore the case of "Mesopotamian religion" to show how a new ancient religion comes into being, and again I follow this new invention through its twentieth-century incarnations. Finally, I consider some of the tensions involved in the study of these ancient religions. Many specialists recognize that religion is a troublesome concept when handling ancient evidence. Yet few scholars are willing to abandon the term. Instead, they have cultivated rhetorical devices to smooth over these conceptual difficulties and make religion seem timeless and universal. I conclude by briefly examining one of these rhetorical tropes, the notion of "embedded religion."

The Origins of the Study of Greek and Roman Religions

Europeans have in some form or fashion been aware of the gods of Greece and Rome continuously from the time of the earliest Christians.[1] From the fifth century until the sixteenth century, most people who thought of Greek and Roman gods regarded them as demonic minions of Satan. This line of thinking dates back at least to the patristic writers. Thus Augustine declared that the Roman pantheon consisted not of "righteous gods" (*dii iusti*) but rather of "impious demons" (*daemones impii*) or "evil spirits" (*maligni spiritus*).[2] Among the more educated population, this view existed alongside (or intermixed with) two others. For some, the Greek and Roman gods were heroic humans of old who had come to be regarded as divine at a very early period (the so-called Euhemerist explanation of the gods, associated especially with Lactantius and Isidore of Seville).[3] For others, the gods and their stories were simply harmless allegorical expressions of virtues and vices.[4] Thus the Greco-Roman pantheon could safely adorn the art and architecture of public spaces (and even churches) throughout Europe, and Christian Neo-Platonists could with clear consciences freely employ deities of Greece and Rome in their symbolic speculations.[5] With the increasing number of newly discovered classical manuscripts and the birth of modern archeology from the time of the Italian Renaissance on came a growing interest in classical antiquity and its many gods. Yet even the great humanists rediscovering ancient Rome regarded its deities as something less than gods.

As we might expect from the preceding chapters, the beginning of critical reflection on these gods as parts of "religions" was tied to the colonial enterprises of European powers. As Europe's reach across the world expanded, the data of explorers, travelers, and missionaries flowed back to Europe. While the focus of these descriptions of far-off peoples and places was their strangeness and difference, the accounts were full of comparisons and contrasts to more familiar concepts. Comparison of the new peoples' beliefs and practices most often centered on how they resembled and differed from Christianity (since a looming concern for many European thinkers was the possibility of spreading the gospel to the New World). The gods of classical antiquity, however, also came to occupy an important place in these accounts, and, as historian Frank E. Manuel put it, "virtually any writing which shed light on 'conformities' between Greco-Roman ritual and the religion of contemporaneous heathen societies, whether people living in a state of civility—the Chinese, the Hindus, the Persians—or savage Negroes and American Indians, helped fashion [a] new view of ancient paganism. . . . To the business agents of the great companies native religious customs seemed important intelligence on the character of the inhabitants with whom they had to deal, and Greco-Roman illustrations were normal forms of communication with the educated directors in Amsterdam and London."[6]

Authors of this type of communiqué presented both general observations about broad similarities between the new peoples and classical antiquity and parallels to specific practices. Such comparative activity went all the way back to the early Spanish explorers in the sixteenth century. I offer just a few examples. The Jesuit missionary José de Acosta gave a general description of the idolatry of the Mexicans in his widely read account from the late sixteenth century:

The *Mexicaines* Idolatrie hath bin more pernicious and hurtfull then that of the *Inguas*, as wee shall see plainer heerafter, for that the greatest part of their adoration and idolatrie was employed to Idols, and not to naturall things, although they did attribute naturall effects to these Idolls, as raine, multiplication of cattell, warre, and generation, even as the Greekes and Latins have forged Idolls of *Phoebus*, *Mercurie*, *Iupiter*, *Minerva*, and of *Mars*. To conclude, whoso shall meerly looke into it, shall finde this manner which the Divell hath used to deceive the Indians to be the same wherewith hee hath deceived the Greekes and Romans, and other ancient Gentiles, giving them to understand that these notable creatures, the Sunne, Moone, Starres, and Elements, had power and authoritie to doe good or harme to men.[7]

Other authors noted more specific points of comparison. Bartolomé de Las Casas peppered his *Apologética Historia* of the New World (probably completed by 1560) with references to classical authors and patristic writers (especially Augustine) who wrote about the gods.[8] His detailed classical learning colored his prose in interesting ways, such as in his description of a figure in a New World temple as "a Serapis."[9] In a work of the late seventeenth century, Richard Blome gave an account of the natives of "Mary-land" in America: "Their Idol they place in the innermost Room of the House, of whom they relate incredible Stories, they carry it with them to the Wars, and ask counsel thereof, as the Romans did of their Oracles."[10]

For Blome and most of his predecessors, the "Idols" found in the Americas were diabolical. In describing the inhabitants of the island of St. Vincent, Blome wrote that they believed "that there are a number of Good and Evil Spirits, the Good being their Gods," and "when their several Priests call upon their several Gods together, as they speak, these Gods, or rather Devils, rail, quarrel, and seem to fight with each other. These Daemons shelter themselves sometimes in the Bones of dead Men," and "Persons of Quality and exquisite Knowledge, who have long lived in *St. Vincent's Island*, do affirm, that the Devils do effectually beat them, and they show on their Bodies the visible marks of the blows."[11] Yet, some writers were beginning to offer different possibilities. Sabine MacCormack, for instance, has traced the transformation of the Incan deity Pachacamac. In 1533, Spanish invaders sacked the pyramid temple of Pachacamac near Lima, destroying the central cult statue and robbing the temple of its gold and silver. Contemporary Spanish reports of the incident focus on the issue of idolatry: "the Christians explained to the Indians the great error in which they had been enveloped, and that he who was talking in that idol was the devil." The leader of the expedition, Hernando Pizarro, "broke the idol in the sight of everyone, told them many things about our holy catholic faith and gave them as armor to defend themselves against the devil the sign of the cross."[12] Near the end of the sixteenth century, José de Acosta, while still firmly convinced of the activity of the devil and demons in the New World, observed that although the natives lacked a word for "god," nevertheless "in trueth they had some little knowledge, and therefore in *Peru* they made him a rich temple, which they called *Pachacamac*, which was the principall Sanctuarie of the realme. And it hath beene saide, this word of *Pachacamac* is, as much to say, as the Creator, yet in this temple they used their idolatries, worshipping the Divell and figures." Acosta reflected on the significance of this acknowledgement of a creator:

> As it is therefore a trueth, comfortable to reason, that there is a soveraigne Lorde and King of heaven, whome the Gentiles (with all their infidelities and idolatries) have not denyed, as wee see in the Philosophy of *Timee* in *Plato*, in the Metaphisickes of *Aristotle*, and in the Aesculape of *Tresmigister*, as also in the Poesies of *Homer* & *Virgil*. Therefore the Preachers of the Gospel have no great difficultie to plant & perswade this truth of a supreame God. . . . But it is hard to roote out of their mindes, that there is no other God, nor any other deitie then one.[13]

Pachacamac had become for Acosta something quite distinct from the devil worshipped in his temple. In the early-seventeenth-century *Commentarios reales* of Garcilaso de la Vega, son of a Spanish conquistador and an Incan princess, Pachacamac found still another manifestation. Garcilaso noted that the Incas worshipped the sun and their kings "with as much Veneration as the ancient Gentiles, such as the *Greeks* and *Romans*, did their *Jupiter, Mars, Venus,* &c.," but at the same time, "they proceeded by the mere light of Nature, to the knowledge of the True Almighty God our Lord, Maker of Heaven and Earth . . . , which they called by the Name of *Pachacamac,* and is a word compounded of *Pacha,* which is the Universe and *Camac,* which is the Soul; and is as much as he that animates the World." Writers who held that "they called the Devil by this Name" were thus quite mistaken:

> Howsoever they are mistaken where they say that the *Indians* gave the name *Pachacamac* to the Devil, for whom they have another Word, which is *Cupay,* which when they utter, they spit, with other signs of Detestation. Notwithstanding this Enemy so far insinuated himself amongst these Infidels, that he caused himself to be worshipped by them by entering into all those things, which they called sacred, or Holy; for he spake to them in their Oracles, their Temples, and the Corners of their Houses, calling himself by the Name of *Pachacamac,* and by this subtilty the *Indians* worshipped every thing through which the Devil spoke, believing it to be a Deity; but had they believed it was the *Cupay,* or Devil, whom they heard, they would certainly have burnt the things through which he spoke.

Garcilaso concluded that in worshipping Pachacamac, "it is evident that the *Indians* held our invisible God to be the Creatour of all things."[14] Thus over the course of roughly a century, and in comparative conversation with the old classical deities, Pachacamac transformed from a demonic idol into the one true Christian god. And Pachacamac would undergo a further change in the eighteenth century, becoming simply the central figure in "The Religion of the Peruvians" in handbooks such as Bernard Picart's *Ceremonies and Religious Customs.*[15]

Related transformations of the ancient pagan gods were occurring simultaneously. As Frank E. Manuel has noted: "With the accumulation of voyage literature and missionary relations and commercial reports, the documents of the ancient world ceased to be mere book learning or source material for theological disputation among rival

Christian sects which vilified each other as heathens. Pagan religion became a living flesh-and-blood reality which was mirrored in contemporary barbarism. . . . The parallel always worked both ways: it infused meaning into the savage rites in the new world, and at the same time it became the key to a reinterpretation of the spirit of the ancients."[16] The close juxtaposition of the classical pantheon and its cults with modern non-Christian worship brought about a more concrete understanding of the ancient deities. The new peoples Europeans encountered had the effect of making the gods and odd worship practices of classical literature seem more like "real options"; Europeans were able to imagine into existence ancient Greeks and Romans acting in ways not unlike these new, contemporary pagans. Just like "Hinduism" and "African religion," then, ancient Greek and Roman "religion" in Europe emerged out of this mix of colonial and missionary interests.[17]

In some ways, the individual Greek and Roman gods were for a short period dissolved into the general "pagan religion" that authors such as Edward Lord Herbert of Cherbury used as the basis for theorizing about the origins of "religion." For example, in Alexander Ross's *Pansebeia*, both "The Religions of the Romans" and "The Religions of the Grecians" are subject headings, but both are judged to be part of "the same Paganism" present in the rest of the ancient world.[18] More erudite students of ancient Greece and Rome in fact left the discussion of the gods to such cross-cultural compilers and theorists.[19] In his widely read handbook on ancient Rome, *Romae Antiquae Notitia: Or, The Antiquities of Rome*, which was first published in 1696, Basil Kennett included a section dedicated to "the Religion of the Romans." Kennett covered the topics of priests, sacrifices, and festivals, but he sidestepped any discussion of the gods: "For it would be very needless and impertinent to enter into a Disquisition about the Deities, a matter that, having its very Foundation in Fiction, is involv'd in so many endless Stories, and yet has employ'd several Pens to explain it."[20] What was central about Roman religion to Kennett was its utility in governing: "That Religion is absolutely necessary to the establishing of Civil Government, is a truth far from being denied by any sort of Persons." He began his discussion of religion by quoting Machiavelli with approval: "For Religion, saith he, produc'd good Laws; good Laws good Fortune; and good Fortune a good end in whatever they undertook. And perhaps he hath not strain'd the Panegyrick too high, when he tells us, That for several Ages together, never was the Fear of God more eminently conspicuous than in that Republick."[21]

In the eighteenth century, such positive valuations of the role of Roman religion in statecraft generated comparisons with Christianity, further contributing to Greek and Roman "religion" coming into being as objects of study. For Enlightenment thinkers put off by the Christian bickering that surrounded them, Greek and Roman "religion" could be shaped into "a self-consciously pagan counter-position to Christianity."[22] The second chapter of Edward Gibbon's *The History of the Decline and Fall of the Roman Empire*, for example, celebrated the tolerant religious practices of the Romans in contrast to the hard-headed intolerance of the Christians. The enlightened skepticism Gibbon attributed to the Romans would shape discussions of Roman religion for two centuries: "The devout polytheist, though fondly attached to his national rites, admitted with implicit faith the different religions of the earth." A footnote followed that specifically contrasted this outlook with Christian attitudes.[23] Gibbon went on to discuss the viewpoint of "the philosophers" of Rome:

> In their writings and conversation, the philosophers of antiquity asserted the independent dignity of reason; but they resigned their actions to the commands of law and custom. Viewing, with a smile of pity and indulgence, the various errors of the vulgar, they diligently practised the ceremonies of their fathers, devoutly frequented the temples of the gods; and sometimes condescending to act a part on the theatre of superstition, they concealed the sentiments of an Atheist under sacerdotal robes. Reasoners of such a temper were scarcely inclined to wrangle about their respective modes of faith, or of worship.[24]

In contrast to this serene picture, Gibbon depicts the "inflexible, and, if we may use the expression, the intolerant zeal of the Christians."[25]

The Christians were, to be sure, less obstinate and zealous than the Jews, from whom they inherited such characteristics, but nonetheless Gibbon's fifteenth and sixteenth chapters (the last two chapters of the first volume) portrayed early Christianity as a kind of antithesis to the benevolent skepticism and open-minded religious atmosphere of the early Roman empire, and not just "native" Roman religion.[26] Indeed, for Gibbon, it was "the aspiring genius of Rome" to be able to absorb the worship practices of foreigners.[27]

The detection of a close relationship between "religion" and the "essence" of a people was a trend that only intensified during the rise of Romanticism and the growth of nationalism in Europe during the nineteenth century, though the nativist element absent in Gibbon would make a strong revival. A renewed European interest in mythology fueled (and was itself fueled by) nationalist concerns.[28] This situation increased interest in ancient "religion" while at the same time provoking a distinct change in attitude toward classical antiquity that favored Greece at the expense of Rome, since the Greeks of antiquity were thought to have a much richer store of mythology (and hence a much richer national spirit) than the ancient Romans.[29] This philhellenism saturated classical studies, particularly work on Greek and Roman "religion," since many thinkers regarded "religion" as especially embodying the "spirit" of a given people (*Volksgeist*).[30] In Hellenic studies, the works of Karl Otfried Müller in the first half of the nineteenth century and Ulrich von Wilamowitz-Moellendorff in the late nineteenth and early twentieth centuries illustrate some of the range of Germanic philhellenism of that era.[31] Müller's *Prolegomena zu einer wissenschaftlichen Mythologie*, published in 1825, along with his *Handbuch der Archäologie der Kunst* (1830), linked the production of Greek art (and *not* Roman imitations) with the particular characteristics of Greek religion, which were expressed especially in mythology.[32] In *Der Glaube der Hellenen*, the second volume of which was published posthumously in 1932, Wilamowitz emphasized continuities between the universalisms of Greek religion and Christianity, linking what he judged the best parts of Christianity with Greek precursors, again taking Greek mythology as the key datum. Unearthing early, or "original," Greek myths became in the nineteenth century an important preoccupation of classicists, one that would persist well into the twentieth century.

In this atmosphere, Roman "religion" suffered in comparison to Greek "religion." For classicists of the nineteenth century and the early twentieth century, Roman "religion" of the historical era consisted merely of borrowed Greek myths and copious external rites devoid of any actual, genuine beliefs, aside from those borrowed second hand from "Oriental religions." The easy tolerance Gibbon had celebrated, these later scholars condemned. The nineteenth century's most acclaimed historian of ancient Rome, Theodor Mommsen, falls into this group.[33] Mommsen admired early "Latin religion" along with Greek religion in the first volume of his monumental *History of Rome*, but his treatment of Roman religion in the subsequent volumes describes a decay of the "pure" and "simple" older "faith." The following sentiments are representative: "The ancient Italian popular faith fell to the ground; over its ruins rose—like oligarchy and despotism rising over the ruins of the political commonwealth—on the one side unbelief, state-religion, Hellenism, and on the other side superstition, sectarianism, the religion of the Orientals."[34] This type of thinking reached its apex in the work of W. Warde Fowler, who traced how a "natural and organic" early Roman household religion, which "in its peculiar way was a real expression of religious feeling," disintegrated through foreign contamination by the time of the Roman republic into an empty formalism and obsession with ritual more dismal even than "the legalism of the Pharisees."[35]

The intense, sometimes obsessive, interest in origins continued to thrive through the close of the nineteenth century. Several landmark studies appeared in the space of little more than a decade. The first edition of J. G. Frazer's *The Golden Bough* was published in 1890.[36] The early twentieth century brought the first edition of Georg Wissowa's *Religion und Kultus der Römer* in 1902 and Jane Harrison's *Prolegomena to the Study of Greek Religion* in 1903.[37] All these works still display a passionate concern for the "original" form of the given "religion," but Wissowa and Harrison together marked a shift that began to see cult and ritual as the central features of "religion" in the classical world.[38]

The mid to late twentieth century marked a period of transition in the study of Greek and Roman religions. The concern for the "original" and "pristine" forms of classical religions perhaps hit its high point with the work of Georges Dumézil, *La religion romaine archaïque*, in 1966, in which this scholar of ancient Indo-European cultures attempted to isolate the most archaic (and thus, of course, most genuine) form of Roman religion.[39] It is, however, the interest in ritual that became fruitful in studies of the later twentieth century. One result of the newfound centrality of ritual in Greek and Roman religions was the more vehement distancing of classical "religions" from Christianity, which was (when distilled into an ideal Protestant form) much more concerned with belief than ritual. Recent classicists have thus, in a way ironically similar to Gibbon, consciously constructed Greek and Roman "religions" as everything that Christianity was not. The historian Moses Finley provides a representative comparison: "How fundamentally alien Greek religion was (to our eyes) is most easily shown by a simple listing. . . . Greek religion had no sacred books . . . , no revelation, no creed. It also lacked any central ecclesiastical organization or the support of a central political organization . . . there could, strictly speaking, be neither Greek orthodoxy nor Greek heresy."[40] The list of differences could go on, and the outlook is perhaps best summed up by the classicist Paul Cartledge, who wrote that "Classical Greek religion is 'other,' desperately foreign to (in particular) post-Christian, monotheistic ways of conceptualizing the divine."[41] I find much of this recent classical scholarship very useful. Its honesty about just how much the ancient Greek and Roman worlds differed from our own has helped me to think in new ways about the ancient world. Yet, such statements of the sheer difference of Greek (and Roman) religion from popular understandings of religion also raise the central question: If these configurations are so utterly different from modern "ways of conceptualizing the divine," if the things that modern people conceive of as "religious" were not so conceived in the ancient worlds and vice versa, then how and why are ancient practices to be recognized as "religion" at all? Before I answer this question, I broaden the scope of the discussion by turning to the invention of Mesopotamian religion.

A Formula for Creating a New Ancient Religion: Mesopotamian Religion

The amalgam described as "Mesopotamian religion" provides an excellent example of the birth and growth of a new "ancient religion." While some of the gods of the ancient Near Eastern world were known by name from the Bible, there was nothing akin to the recovery of classical sources for Greek and Roman gods that had occurred during the Italian Renaissance. Nevertheless, the notion of "ancient Mesopotamian religion" was already beginning to form in the seventeenth century. It existed as a kind of shell, a basic outline that could not really be filled out largely because of a lack of evidence. The situation is evident in the sprawling book of Alexander Ross already mentioned, *Pansebeia*, which was first published in 1653. Ross has a short section devoted to "The Religions of the Ancient Babylonians," which proceeds in his typical question-and-answer format: *"What kinde of Religious, or rather, Superstitious Government was there among the Ancient* Babylonians? They had their Priests, called *Chaldeans*, and *Magi*, who were much addicted to Astrology and Divination. . . . They worshipped divers Gods, or Idols rather; the two Chief were *Belus*, or *Bel*, or *Baal*, by whom they meant *Jupiter*; and the other was *Astaroth*, or *Astarte*, by which *Juno* was understood."[42] Ross continues for another page in this mode of equating the various gods. At the close of his discussion of the topic, he cites his sources: "See Diodorus, Philostratus, Eusebius, Scaliger."[43] That is, the sources were classical and patristic authorities along with the work of Joseph Justus Scaliger, the sixteenth-century polymath who had coordinated and synthesized the calendrical systems of different ancient cultures. Even though firsthand knowledge of Mesopotamian sources was almost totally lacking, these classical sources and the emerging framework of World Religions allowed the basic contours of what would become "Mesopotamian religion" to be set in place. It was immaterial whether or not the primary source evidence that emerged in the eighteenth and nineteenth centuries would show that such a category was native to ancient Mesopotamian civilizations. Mesopotamian religion as a concept had been created, and it was only a matter of time until data would be provided to fill in the blanks.

European travelers and missionaries in the seventeenth century had begun to send artifacts from Mesopotamia back to Europe.[44] By the early eighteenth century, cuneiform inscriptions were beginning to be published in learned journals, but no one was able to read them. The academic discipline of Assyriology, then, did not emerge in Europe until the middle of the nineteenth century when systems of cuneiform writing began to be decoded and systematic excavations commenced in the Middle East. The actual decipherment of Assyrian cuneiform is generally credited to Henry Creswicke Rawlinson, a British lieutenant serving with the East India Company.[45] Having learned Persian, Arabic, and Hindi in the course of his service in India, Rawlinson was in 1835 sent to act as a military advisor to the Persian government. During that year, he began to study cuneiform inscriptions, including the trilingual Behistun Rock Inscription. Over the next decade, and in the course of military exploits in Afghanistan and elsewhere, Rawlinson managed to decode the Old Persian portion of the Behistun Inscription, paving the way for understanding the use of the cuneiform in other languages.[46] Also in the early 1840s the French and British began systematic archeological expeditions in the region of present-day Iraq. A wealth of new material made clearer the relevance of Mesopotamian culture for the understanding of biblical narratives, which in turn increased philanthropic financial support for further archeological excavations as well as the creation of professorships in Assyriology at major universities.

As is clear from Rawlinson's story, the development of Assyriology was subject to its own set of colonial dynamics. The raw materials upon which the discipline was built (cuneiform tablets and other inscribed artifacts) needed to be excavated and removed from sites in Mesopotamia. From 1850 to 1950, institutions in Europe and the United States sponsored archeological expeditions that brought (literally) tons of texts into Western libraries and museums. As these newly discovered artifacts were interpreted, a vocabulary and conceptual apparatus were already established, including the concept of "Mesopotamian religion," such that ancient data could simply be slotted into place. Again, I mean this quite literally. At the British Museum, for instance, cuneiform tablets were labeled with a system of letters to identify their contents (H for history, R for religion) and filed away accordingly.[47]

By 1898, Professor of Semitic Languages Morris Jastrow could write a synthetic work, *The Religion of Babylonia and Assyria*, which ran to 701 pages, plus bibliography and index. The book made impressive use of the new textual discoveries and archeological reports. It was divided into three sections (gods, religious literature, and religious architecture) followed by an assessment of "the influence exerted by the religion of Babylonia and Assyria," said to be measured in three areas: "doctrines, rites, and ethics."[48] Thus in the early twentieth century, the study of "Mesopotamian religion" was on its way to gaining a footing equal to that of the other major religions. *The Religion of Babylonia and Assyria* was part of a series, of which Jastrow himself was the editor, called "Handbooks on the History of Religions."[49]

The continued study of "Mesopotamian religion" in the twentieth century can helpfully illustrate what often counts as "advances" in the study of an ancient religion. Such studies tend to change as popular notions of religion change. While Jastrow's "Mesopotamian religion" consisted of gods, religious literature, religious architecture, doctrines, rites, and ethics, later treatments of the topic would keep pace with the growing interest in "religious experience" heralded by studies such as those of William James and Rudolf Otto already mentioned. The Assyriologist Niek Veldhuis has recently discussed the use of "religion" in the field of Mesopotamian studies by contrasting the approaches of two highly influential Assyriologists of the twentieth century, Thorkild Jacobsen and Leo Oppenheim.[50] Veldhuis's main goal is to stress the differences between the two, and he is surely justified in doing so: Jacobsen had no qualms about reconstructing complex Mesopotamian religious systems, whereas Oppenheim's view was summarized in his chapter subtitle "Why a 'Mesopotamian Religion' Should Not Be Written."[51] What I want to point out, however, is that despite their different approaches, Jacobsen and Oppenheim shared some very basic assumptions about "religion." In keeping with popular twentieth-century characterizations of "religion," both focused on religion as individuals' personal experiences, and both saw religion as a matter of "feelings." Because Jacobsen and Oppenheim are often seen as representing diametrically opposed approaches to Mesopotamian religion, the demonstration of their shared assumptions helps to show the rather narrow confines that the concept of religion establishes for the interpretation of ancient evidence.

Oppenheim and Jacobsen do not frequently appear in each other's footnotes, but each was well aware of the other's work. The two had a tumultuous working relationship for more than a decade at the University of Chicago's Oriental Institute during the production of the Chicago Assyrian Dictionary. One can get the flavor of their rapport from this excerpt from a statement of Oppenheim to the Oriental Institute in 1959: "Dr. Jacobsen loves to profess—and that at [sic] nauseam—that my scholarly thinking is not as deep as his, nor is, for that matter, anybody else's. This, I have found out, means in simple terms that Dr. Jacobsen considers his arguments so wonderful and convincing that he expects all his colleagues to accept them as the only and god-revealed divinely inspired truth" (strike-out in the original).[52] That the scholarship of the two should be in opposition at a rhetorical level is thus not surprising, but their mutual animosity renders their similarities all the more interesting.

I begin by briefly summarizing the approaches of these two scholars. Jacobsen unapologetically began his book-length treatment of

Mesopotamian religion with an appeal to the universality of religion as described by Rudolf Otto's notion of the *mysterium tremendum et fascinosum*.[53] Very similar appeals to Otto and William James introduce the substance of his programmatic essays on Mesopotamian religion.[54] This opening statement from *The Treasures of Darkness* is characteristic of the way Jacobsen wrote about "religion": "Basic to all religion—and so also to ancient Mesopotamian religion—is, we believe, a unique experience of confrontation with power not of this world. Rudolf Otto called this confrontation 'Numinous' and analyzed it as the experience of a *mysterium tremendum et fascinosum*, a confrontation with a 'Wholly Other' outside of normal experience and indescribable in its terms."[55] According to Jacobsen, Mesopotamian religion was just like "all religion"; it consisted of the individual's experience of "the Numinous," which is, by definition, indescribable. Jacobsen followed this statement with an extended account of the development of Mesopotamians' changing reactions to "the Numinous" from the fourth millennium through the second millennium B.C.E.[56] It is a grand synthesis. For my purposes, however, most intriguing are his reflections on his own project. He claimed that he wanted to isolate "the forms of approach to 'the Numinous' generally available" at a given time.[57] To take but one example, Jacobsen argued that during the fourth millennium, since Mesopotamians were principally concerned with the rhythms of rural life and staving off famine, the experience of "the Numinous" consisted of worship of Dumuzi and other gods as providers and gods of fertility. During the third millennium, the dramatically increased importance of the "secular" office of king opened up a new form of "approach" to "the Numinous" for Mesopotamians: "this new concept of the ruler, though purely secular in origin, actually provided an approach to central aspects of the Numinous which had not been readily suggestible before: the aspects of tremendum as 'majesty' and 'energy.'"[58] So, for Jacobsen, "the Numinous" is always and everywhere the same; it exists outside all cultural contingencies.[59] In his reading, religion involves an ever-present and unchanging "Numinous" to which humans react. His book and essays trace the changing human reactions to this universal, unchanging, and indescribable thing. His sweeping descriptions of these personal experiences are what constitute "Mesopotamian religion."

In contrast to Jacobsen's presentation, Oppenheim's approach seems much more restrained. Oppenheim claimed that a systematic account of the type that Jacobsen offered was simply not possible. As we will see, however, his reasoning for not wanting to write a "Mesopotamian religion" was based on a concept of "religion" quite similar to that of Jacobsen—a focus on individual "experience." Oppenheim demurred from the project of writing a "Mesopotamian religion" for two reasons: "the nature of the available evidence, and the problem of comprehension across the barriers of conceptual conditioning."[60] On the first point, he argued that the surviving evidence does not provide data for "religion." For instance, the many extant Mesopotamian prayers "contain no indication of an emotion-charged preference for a specific central topic such as, for example, the individual in relation to spiritual or moral contexts of universal reach, the problem of death and survival, the problem of immediate contact with the divine, to mention here some *topoi* that might be expected to leave an imprint on the religious literature of a civilization as complex as the Mesopotamian."[61] Thus, his problem with the evidence was not so much its fragmentary nature as its failure to answer the questions raised by the modern notion of religion (note the assumption that "religious literature" was presented as a self-evident category). Oppenheim "expected" religion in "a civilization as complex as the Mesopotamian," but he was disappointed that the extant evidence simply did not give him insight into the particular Mesopotamian manifestation of the universal religious experience of the "common man."[62] He saw a similar problem with using Mesopotamian "myths" as evidence for "religion" because they did not directly express the "religious experience" of individuals. He wrote that Mesopotamian myths "form something like a fantastic screen, enticing as they are in their immediate appeal, seductive . . . but still a screen which one must penetrate to reach the hard core of evidence that bears directly on the forms of religious experience of Mesopotamian man."[63] Again, it is not the case that religion was an invalid category for Oppenheim. Rather, religious experience, "the hard core of evidence" in his terms, was just too difficult for modern scholars to reach.

Oppenheim's second reason for shying away from a "Mesopotamian religion" is summed up in the phrase "conceptual difficulties." It is not polytheism in and of itself, said Oppenheim, that constitutes the unbridgeable gap between our world and that of ancient Mesopotamians. Rather, the problem was the "plurality of intellectual and spiritual dimensions" of "the higher polytheistic religions": "This conceptual barrier, in fact, is more serious an impediment than the reason usually given, the lack of data and specific information. Even if more material were preserved, and that in an ideal distribution in content, period, and locale, no real insight would be forthcoming—only more problems. Western man seems to be both unable and, ultimately, unwilling to understand such religions except from the distorting angle of antiquarian interest and apologetic pretenses."[64] For Oppenheim, "Mesopotamian religion" was an entity "out there" in antiquity; it is just that scholars lack either the conceptual tools or the willpower to excavate it properly.[65] Oppenheim, then, did not oppose writing about "Mesopotamian religion" on the grounds that the category of religion is inappropriate for the culture he studies. Indeed, in 1950, he wrote a synthetic piece titled simply "Assyro-Babylonian Religion" for a collection on "forgotten" and "living primitive" religions.[66] Instead, he was concerned that modern investigators cannot accurately grasp a polytheistic religion. He was, moreover, just as interested in "religious experience" as Jacobsen. To be sure, the two men had reached radically different conclusions about Mesopotamian religious experience. The following two quotations highlight those differences. Oppenheim, in the context of discussing Mesopotamian prayers, had concluded that

> the influence of religion on the individual, as well as on the community as a whole, was unimportant in Mesopotamia. No texts tell us that ritual requirements in any stringent way affected the individual's physiological appetites, his psychological preferences, or his attitude

toward his possessions or his family. His body, his time, and his valuables were in no serious way affected by religious demands. . . . He lived in a quite tepid religious climate within a framework of socioeconomic rather than cultic co-ordinates. . . . Manifestations of religious feelings, as far as the common man is concerned, were ceremonial and formalized rather than intense and personal.[67]

Compare Jacobsen's formulation:

> The religious framework thus affected and conditioned life in ancient Mesopotamian society intensely and on all levels. It may be assumed that, as in most societies, the majority of men in ancient Mesopotamia had normal aptitude for, and sensitivity to, religion and religious values. Occasional individuals lacking in such normal sensitivity, who could see in religion only meaningless restrictions on their personal inclinations, will of course have been found, perhaps especially among the slaves and brutalized poor. To balance them the civilization seems to have had an unusually large number of highly sensitive minds, religiously creative poets, thinkers, and priests. Mesopotamian religious literature at its best is the literature of a people highly gifted in religion, capable of profound religious insights and of finding profound and moving expression of them.[68]

Despite these drastically different takes on the evidence, both Jacobsen and Oppenheim center on individuals' "religious experience" or "feelings" as the locus of "Mesopotamian religion." This focus on interiority and personal experience is a distinctly modern take on the ancient evidence.[69] Like Greek and Roman religions, ancient Mesopotamian religion turns out to be very much a modern entity.

Making Something New Old Again; or, Why Religion Seems Like a Natural Category

Like Jacobsen and Oppenheim, the overwhelming majority of scholars in ancient history simply assume the universality of religion. Yet as I pointed out at the beginning of Chapter 2, many specialists working on a variety of ancient cultures are well aware that religion was not a concept native to the cultures they study. As we saw earlier in this chapter, many scholars of classical Greece and Rome have recently come to stress the great differences between typical modern conceptions of religion and what went on in the ancient Mediterranean world. For the most part, though, even these historians still write as though religion was in fact a concept native to the ancient world. How and why do they do so?

One of the dominant means of talking about "religion" in ancient Mediterranean cultures is through the use of the terminology of "embeddedness." It is quite common to read that religion "was embedded in all aspects of ancient life."[70] Indeed, this trope of "embedded religion" is ubiquitous in recent studies of ancient "religion." The authors who employ it argue that the behaviors modern people generally collect under the heading of "religion" did not compose a well-defined category in ancient Mediterranean antiquity. Rather, "religion was embedded" in many or all aspects of ancient cultures. The use of this notion of embeddedness is salutary insofar as it helps to emphasize that categories post-Enlightenment thinkers often regard as distinct (such as politics, economics, and religion) were *not* distinct in the ancient world. Yet, such terminology also presents problems. I want to emphasize that I do not see the following critique as overturning or dismissing the important work of the scholars who have employed such tropes. Instead, I would argue that the following observations carry these scholars' insights to what I view as their logical conclusions. With that caveat in mind, it is useful to recall the discussion of descriptive and redescriptive uses of "religion" from Chapter 1. The authors who use the trope of "embedded religion" generally write in a descriptive register (they present themselves as giving an accurate account of an ancient culture). Yet, their use of the idea that "religion was embedded" in the social structures of the ancient world suggests that "religion" is in fact a redescriptive term (ancient people did not recognize religion as a distinct sphere of life). The trope of "embedded religion" can thus produce the false impression that "religion" is a descriptive concept rather than a redescriptive concept for ancient cultures (that is, there really is something "out there" in antiquity called "Greek religion" that scholars are simply describing rather than creating). By permitting this slippage between descriptive and redescriptive uses of "religion," the rhetoric of "embedded religion" allows historians to have their cake and eat it, too. They can (correctly) recognize that religion was not a concept in ancient cultures, but they can continue speaking as if it were. The result of such techniques for speaking about antiquity is the reinscription of religion as something eternally present in all cultures.[71]

Conclusion

Although the Greeks, Romans, Mesopotamians, and many other peoples have long histories, the stories of their respective "religions" are of recent pedigree. The formation of "ancient religions" as objects of study coincided with the formation of religion itself as a concept in the sixteenth and seventeenth centuries. It thus makes a good deal of sense that some of these "ancient religions" have come to seem strangely foreign to modern notions of religion. Even in the face of this growing sense of discomfort with the concept of religion, the vast majority of scholars continue discussing "ancient religions." I suspect this persistence is due to their unwillingness or inability to contemplate certain kinds of difference. The cultural critic Russell T. McCutcheon has aptly summarized the state of affairs:

> Just as the concepts nation or nation-state—let alone individual or citizen—are today so utterly basic, even vital, to many of our self-understandings and our ability to self organize that we routinely cast them backward in chronological time and outward in geographic space, so too it is difficult *not* to understand, say, ancient Romans or Egyptians as having a "religion." After all, common sense tells us that religion is a human universal. But . . . there is something at stake in so easily projecting, in this case, backward in history or outward in culture our local classification, for along with its ability to organize certain sets of human behaviors comes attendant socio-political implications. By means of such projection we may be doing something more than neutrally or passively classifying the world around us; instead, by means of such classifications, we may very well be actively presenting back to ourselves the taxonomies that help to establish our own contingent

and inevitably provincial social world as if their components were self-evident, natural, universal, and necessary.[72]

It is hard to overstate the importance of this point. If we want to go on talking about ancient Mesopotamian religion, ancient Greek religion, or any other ancient religion, we should always bear in mind that we are talking about something modern when we do so. We are not naming something any ancient person would recognize. In our current context, we organize our contemporary world using the concepts of religious and secular. Furthermore, we carve up the religious side of that dichotomy into distinct social groups, the World Religions. Intentionally or not, when we bring this vocabulary to ancient sources, baggage comes along with it. I am advocating that we admit to and embrace this fact. Religion is a modern category; it may be able to shed light on some aspects of the ancient world when applied in certain strategic ways, but we have to be honest about the category's origins and not pretend that it somehow organically and magically arises from our sources. If we fail to make this reflexive move, we turn our ancient sources into well-polished mirrors that show us only ourselves and our own institutions.

CONCLUSION: AFTER RELIGION?

I have argued that the idea of religion is not as natural or universal as it is often assumed to be. Religion has a history. It was born out of a mix of Christian disputes about truth, European colonial exploits, and the formation of nation-states. Yet the study of religion as an academic discipline has proceeded largely on the assumption that religion is simply a fact of human life and always has been. Since this assumption is so problematic, the question arises: How should the study of religion move forward? I am neither a prophet nor a prescription writer, but I would be remiss not to offer a few thoughts on this question by way of conclusion. I offer them as possible directions of exploration that I think could yield interesting results. I hope that these thoughts, and this book as a whole, will provoke some valuable conversations about how we can speak about religion in a more informed way.

One useful way of proceeding would be to bear in mind two sets of distinctions. The first is the distinction between ancient worlds (in which the notions of religion and being religious did not exist) and modern worlds (in which ideas of religion produced from the sixteenth to the nineteenth century have come to structure everyday life in many parts of the world). The second distinction is that between descriptive and redescriptive usages of religion, which I discussed in Chapter 1.

Let me begin, then, with the present day. Many scholars have acknowledged that Christian assumptions have been a part of most definitions of religion. There is, however, a widespread conviction that the history of religious studies has brought about a progressive purging of those Christian assumptions such that religion has become a more and more universally valid descriptive category. According to this scenario, religion has become more democratized and more useful for cross-cultural application by being redefined in less overtly Christian ways (for example, by replacing God or gods with Ultimate Concerns as the focal point of religion).[1] Such efforts to produce "better definitions" of religion, or "more cross-culturally valid" definitions of religion seem to me to be misguided. Benson Saler has advised his fellow anthropologists that what is needed is not a "better" or "more inclusive" definition of religion. He writes, "Religion is a word that has traditional meanings for us and for the audience for which we write, and by so widening or otherwise altering what it includes, it may well cease to have much utility as a research and literary tool."[2]

I agree with Saler's analysis and think that a more productive path would be to study just what is at stake for those who think it is important to adhere to this or that *particular* definition of religion. Jonathan Z. Smith, for example, has focused attention on the ways that government entities in the United States determine what does and does not get to count as religion through an examination of Supreme Court cases.[3] This kind of approach has more potential for generating useful insights. What sorts of interests are involved in such decisions of defining religion? *Who* is doing the defining and *why?* In other words, a good focus for those who would study "religion" in the modern day is keeping a close eye on the *activity* of defining religion and the *act* of saying that some things are "religious" and others are not.[4]

Such an approach means giving up on the essentialist project of finding "the" definition of religion. Such a reorientation in the study of religion would also allow for a more playful approach to second-order, redescriptive usages of religion. Religion could be deployed in nonessentialist ways to treat something as a religion for the purposes of analysis. Such a move would shift our mode of discourse. We would no longer ask the question "Is phenomenon X a religion?" Rather, we would ask something like "Can we see anything new and interesting about phenomenon X by considering it, for the purpose of study, as a religion?" Take the example of capitalism. If we pose the question "Is capitalism a religion?" we fall into the old trap of seeing how many characteristics capitalism shares with modern Protestant Christianity and debating whether the number is sufficient such that capitalism should receive the designation of religion. If we shift away from the essentialist standpoint, we might ask different questions, such as "How might we understand human behavior differently if we, as a thought exercise, regard capitalism as a religion?" Such an inquiry could provoke a series of strategic comparisons involving gods and invisible market forces, catechumens reciting creeds and advertisers' sloganeering. This kind of exercise helps us see phenomena in new ways and should be encouraged.[5] I think, then, there is still a place for "the study of religion" in the modern world, provided that those doing the study adopt a self-conscious and critical attitude that has often been lacking.[6]

But what of the ancient world, which has provided much of the focus for this book? Here I think matters are a bit more complicated. Ancient peoples were not in the business of dividing aspects of their lives into "religious" and "not religious," so the approach to studying religion in the modern word that I just outlined would not be very effective when applied to ancient evidence. Are there other possibilities? I have had the good fortune of presenting portions of this work to audiences who have pondered this difficult question with me. On one of those occasions, the historian Edwin Judge suggested a three-step procedure to follow when one encounters the word "religion" in a translation of an ancient text. First, cross out the word whenever it occurs. Next, find a copy of the text in question in its original language and see what word (if any) is being translated as "religion." Third, come up with a different translation: "It almost doesn't matter what. *Anything* besides 'religion'!" According to Judge, simply allowing "religion" to stand in an ancient text leads to a kind of "miasma of thought" that prevents one from seeing how ancient people might have organized their worlds.[7]

I find this approach sensible, with regard to the issue of translation. It is important, however, to distinguish between issues of translation and issues of historiography. Judge's rules about translation apply to what I have been calling the descriptive process—the attempt to reproduce the classifications of the group of people being studied. At this level, religion has no place in the study of the ancient world. Ought we then abandon the study of religion in antiquity altogether? Such an approach seems unhelpful to me. All of our words and conceptual tools have histories. In this book, I have interrogated the word "religion," and in doing so, I have been somewhat cavalier in my use of other words such as "culture," "society," and "ethnicity," to name just three. All these terms could (and should) be subjected to the kind of scrutiny that I have applied to "religion."[8] But all these terms also form important parts of the vocabulary that historians use all the time. To simply jettison them wholesale is impractical and out of keeping with the Wittgensteinian approach to language that I have advocated elsewhere in this book. Words are social products, and as such, they never offer perfect clarity. But a greater degree of self-consciousness about the words we use is definitely something to be desired.

Thus, I do think that religion can be used as a redescriptive concept for studying the ancient world. The question then becomes: What sort of definition or theory of religion should be used for this redescriptive project? And so we return to that slippery issue of what we *mean* by religion. In the first chapter, I noted that when pressed to define religion, most people offer definitions that amount to "anything that sufficiently resembles modern Protestant Christianity." Notice, however, that this common use of "religion" occurs *in the context of being asked to define the term.* Now I want to think for a moment about what people do when we are not playing the particular game of defining religion. How is the word "religion" used in a more mundane sense when people are not put on the spot and asked to engage in the language game of providing definitions? In those situations, religion seems to be used mostly to discuss things involving gods or other superhuman beings and the technologies for interacting with such beings. Is a definition like this one tenable for the study of antiquity? At first glance, such a definition appears simplistic and obviously a poor fit for many non-Western and ancient cultures. If, however, one's definition of religion is explicitly and emphatically *redescriptive*, there is nothing wrong with the definition "not fitting" the frameworks present in other cultures. Indeed, as Jonathan Z. Smith has pointed out, "It is the very distance and difference of religion as a second-order category that gives it cognitive power."[9] In fact, the use of this type of definition of religion for the study of antiquity has been proposed by Stanley Stowers.[10] His advice is as follows: "The theory/definition ought to be explicitly a second-order conception designed for and justified by its usefulness in scholarly enquiry. At the same time certain advantages for such enquiry attach to theories that bear some continuity with 'religion,' 'the things of the gods,' or whatever folk concepts that mostly overlap with our modern Western concepts."[11] When Stowers writes that "the definition ought to be an explicitly second-order conception," he seems to me to take for granted something very much like the arguments put forth in this book. It is my impression, however, that many scholars do not take this starting point for granted, and it is therefore a point worth dwelling on more than Stowers does. This is one reason I have been at pains throughout this book to emphasize that religion is not a universally applicable first-order concept that matches a native discursive field in every culture across time and throughout history. If we are going to use religion as a second-order, redescriptive concept, we must always be explicit that we are doing so and avoid giving the impression that religion really was "out there" "embedded in" or "diffused in" the ancient evidence. The problem with using "religion" to talk about the ancient world is not anachronism. All of our concepts are modern and hence anachronistic when applied to the ancient world. The problem is that we so often suffer from a lack of awareness that we are being anachronistic. Informed and strategic deployment of anachronism, on the other hand, can have unexpected and thought-provoking results.[12]

Thus, I do think the use of religion as an explicitly second-order or redescriptive concept has a place in the study of antiquity. That leaves us with the final question of what to do about our *descriptive* accounts of the ancient world. If we follow Judge's dictum and do not allow ourselves to invoke the concept of religion in our descriptive accounts, we will force ourselves to think outside our usual categories. This is a very healthy practice, but it also leads almost immediately to another question: How in practical terms can we accomplish this sort of defamiliarization? First, it is crucial to understand that this is not simply a problem of finding another concept or word that covers the same ground as "religion," of finding a better word for it. The whole point is that, in antiquity, there never was any "it" there to begin with. The different type of descriptive accounts that I have in mind would allow what we have been calling "ancient religions" (that is, the contents of all those books called *Mesopotamian Religion, Religions of Rome, Ancient Greek Religion*, etc.) to be disaggregated and rearranged in ways that correspond better to ancient peoples' own organizational schemes. What we will produce with such a procedure is not a "replacement" for religion; it will be something altogether different. We will end up not with slightly tweaked books on ancient Greek religion or on Roman religion, but with books on Athenian appeals to ancestral tradition, Roman ethnicity, Mesopotamian scribal praxis, Christian and Muslim heresiological discourses, and other topics that will encapsulate and thoroughly rearrange those bits and pieces of what we once gathered together as "ancient religions."[13]

NOTES

Introduction

1. Linguists classify Khasi as part of the Mon-Khmer branch of the family of Austro-Asiatic languages (the Bengali language, on the other hand, is classified as Indo-Aryan). It is unclear when the term *niam* entered the Khasi vocabulary and when it came to be used as an equivalent for "religion," since Khasi seems to have had no stable written form until the early nineteenth century, when British and Bengali Christian missionaries began to produce tracts in the Khasi language written in Bengali characters. By the middle of the nineteenth century, Presbyterian missionaries had begun a concerted effort to print Christian materials in Khasi using Roman characters, which eventually became the standard format for written Khasi. For a concise discussion of the history of the language, see I. M. Simon, "The Khāsi Language: Its Development and Present Status," *Contributions to Asian Studies* 11 (1978): 167–80. On the classification of Khasi, see Paul Sidwell, *Classifying the Austroasiatic Languages: History and State of the Art* (Munich: Lincom Europa, 2009), 98–106.

2. For a brief summary and important critique of recent efforts to study religion and human evolution, see Maurice Bloch, "Why Religion Is Nothing Special But Is Central," *Philosophical Transactions of the Royal Society B* 363 (2008): 2055–61.

3. In French, one may turn to Michel Despland, *La religion en occident: Évolution des idées et du vécu*, repr. ed. (Montreal: Fides, 1988 [1979]), who examines the concept of religion in a large number of authors from the standpoint of the philosophy of religion. Ernst Feil's monumental *Religio: Die Geschichte eines neuzeitlichen Grundbegriffs*, 4 vols. (Göttingen: Vandenhoeck and Ruprecht, 1986–2007), proceeds in a fashion similar to Despland's book but in a much more thorough way and has all the benefits and drawbacks of its genre—the multivolume German magnum opus. In Italian, related topics are treated in Dario Sabbatucci, *La prospettiva storico-religiosa: fede, religione e cultura* (Milan: Saggiatore, 1990).

4. Wilfred Cantwell Smith, *The Meaning and End of Religion: A New Approach to the Religious Traditions of Mankind*, repr. ed. (Minneapolis, Minn.: Fortress, 1991 [1963]), 51.

5. Ibid., 19.

6. The reference is to Plato, *Republic* 615c (*eis de theous asebeias te kai eusebeias kai goneas*); translation and italics are my own. I cite from the edition of S. R. Slings, *Platonis Rempublicam* (New York: Oxford University Press, 2003).

7. The reference is to the historian Dionysius of Halicarnassus, who lived in the first century B.C.E., in his *Roman Antiquities* 8.44 (*tēs pros to genos eusebeias*). I cite from the edition of Cary in the Loeb Classical Library, *The Roman Antiquities of Dionysius of Halicarnassus*, 7 vols. (London: William Heinemann, 1945). It is perhaps not surprising that this term of proper regard for social hierarchies is most often translated into Latin as *pietas*, and it appears parallel to *dharma* in the inscriptions of the Indian ruler Ashoka (third century B.C.E.). See the Greek text edited by G. Pugliese Carratelli et al., *A Bilingual Graeco-Aramaic Edict by Aśoka: The First Greek Inscription Discovered in Afghanistan* (Rome: Istituto Italiano per il Medio ed Estremo Oriente, 1964).

8. Talal Asad, "Reading a Modern Classic: W. C. Smith's *The Meaning and End of Religion*," *History of Religions* 40 (2001): 205–22. The remainder of Asad's quotation is dense but bears repeating: "Religion has been part of the restructuration of practical times and spaces, a rearticulation of practical knowledges and powers, of subjective behaviors, sensibilities, needs, and expectations in modernity. But that applies equally to secularism, whose function has been to try to guide that rearticulation and to define 'religions' in the plural as a species of (non-rational) belief. . . . Secularist ideology, I would suggest, tries to fix permanently the social and political place of 'religion'" (221).

9. See the discussion in Jan N. Bremmer, "Secularization: Notes toward a Genealogy," in *Religion: Beyond a Concept*, ed. Hent de Vries (New York: Fordham University Press, 2008), 432–37.

10. See John E. Stambaugh, "The Functions of Roman Temples," *Aufstieg und Niedergang der römischen Welt* 2.16.1 (1978): 554–608.

11. See Matt. 22:15–22, Mark 12:13–17, Luke 20:20–26, and Logion 100 in the *Gospel of Thomas*. Among early Christians, the passages from the canonical gospels were sometimes read in light of 1 Tim. 2:1–2. According to the Christian teacher Justin Martyr, who wrote in Rome in the middle of the second century, Caesar was entitled not only to taxes, but also to prayers to the Christian god on the emperor's behalf. Alternatively, in the fourth century, Ambrose of Milan understood the passage to be an exhortation to give up all property and take up an ascetic life.

For easy reference, see the sources gathered in Arthur Just, Jr., *Ancient Christian Commentary on Scripture: Luke* (Downers Grove, Ill.: InterVarsity, 2003), 310–11.

12. Peter Harrison, *"Religion" and the Religions in the English Enlightenment* (Cambridge: Cambridge University Press, 1990), 174.

13. For the moment, I will simply provide a list of authors whose work on the development of the concept of religion I have found especially helpful (individual works will be noted in the course of the book): Talal Asad, Jan Bremmer, William T. Cavanaugh, David Chidester, Michel Despland, Ernst Feil, Timothy Fitzgerald, Peter Harrison, Richard King, Craig Martin, Tomoko Masuzawa, Russell McCutcheon, Jonathan Z. Smith, Wilfred Cantwell Smith, Guy Stroumsa, and Sarah Thal. Three other projects have been less influential, but they still ought to be mentioned in this context: S. N. Balagangadhara, *"The heathen in his blindness": Asia, the West, and the Dynamic of Religion* (Leiden: Brill, 1994); Daniel Dubuisson, *The Western Construction of Religion: Myths, Knowledge, and Ideology*, trans. William Sayers (Baltimore, Md.: Johns Hopkins University Press, 2003 [French ed. 1998]); and Hans G. Kippenberg, *Discovering Religious History in the Modern Age*, trans. Barbara Harshav (Princeton, N.J.: Princeton University Press, 2002 [German ed. 1997]).

14. As I was finishing revisions to this book, I was alerted to the existence of William T. Cavanaugh's book *The Myth of Religious Violence* (New York: Oxford University Press, 2009). His chapter titled "The Invention of Religion" surveys some of the same evidence that I cover here in Chapters 5 and 6. This is not surprising, given that we seem to share a common starting point in the work of Wilfred Cantwell Smith and that I have made use of some of Cavanaugh's earlier articles. It is encouraging to see that he has reached conclusions similar to mine.

15. See Pim den Boer, "Europe to 1914: The Making of an Idea," in *The History of the Idea of Europe*, ed. Kevin Wilson and Jan van der Dussen (London: Routledge, 1995), 13–82.

1. What Do We Mean by "Religion"?

1. *Jacobellis v. Ohio*, 378 U.S. 184 (1964), available at http://caselaw.lp .findlaw.com/scripts/getcase.pl?court=us&vol=378&invol=184 (accessed 25 May 2011).

2. Eric J. Sharpe, *Understanding Religion* (New York: St. Martin's, 1983), 46–48. I am not the first to observe the applicability of Justice Stewart's remarks to attempts at defining religion; see, for example, Russell

T. McCutcheon, "Religion, Ire, and Dangerous Things," *Journal of the American Academy of Religion* 72 (2004): 173–93, at 186.

3. Eric J. Sharpe, *Comparative Religion: A History*, 2nd ed. (La Salle, Ill.: Open Court, 1986 [1975]), 318.

4. There are a number of good summaries of the major attempts at defining and explaining "religion." The best starting place is Russell T. McCutcheon, *Studying Religion: An Introduction* (London: Equinox, 2007).

5. Jonathan Z. Smith, "Religion, Religions, Religious," first published in *Critical Terms for Religious Studies*, ed. Mark C. Taylor (Chicago: University of Chicago Press, 1998), 269–84, and later reprinted in Jonathan Z. Smith, *Relating Religion: Essays in the Study of Religion* (Chicago: University of Chicago Press, 2004), 179–96. The quotation here is from the latter, p. 193. The reference is to the appendix of Leuba's *A Psychological Study of Religion: Its Origin, Function, and Future* (New York: Macmillan, 1912), 339–63.

6. See Bruce Lincoln, *Holy Terrors: Thinking about Religion after September 11*, 2nd ed. (Chicago: University of Chicago Press, 2006 [2003]).

7. Clifford Geertz, "Religion as a Cultural System" in *Anthropological Approaches to the Study of Religion*, ed. Michael Banton (New York: Frederick A. Praeger, 1966), 1–46, quotation from 4. The piece was reprinted as chapter 4 of Geertz, *The Interpretation of Cultures* (New York: Basic Books, 1973).

8. In much of this criticism, Lincoln follows Talal Asad. See Asad, *Genealogies of Religion: Discipline and Reasons of Power in Christianity and Islam* (Baltimore, Md.: Johns Hopkins University Press, 1993), 27–54.

9. Lincoln, *Holy Terrors*, 1.

10. Ibid., 5–7. As I say, there is much to admire in this careful definition, but Lincoln's repeated reference in the definition to "religious discourse" raises a question: How does he know what counts as religious if he has yet to define "religion"?

11. Ittai Gradel's parenthetical addition to his definition of "religion" is another good example of this phenomenon: "The most useful definition, in my view, interprets the concept of 'religion' as defined by action of dialogue—sacrifice, prayer, or other forms of establishing and constructing dialogue—between humans and what they perceive as 'another world,' opposed to and different from the everyday sphere in which men function. Typically, this 'other world' is a realm of gods or God (but not necessarily so: academic Buddhism, which most scholars are loath to exclude from the concept, does not operate with gods)" (*Emperor Worship*

and Roman Religion [Oxford: Clarendon, 2002], 5). One can see the logic clearly at work: scholars commonly call Buddhism a religion, so a definition of religion must not exclude Buddhism.

12. Ludwig Wittgenstein, *Philosophical Investigations: The German Text with a Revised English Translation*, 3rd ed., trans. G. E. M. Anscombe (Oxford: Blackwell, 2001), 18 (section I.43). My use of Wittgenstein is not entirely orthodox. For a sound defense of this kind of "pragmatic" reading of Wittgenstein, see Richard Rorty, "Wittgenstein and the Linguistic Turn," in *Philosophy as Cultural Politics: Philosophical Papers*, Vol. 4 (Cambridge: Cambridge University Press, 2007), 160–75.

13. This working notion of "religion" bears a strong resemblance to the type of definition that Benson Saler developed in his important study *Conceptualizing Religion: Immanent Anthropologists, Transcendent Natives, and Unbounded Categories* (Leiden: Brill, 1993). Saler advocates a polythetic definition of religion, relying on Wittgenstein's notion of family resemblances. He also invokes prototype theory in order to prevent the polythetic classification from being too free-floating. The prototypes he chooses are Christianity, Judaism, and Islam. I differ from Saler in that I regard the concepts of Judaism and Islam as having been (to a large degree) constructed in the mold of Christianity by heresiologists and Christian thinkers. On this point, see Catherine Bell, "Paradigms behind (and before) the Modern Concept of Religion," *History and Theory* 45 (2006): 27–46, esp. 31.

14. Karen Armstrong, *Islam: A Short History* (London: Phoenix, 2001), ix.

15. *Abington School District v. Schempp*, 374 U.S. 203 (1963), available at http://caselaw.lp.findlaw.com/scripts/getcase.pl?court=us&vol=374&invol=203 (accessed 18 April 2011). In this case the justices stressed that government institutions should not be involved in things such as prayer and scripture reading; these practices were to be private.

16. The ruling is attributed to Marcian (*Institutes* Book 3) and is preserved in Justinian's *Digest* 1.8.6. See the Latin edition of Theodor Mommsen et al., *Corpus Iuris Civilis*, 3 vols. (Berlin: Weidmann's, 1928–1929). The English translation is that of Alan Watson, *The Digest of Justinian*, rev. ed. (Philadelphia: University of Pennsylvania Press, 1998).

17. John L. Esposito, Darrell J. Fasching, and Todd Lewis, *World Religions Today*, 3rd ed. (New York: Oxford University Press, 2009), 39.

18. Ibid., 16.

19. The roots of this practice are informative. The 1535 edition of Ephraim Pagitt's *Christianographie* contains a map of Europe, Asia, Africa, and India labeled not with different religions, but with the different types of

Christians believed to inhabit each area. See Pagitt, *Christianographie, Or The Description of the multitude and sundry sorts of Christians in the World not subject to the Pope With their Unitie, and how they agree with us in the principall points of Difference betweene us and the Church of Rome* (London: Matthew Costerden, 1635). For reproductions and discussion of two more familiar "World Religions" maps of the nineteenth century, see Christoph Auffarth, "'Weltreligion' als ein Leitbegriff der Religionswissenschaft im Imperialismus," in *Mission und Macht im Wandel politischer Orientierungen: Europäische Missionsgesellschaften in politischen Spannungsfeldern in Afrika und Asien zwischen 1800 und 1945*, ed. Ulrich van der Heyden and Holger Stoecker (Stuttgart: Franz Steiner, 2005), 17–36.

20. For further discussion and criticism of assertions that the ability to "be religious" preceded the notion of "religion," see Russell T. McCutcheon, "Religion before 'Religion'?," in *Chasing Down Religion: In the Sights of History and the Cognitive Sciences. Essays in Honor of Luther H. Martin*, ed. Panayotis Pachis and Donald Wiebe (Thessaloníki: Barbounakis, 2010), 285–301.

21. See Reginald Pecock,*The Repressor of Over Much Blaming of the Clergy*, 2 vols., ed Churchill Babington (London: Longman, Green, Longman, and Roberts, 1860), 2.521.

22. On the history of the vocabulary of "emic" and "etic" and its relationship to notions of "description" and "redescription," see Russell T. McCutcheon's introduction to *The Insider/Outsider Problem in the Study of Religion: A Reader*, ed. Russell T. McCutcheon (London: Cassell, 1999), 15–17.

23. Saler, *Conceptualizing Religion*, 70.

24. Wittgenstein, *Philosophical Investigations*, 100 (section I.383).

25. I believe Wittgenstein's earlier work suffered from this presumption. In his *Tractatus Logico-Philosophicus* (trans. C. K. Ogden [London: Keegan paul, Trench, and Trubner, 1922]) he wrote: "There is indeed the inexpressible. This *shows* itself; it is the mystical" (section 6.522, 187). I like to think of the *Philosophical Investigations* as Wittgenstein's meditation on the wrongheadedness of these sentiments.

26. See the superb discussion of this topic by Robert H. Sharf, "Experience," in *Critical Terms for Religious Studies*, ed. Mark C. Taylor (Chicago: University of Chicago Press, 1998), 94–115.

27. Russell T. McCutcheon, *Manufacturing Religion: The Discourse on Sui Generis Religion and the Politics of Nostalgia* (New York: Oxford University Press, 1997), 109–11.

2. *Lost in Translation*

1. Joseph A. Adler (revising and expanding Daniel L. Overmyer), "Chinese Religion: An Overview," in *Encyclopedia of Religion*, 2nd ed., ed. Lindsay Jones (Detroit: Macmillan, 2005), 3.1580–1613, quotation from 3.1580.

2. Lars Kirkhusmo Pharo, "The Concept of 'Religion' in Mesoamerican Languages," *Numen* 54 (2007): 28–70, quotation from 28. Examples like these could be multiplied for cultures across the globe and through time. To take just one more instance, Christiane Zivie-Coche writes in the preface to *Gods and Men in Egypt: 3000 BCE to 395 CE*, trans. David Lorton (Ithaca, N.Y.: Cornell University Press, 2004 [French ed. 1991]), that in ancient Egyptian languages, "there was no equivalent of our word religion. The Egyptians undoubtedly had no need to forge such a concept, for the domain of the religious was in no way delimited and assigned to a precise place in their life" (ix).

3. In dictionaries of modern Hebrew, the word *dath* is sometimes given as an equivalent of "religion." See, for example, Avraham Zilkha, *Modern English-Hebrew Dictionary* (New Haven, Conn.: Yale University Press, 2002). But one only very rarely sees this word rendered as "religion" when it occurs in ancient texts (it is in fact a Persian loan word and a relative latecomer to ancient Hebrew, first appearing in Esther, Ezra, and Daniel).

4. Certainly the most widely cited and influential book in English is Wilfred Cantwell Smith's *The Meaning and End of Religion*. More thorough, however, are Michel Despland, *La religion en occident* and Ernst Feil, *Religio*. Also worth consulting is the summary in F. Max Müller, *Natural Religion: The Gifford Lectures delivered before the University of Glasgow in 1888* (London: Longmans, Green, 1889), 36–50. For my examples in this chapter, I have drawn freely on the work of these authors.

5. There are those who vigorously maintain that religion was a native concept for Romans. See, for example, the passionate case made by Giovanni Casadio, "*Religio* versus Religion," in *Myths, Martyrs, and Modernity: Studies in the History of Religions in Honour of Jan N. Bremmer*, ed. Jitse Dijkstra et al. (Leiden: Brill, 2010), 301–26. His argument is typical of such studies, in that it proceeds by using words like "religious," "supernatural," and "experience" as if they were simple and unproblematic.

6. *Curculio* 349–50. I cite from the edition and translation of Paul Nixon, *Plautus with an English Translation*, 5 vols. (London: William Heinemann, 1917).

7. *The Woman of Andros* 940–41. I cite from the edition and (slightly adapted) translation of John Barsby, *Terence The Woman of Andros, The*

Self-Tormentor, The Eunuch (Cambridge, Mass.: Harvard University Press, 2001). I owe these references to Émile Benveniste, *Indo-European Language and Society*, trans. Elizabeth Palmer (London: Farber and Farber, 1973 [French ed. 1969]), 520.

8. *On the Nature of the Gods* 3.2.5, repr. ed. (London: Heinemann, 1972 [1933]).

9. Clifford Ando, "Introduction: Religion, Law and Knowledge in Classical Rome," in *Roman Religion*, ed. Clifford Ando (Edinburgh: Edinburgh University Press, 2003), 2–3. Ando points out that other modern translations similarly gloss the difficulty. In the Oxford World's Classics edition, Patrick Gerard Walsh translates: "I have never regarded any of these constituents of our religion with contempt" (*Cicero: On the Nature of the Gods* [Oxford: Oxford University Press, 1998]), 109.

10. Livy, writing in the early days of the Roman empire, employs the term similarly: *Numa in pace religiones instituisset*, "in peacetime Numa had instituted *religiones*" (1.32.5). In the Loeb edition, B. O. Foster translates "Numa had instituted religious practices in time of peace" (Cambridge, Mass.: Harvard University Press, 1919).

11. Cicero, *Against Verres* 2.5.34. I cite from the Loeb edition of L. H. G. Greenwood, *Cicero: The Verrine Orations*, 2 vols. (London: William Heinemann, 1935).

12. I cite the Loeb edition of W. H. D. Rouse, *Lucretius: De rerum natura*, rev. ed. (Cambridge, Mass.: Harvard University Press, 1975 [1924]). Biographical data on Lucretius is scanty. He probably wrote *On the Nature of Things* in the middle of the first century B.C.E. If a difficult passage in one of Cicero's letters to his brother Quintus (2.10 in the Oxford edition) actually refers to *On the Nature of Things*, it would be possible to say with more precision that the poem must have been published before 54 B.C.E. A brief contextualization of Lucretius and his work is available in E. J. Kenny, *Lucretius* (Oxford: Clarendon, 1977).

13. *On the Nature of Things* 1.63 (*oppressa gravi sub religione*) and 1.82–83. See also 1.101: "so potent was *religio* in persuading to evil deeds" (*tantum religio potuit suadere malorum*).

14. Ibid. 1.932 and 4.7. The original 1924 Loeb edition translated *religionum* here as "religion," but the 1975 edition revised the translation to "superstition."

15. Ibid. 5.82–88 and 6.58–64.

16. I have found a few occurrences of this sense of the term in Christian authors, but the context invariably involves a critique of Epicureans.

17. W. C. Smith (*The Meaning and End of Religion: A New Approach to the Religious Traditions of Mankind*, repr. ed. [Minneapolis, Minn.: Fortress, 1991 (1963)], 208, n. 22) also notes a curious usage in two letters of Cyprian, the mid-third-century bishop of Carthage, in which *religio* seems to mean "the structural organization of the church": *et promouebitur quidem, cum deus permiserit, ad ampliorem locum religionis suae* ("For, God permitting, he will undoubtedly be promoted to a more exalted ecclesiastical station," 40.1.3); and in Letter 55: *cunctis religionis gradibus ascendit* ("climbing up through every grade in the Church's ministry," 55.8.2). The Latin text is that of G. F. Diercks, *Sancti Cypriani Episcopi Epistularium* (Turnhout: Brepols, 1994). The English translation is that of G. W. Clarke, *The Letters of St. Cyprian of Carthage* (New York: Newman, 1984–1989).

18. The main action of *Octavius* takes place at Ostia in Italy; the content of the treatise bears a strong resemblance to some of Tertullian's work (so some scholars favor a North African provenance), but the direction of influence (if such exists) is not clear. There is thus uncertainty regarding both the date and the place of composition. See Simon Price, "Latin Christian Apologetics: Minucius Felix, Tertullian, and Cyprian," in *Apologetics in the Roman Empire: Pagans, Jews, and Christians*, ed. Mark Edwards et al. (Oxford: Oxford University Press, 1999), 105–29. The Latin text is drawn from the edition of Bernhard Kytzler, *M. Minuci Felicis Octavius* (Leipzig: Teubner, 1982). The English translations are slightly adapted from those of Rudolph Arbesmann in *Tertullian: Apologetical Works and Minucius Felix: Octavius* (New York: Fathers of the Church, 1950).

19. *Octavius* 6.

20. The same type of ambiguity found in the passage cited above from Cicero (*On the Nature of the Gods* 3.2.5) exists in Minucius Felix (the difference between *religio* as a rite and *religio* as a collection of rites). In *Octavius* 7, the character Caecilius speaks of the establishment of the rites of every *religio* (*initiasse ritus omnium religionum*). Minucius Felix also provides an instance of the kind of usage of *religio* that appears in Lucretius. In *Octavius* 5, Caecilius relates an Epicurean materialistic story of the universe's make-up and then asks, "What reason, then, is there for *religio*, for terror and excessive dread of the divine?" (*unde haec religio, unde formido, quae superstitio est?*). In this instance, *religio* and *superstitio* seem to be synonymous. At the conclusion of chapter 13, however, the character Caecilius contrasts *superstitio* and *religio*. Finally,

Minucius can even say that a person "had" *religio: Mancinus religionem tenuit* (*Octavius* 26).

21. On Tertullian in general, see Timothy David Barnes, *Tertullian: A Historical and Literary Study* (Oxford: Clarendon, 1985).

22. *Against the Jews* 4.6. I refer to the text of E. Kroymann in *Quinti Septimi Florentis Tertulliani Opera: Pars II* (Turnhout: Brepols, 1954).

23. *Octavius* 1. At the conclusion of the final speech by Octavius, a third term, "impiety," joins in the comparison: "Superstition should be repressed, impiety done away with, and *vera religio* kept untouched" (*cohibeatur superstitio, inpietas expietur, vera religio reservetur, Octavius* 38).

24. Ibid. 29.

25. *Apology* 24. In this instance, *vera religio* stands against the singular *romana religio* (*Apology* 24.1–2), but Tertullian elsewhere speaks of the plural *romanae religiones* (*Apology* 26.2). I refer to the Latin text of E. Dekkers in *Quinti Septimi Florentis Tertulliani Opera: Pars I* (Turnhout: Brepols, 1954).

26. *Against the Pagans* 1.25. See also 2.72 for a similar use. The Latin text is that of Concetto Marchesi, *Arnobii Adversus Nationes Libri VII*, 2nd ed. (Turin: Società per Azione G. B. Paravia, 1953). The English translation is that of George E. McCracken, *Arnobius of Sicca: The Case against the Pagans*, 2 vols. (Westminster, Md.: Newman, 1949). Arnobius probably wrote in Sicca in North Africa. For discussion and a basic bibliography, see Michael Bland Simmons, *Arnobius of Sicca: Religious Competition in the Age of Diocletian* (Oxford: Clarendon, 1995).

27. Elsewhere, however, Arnobius uses the shift from plural to singular to contrast the many ways of worshipping the gods and the one genuine way of worship established by Christ, who led Christians from *falsis religionibus* to *religionem veram* (*Against the Pagans* 1.38; see also 2.2 and 2.72).

28. *Against the Pagans* 1.57, my translation. See also 2.70, where Arnobius again refers to Christians' plural *religiones* (*religionum nostrarum*).

29. Lactantius's surviving works come from the early part of the fourth century; he was likely a student of Arnobius. For Latin texts of Lactantius, I use the editions of Samuel Brandt and Georgius Laubmann, *L. Caeli Firmiani Lactanti: Opera Omnia*, 3 vols. (Vienna/Leipzig: F. Tempsky/G. Freytag, 1890–1897). The English translation here is that of Mary Francis McDonald, *Lactantius: The Divine Institutes Books I–VII* (Washington, D.C.: Catholic University of America Press, 1964). For a succinct recent treatment of Lactantius, see the introduction to the translation of Anthony Bowen and Peter Garnsey, *Lactantius: Divine Institutes* (Liverpool: Liverpool University Press, 2003).

30. For the contrast of *vera religio* with the plural *falsae religiones,* see *Divine Institutes* 1.23.6–7; for contrast with the singular *falsa religio,* see *Divine Institutes* 2.3.17–20. The phrase *falsae religiones* in Lactantius seems to be synonymous with the phrase *profanae religiones* in Firmicus, a Christian author of the middle of the fourth century who wrote a tract that carries the title *De errore profanarum religionum.* For the Latin text, see Robert Turcan, *Firmicus Maternus: L'erreur des religions paiennes* (Paris: Les belles lettres, 1982). For the phrase *profanae religiones,* see *De errore* 6.1 and 17.4. Just as Lactantius can interchange the plural *falsae religiones* with the singular *falsa religio,* Firmicus also refers to the singular *profana religio* (*De errore* 21.1). The meaning of all of these phrases seems to be "incorrect worship"—worship that is not directed to the Christian god.

31. *Divine Institutes* 1.20.21, translation slightly adapted. Lactantius also refers to Christian practice as "our *religio*" (*nostra religio,* which is synonymous with *dei cultus,* in *Divine Institutes* 5.20.26–30) or "the *religio* of God" (*religionis suae, Divine Institutes* 5.18.11).

32. Book 4 of the *Divine Institutes* is dedicated to justifying this claim. As he phrases the point in 4.3: "Where, therefore, is *sapientia* joined with *religio?* There, namely, where one God is adored, where life and every act is referred to one head and the Supreme Being, and finally, the same ones are the doctors of wisdom who are also the priests of God" (*ubi ergo sapientia cum religione coniungitur? ibi scilicet ubi deus colitur unus, ubi vita et actus omnis ad unum caput et ad unam summam refertur, denique idem sunt doctores sapientiae qui et dei sacerdotes*). In *Divine Institutes* 7.7.12, a discussion about philosophers and their opinions, *religio* is nearly synonymous with *philosophia,* when "doctrines" are said to be "in" *religio* (*haec vero propria est in nostra religione doctrina*).

33. *Divine Institutes* 1.17.13 (*tanta religione constrictus abnuere non potuit*).

34. Ibid. 1.16.3. The meaning must be nearly the same when Lactantius claims (in *Divine Institutes* 1.17.4) that Cicero destroyed all *religiones* (*nam totus liber tertius de natura deorum omnes funditus religiones evertit ac delet*). In 4.28.11, however, he claims that "*religio* is a worship of the true; *superstitio* of the false. And it is important, really, why you worship, not how you worship or what you pray for" (*religio veri cultus est, superstitio falsi. et omnino quid colas interest, non quemadmodum colas aut quid precere*).

35. *The Wrath of God* 8.1.2. The English translation is that of Mary Francis McDonald, *Lactantius: The Minor Works* (Washington, D.C.: Catholic University of America Press, 1965). See also *Divine Institutes* 1.11.5, in

which *religio* stands in a list with prayers, hymns, shrines, and statues (*religio ipsa et precationes et hymni et delubra et simulacra*). Lactantius calls the *religio* of heaven (*religio caelestis*) genuine worship (*verus cultus, Divine Institutes* 6.2.13; see also the phrase *dei cultum religionemque* in 7.22.14). He also places *religio* parallel to the verbal formulae involving *colere*, "to worship" (e.g., *Divine Institutes* 1.15.7), and in his discussion of Numa's institution of traditional Roman practices (*Divine Institutes* 1.22), Lactantius uses the plural *religiones*, just as Livy had done centuries earlier.

36. *Divine Institutes* 2.18.2. Later in the same discussion, Lactantius phrases the point in another way: "There is no *religio* in statues but rather a mockery of *religio*" (*non religio in simulacris, sed mimus religionis est*).

37. W. C. Smith sees the composition of *De vera religione* as evidence of Augustine's special interest in one "highly important" sense of the term (*The Meaning and End of Religion*, 28). I do not detect anything significant in Augustine's use of the term. For the text of *De vera religione*, I refer to the edition of K.-D. Daur in *Sancti Aurelii Augustini: De doctrina christiana, De vera religione* (Turnhout: Brepols, 1962). For an English translation, see John H. S. Burleigh, *Augustine: Earlier Writings* (Philadelphia: Westminster, 1953), 218–83.

38. I cite the edition of Almut Mutzenbecher, *Sancti Aurelii Augustini: Retractationum libri II* (Turnhout: Brepols, 1984). Augustine expresses a similar sentiment more elliptically in *De vera religione* 1.

39. Although the plural term *religiones* is not frequent, Augustine's other usages here imply multiple possible *religiones:* "In Christian times there can be no doubt at all as to which *religio* is to be received and held fast" (*Christianis temporibus quaenam religio potissimum tenenda sit . . . non esse dubitandum*), *De vera religione* 3.

40. *De vera religione* 108–10. The objects of worship to be avoided include human works (*humanorum operum cultus*), beasts (*cultus bestiarum*), the deceased (*cultus hominum morturorum*), demons (*cultus daemonum*), lands and waters (*terrarium cultus et aquarum*), and several others.

41. Ibid. 112. Augustine emphasizes the contrast between the worship of the one god and idolatry throughout the work. He claims that the avoidance of idolatry is *perfecta religio* (*De vera religione* 19).

42. *City of God* 10.1. I cite from the Loeb Classical Library edition of David S. Wiesen, *Saint Augustine: The City of God against the Pagans* (London: William Heinemann, 1968). I have slightly adapted Wiesen's translation. This passage comes in the context of similar complaints about the

adequacy of other words (like *cultus* and *pietas*) for expressing Christian piety. He ends up settling upon a Greek word, *latreia*, as the least unsatisfactory option.

43. The word *religio* translates the Hebrew *ḥuqqah* in five instances (the Greek translation of the Septuagint is given in parenthesis): Exod. 12:43 (*nomos*), Exod. 29:9 (*hierateia*), Num. 19:2 (*diastolē*), Lev. 7:36 (*nomimon*), and Lev. 16:31 (*nomimon*). It also translates the Hebrew *avodah* (labor, service) at Exod. 12:26 (*latreia*). In 2 Macc. 6:11, *religio* translates the Greek phrase *to eulabōs echein*. In two intriguing passages in Esther (8:17 and 9:27), the translation is too free to coordinate single terms among the Latin, Hebrew, and Greek.

44. See Michel Despland, *La religion en occident: Évolution des idées et du vécu*, repr. ed. (Montreal: Fides, 1988 [1979]), 51–121, and Peter Biller, "Words and the Medieval Notion of Religion," *Journal of Ecclesiastical History* 36 (1985): 351–69.

45. *Ad ecclesiam* 4.1 and 4.5. See the edition of Georges Lagarrigue, *Salvien de Marseille: Oeuvres* (Paris: Éditions du Cerf, 1971). I owe the references to Charles Du Fresne Du Cange, *Glossarium Mediae et infimae latinitatis*, repr. ed. (Paris: Librairie des sciences et des arts, 1938), although these references are incorrectly assigned to Book 3 of *Ad ecclesiam*.

46. *Historia Compostellana* 1.5.1. I cite the edition of Emma Falque Rey, *Historia Compostellana* (Turnhout: Brepols, 1988). I owe this reference to the entry for *religio* in Albert Blaise, *Dictionnaire Latin-Français des auteurs du Moyen-Age* (Turnhout: Brepols, 1975).

47. This particular meaning of the term, "a state of life bound by monastic vows; the condition of one who is a member of a religious order," is the first definition listed in the *Oxford English Dictionary*, which traces this usage in English back to the thirteenth century. The *Middle English Dictionary*, ed. Robert E. Lewis (Ann Arbor: University of Michigan Press, 1985), gives the primary definition of *religioun* as "a religious order, a community of monks, nuns, friars, canons or others living by a religious rule of life," with examples from the early thirteenth century through the end of the fifteenth century.

48. At 6352. Cited from *The Works of our Ancient, Learned, & Excellent English Poet, Jeffrey Chaucer, As they have lately been Compar'd with the best Manuscripts*, ed. Thomas Speght (London, 1687), 247–48. The reference is drawn from the *Oxford English Dictionary*.

49. See the edition of Roberto Busa, *S. Thomae Aquinatis: Opera omnia* 2 (Stuttgart: Frommann-Holzboog, 1980). See further the entry for *religio*

in *A Lexicon of St. Thomas Aquinas*, ed. Roy J. Deferrari, M. Inviolata Barry, and Ignatius McGuiness (Baltimore, Md.: Catholic University of America Press, 1948).

50. See the authors treated in Despland, *La religion en occident*, 123–42.

51. I cite from the edition of James E. Biechler and H. Lawrence Bond, *Nicholas of Cusa on Interreligious Harmony: Text, Concordance and Translation of De Pace Fidei* (Lewiston, N.Y.: Edwin Mellen, 1990).

52. The phrase occurs at *De pace fidei* 1.6. Similar sentiments appear throughout the work.

53. For a reading of the work as "interreligious dialogue," see James E. Biechler, "Interreligious Dialogue," in *Introducing Nicholas of Cusa: A Guide to a Renaissance Man*, ed. Christopher M. Bellitto et al. (New York: Paulist Press, 2004), 270–96.

54. These words are the heading for the fourth chapter. I cite a reprint of the Basel edition of 1576, *Marsilio Ficino: Opera Omnia*, repr. ed. (Turin: Bottega d'Erasmo, 1959), 34 (p. 4 in the original).

55. I cite the Latin edition of Rudolf Gwalther and Leo Jud, *Opera D. Huldrychi Zuinglii* (Zurich: Christoph Froschauer, 1545). The English translation is from the edition of Samuel Macauley Jackson and Clarence Nevin Heller, *Commentary on True and False Religion* (Durham, N.C.: Labyrinth, 1981).

56. The work was originally published in Dutch in 1622 in a verse version. A Latin edition appeared in 1627 and was followed by numerous translations. See Jan-Paul Heering, "Hugo Grotius' *De Veritate Religionis Christianae*," in *Hugo Grotius: Theologian: Essays in Honour of G. H. M. Posthumus Meyjes*, ed. Henk J. M. Nellen and Edwin Rabbie (Leiden: Brill, 1994), 41–52. For a more expansive contextualization of this work, see Heering, *Hugo Grotius as Apologist for the Christian Religion: A Study of His Work De Veritate Religionis Christianae*, trans. J. C. Grayson (Leiden: Brill, 2004 [Dutch ed. 1992]).

57. Symon Patrick, trans., *The Truth of Christian Religion in Six Books* (London: Rich, Royston, 1683), 52. For the Latin, I consulted Hugo Grotius, *De Veritate Religionis Christianae*, 2nd ed. (Leiden: Ioannis Maire, 1629), 63.

58. See further Smith, *The Meaning and End of Religion*, 39–40.

59. At the close of the seventeenth century, one could still talk about "methods of religion" rather than individual "religions." See John Edwards, *POLUPOIKILOS SOPHIA: A Compleat History or Survey of all the Dispensations and Methods of Religion* (London, 1699). When the plural

does occur in this work, it is paired with "idolatry" ("the World was then full of Idolatry and false Religions," 533), which is in keeping with the church fathers' use of *religiones*.

60. I cite from the edition of Raymond Kilbanksy and J. W. Gough, *Epistola de Tolerantia: A Letter on Toleration* (Oxford: Clarendon, 1968), 68.

61. The bibliography on *thrēskeia* is much slimmer than that on *religio*. To my knowledge, the only systematic treatments of the term are to be found in Joseph Christiaan Antonius Van Herten, thrēskeia eulabeia hiketēs. *Bijdrage tot de kennis der religieuze terminologie in het Grieksch* (Amsterdam: H. J. Paris, 1934), 1–27; Karl Ludwig Schmidt, "*thrēskeia, thrēskos, ethelothrēskeia*," in *Theological Dictionary of the New Testament*, ed. and trans. Geoffrey W. Bromiley (Grand Rapids, Mich.: Eerdmans, 1964–1977), 3.155–59; and Laurence Foschia, "Le nom du culte, *thrēskeia*, et ses dérivés à l'époque impériale," in *L'hellénisme d'époque romaine: Nouveaux documents, nouvelles approches (Ier s.a.C.—IIIe s.p.C.)*, ed. Simon Follet (Paris: de Boccard, 2004), 15–35. My thanks to Rachel Yuen-Collingridge for bringing the latter to my attention. The program of the sixteenth Congress of the International Association for the History of Religions held in 1990 mentions a paper given by Stella Georgoudi with the title "A propos du terme *thrēskeia*: d'Hérodote à la Grèce moderne," but I have been unable to obtain a copy of this paper.

62. Herodotus uses the word two times (in the Ionic form *thrēskēïē*), at 2.18 and 2.37; see also the two occurrences of the verbal form *thrēskeuō* in 2.64. I cite from the Loeb edition of A. D. Godley, repr. and rev. ed., 4 vols. (Cambridge, Mass.: Harvard University Press, 1981 [1926]).

63. *The Embassy to Gaius* 296–98. I cite from the edition of F. H. Colson, *Philo: The Embassy to Gaius*, repr. ed. (London: Harvard University Press, 1991 [1962]).

64. The term also occurs in James 1:26–27 and Acts 26:5, where the meaning is something along the lines of "manner of worship." I am indebted to G. Anthony Keddie of the University of Texas for pointing out the connection between the phrase "sect [*hairesin*] of our *thrēskeia*" in Acts 26:5 and the action associated with such *haireseis* in Acts 24:14, namely, worshipping (*latreuō*). The unique compound word *ethelothrēskeia* in Col. 2:23 is rendered in the Vulgate as *superstitio*.

65. Josephus, *Judean Wars* 1.150. For the writings of Josephus, I rely on the text of Benedictus Niese, *Flavii Iosephi Opera*, repr. ed., 7 vols. (Berlin: Weidmannos, 1955 [1885–1895]).

66. Josephus, *Judean Antiquities* 12.253 and *Judean Wars* 4.275.

67. Translating the syntax quite literally, one would speak of Abraham's *"thrēskeia* directed toward" his god *(tēs peri auton thrēskeias)* *(Judean Antiquities* 1.223). See also *Judean Wars* 2.198.

68. Josephus, *Judean Wars* 1.146.

69. Ibid. 5.190–214.

70. Origen, *Against Celsus* 2.8. I cite from the edition of Paul Koetschau, *Die Schrift vom Martyrium Buch I–IV gegen Celsus* (Leipzig: J. C. Hinrichs'sche, 1899). Translations are my own.

71. *Life of Constantine* 3.53. I cite the edition of Ivar A. Heikel, *Über das Leben Constantins* (Leipzig: J. C. Hinrichs'sche, 1902). Translations are my own.

72. *Demonstratio* 2.3.106. I cite the edition of Ivar A. Heikel, *Die Demonstratio Evangelica* (Leipzig: J. C. Hinrichs'sche, 1913). Translations are my own.

73. For a classic reflection on what exactly the "edict" is, see Norman H. Baynes, *Constantine the Great and the Christian Church*, 2nd ed. (Oxford: Oxford University Press, 1977), 69–74.

74. See Eusebius, *Church History* 10.5, and Lactantius, *On the Deaths of the Persecutors* 48. For Eusebius, I use the edition of Eduard Schwartz, *Die Kirchengeschichte*, 3 vols. (Leipzig: J. C. Hinrichs'sche, 1903–1909). For Lactantius, I use the edition of Brandt and Laubmann. Translations are my own, loosely based on both the Greek and Latin texts.

75. See Ramsay MacMullen, *Constantine* (London: Weidenfeld and Nicolson, 1970), 92–95.

76. See the entry for *thrēskeia* in Kurt Latte, ed., *Hesychii Alexandrini lexicon* (Copenhagen and Berlin: Munksgaard and de Gruyter, 1953–2009).

77. See the entry for *thrēskeia* in Ada Adler, ed., *Suidae Lexicon* (Leipzig: Teubner, 1931).

78. *Bibliotheca* 40.31, 55.2, 79.17, 80.14, and 98.4. For the text, I consulted the edition of René Henry, *Photius: Bibliothèque* (Paris: Les belles lettres, 1959).

79. For the complicated history of this work, see the discussion in Chapter 4. For the topic at hand, I cite from G. R. Woodward and H. Mattingly's edition of the work in the Loeb Classical Library, which first appeared in 1914 and has been updated and reprinted numerous times (*St. John Damascene: Barlaam and Ioasaph* [London: William Heinemann, 1967]).

80. *Barlaam and Ioasaph* 24.204.

81. Ibid. 4.22–23.

82. The terminology of *thrēskeia* in the Byzantine era in particular awaits a detailed study. The concept of religion has forced even thoughtful stu-

dents of Byzantine literature into confused and confusing statements. For instance, in an article in which he regularly renders *thrēskeia* as "religion," Daniel J. Sahas has concluded that "for the Byzantines religion is neither a *thing* nor *one* thing; Religion is a 'they.' Religion is a people and the way they are known and can be identified, ethnically, nationally, and traditionally. . . . A people constitutes a religion and religion is the totality of manifestation of a people's life, culture, conduct, tradition and eschatological mission. Thence notions such as 'Church' or 'State,' or religion and secularism seem to be . . . non-viable distinctions" ("The Notion of 'Religion' with Reference to Islam in the Byzantine Anti-Islamic Literature," in *The Notion of "Religion" in Comparative Research: Selected Proceedings of the XVIth Congress of the International Association for the History of Religions*, ed. Ugo Bianchi [Rome: "L'Erma" di Bretscneider, 1994], 523–30, quotation from 527). It would seem that "religion" is not a very helpful term for discussing such cultures.

83. I should note at the outset of this discussion that I am not a specialist in Arabic. My citations from the Qur'an are drawn from the *Quranic Arabic Corpus*, an online annotated linguistic resource for the Qur'an (http://corpus.quran.com/, accessed 25 May 2011).

84. My references are drawn from *The Koran* (London: Penguin, 2003), translated and with notes by N. J. Dawood.

85. Patrice C. Brodeur, "Religion," in *Encyclopaedia of the Qur'ān*, Vol. 4, ed. Jane Dammen McAuliffe (Leiden: Brill, 2004), 395–98.

86. For a general survey of translations of the Qur'an, see Hartmut Bobzin, "Translations of the Qur'ān," in *Encyclopaedia of the Qur'ān*, Vol. 5, ed. Jane Dammen McAuliffe (Leiden: Brill, 2006), 340–58.

87. Alexander Ross, *The Alcoran of Mahomet, translated out of Arabique into French; by the sieur Du Ryer, Lord of Malezair, and resident for the King of France, at Alexandria. And newly Englished, for the satisfaction of all that desire to look into the Turkish vanities* (London, 1649). A second edition appeared in 1688 and carried the more detailed title: *The Alcoran of Mahomet, translated out of Arabick into French, by the Sieur Du Ryer, Lord of Malezair, and resident for the French king, at Alexandria. And newly Englished, for the satisfaction of all that desire to look into the Turkish vanities. To which is prefixed, the life of Mahomet, the prophet of the Turks, and author of the Alcoran. With A needful caveat, or admonition, for them who desire to know what use may be made of, or if there be danger in reading the Alcoran* (London: Randal Taylor, 1688). My citations come from the 1649 edition.

88. On the reception of *The Alcoran of Mahomet*, see Nabil Matar, "Alexander Ross and the First English Translation of the Qur'ān," *Muslim World* 88 (1998): 81–92.

89. Ross's edition is not divided into Sura and verse. Page numbers refer to the 1649 edition.

90. Sura 9:33 is one of several passages of the Qur'an preserved in Greek in the ninth- or tenth-century writings of Nicetas of Byzantium. Here, *dīn* is rendered (both times) by the Greek word *pistis*. I have consulted Karl Förstel's edition, *Niketas von Byzanz, Schriften zum Islam* (Würzburg: Echter Verlag, 2000), 90–91.

91. For the French, I consulted a later edition of du Ryer, *L'Alcoran de Mahomet: Translaté d'Arabé en François* (Paris: Antoine de Sommaville, 1672). The edition is not divided into Sura and verse; page references are to this edition. The readings that underlie Ross's English are as follows: Sura 5:3 "Le jour viendra que j'accompliray vostre loy, & que ma grace sera abondamment sur vous, la loy de salut est la loy que je vous veux donner" (p. 82); Sura 3:19: "La loy de salut est la loy agreable à sa divine Majesté" (p. 40); Sura 9:33: "Il a envoyé son Prophete pour conduire le peuple au droit chemin, pour prescher la loy de verité, & pour la faire paroitre par dessus toutes les autres loix du monde contre la volonté des idolatres" (p. 150); Sura 30:30–32: "Embrasse la loy de salut, Dieu l'a étably pour la faire observer aux hommes, elle ne reçoit point d'alterations, mais le plus grand' partie du monde ne le connoist pas: craignez Dieu, faites vos oraisons au temps ordonné, ne soyez pas semblables à ceux qui disent que Dieu a un compagnon, ny semblables à ceux qui sont à present au nombre des heretiques, & qui estoient auparavant des vostres; chaque secte se plaist en ses opinions" (p. 317).

92. See Theodore Bibliander, *Machumetis Saracenorum principis eiusque successorum vitae, doctrina, ac ipse Alcoran* (Zurich[?], 1550 [1543]). Sura 30:30, for example, begins with the following: *Cor tuum benivole verte ad legem divinam, immutabilem, omnibus divinitus missam gentibus. Haec est enim lex recta, licet pluribus nesciis* (p. 128 of the 1550 edition).

93. For technical etymological discussions, see Arthur Jeffery, *The Foreign Vocabulary of the Qur'ān*, repr. ed. (Leiden: Brill, 2007 [1938]), 131–33 (*dīn*) and 268–69 (*milla*). For a survey of occurrences of *dīn* in the Qur'an arranged into Régis Blachère's proposed chronological stratification of the suras, see Yvonne Yazbeck Haddad, "The Conception of the Term *dīn* in the Qur'ān," *Muslim World* 64 (1974): 114–23.

94. Louis Gardet, "dīn," in *Encyclopaedia of Islam*, Vol. 2, ed. B. Lewis at al. (Leiden: Brill, 1965), 293–96. The quotations I discuss here are from p. 293.

95. I should note that the word "religion" is not absent in du Ryer and Ross. Both translations are prefaced with a short "Summary of the Religion of the Turks," and in Ross's translation "religion" is used on a few occasions to render *dīn*, but it also translates *umma* and *milla*.

96. The translation follows that of Dawood, but Dawood renders *dīn* as "religion" (Ross again uses "Law").

97. The translation follows that of Dawood, but Dawood renders *dīn* as "religion" and leaves *islām* untranslated (Ross uses "Law" and "Law of Salvation," respectively).

98. Haddad, "The Conception of the Term *dīn*," 121.

99. See Stephen J. Davis, Samuel Noble, and Bilal Orfali, *A Disputation over a Fragment of the Cross: A Medieval Arabic Text from the History of Christian-Jewish-Muslim Relations in Egypt*, forthcoming. My sincere thanks to Stephen Davis for bringing this text to my attention and to all the authors for allowing me to consult this work before its publication.

100. The word *milla* occurs fifteen times in the Qur'an, far less frequently than *dīn*, which appears more than ninety times. The word *umma* occurs more than sixty times, but it is most often translated as "nation" or "community."

101. Frederick Mathewson Denny, "The Meaning of 'Ummah' in the Qur'ān," *History of Religions* 15 (1975): 34–70, quotation from 58.

102. Jacques Waardenburg, *Muslims and Others: Relations in Context* (Berlin: de Gruyter, 2003), 17. I find it curious that, given this statement, Waardenburg persists in referring to Muhammad's formation of "a religion." I should also point out that he has his own views about the development of the notion of *dīn* and would quite likely object to aspects of my discussion (*Muslims and Others*, 99–107).

103. In his article on "dīn" in *The Encyclopaedia of Islam*, Gardet is at pains to show that *dīn* differs from the Latin *religio*, but the notion of *religio* that concerns Gardet is an essentialist definition determined by the speculative etymologies of *religio*, not by any actual usages of the term.

3. Some (Premature) Births of Religion in Antiquity

1. Wilfred Cantwell Smith, *The Meaning and End of Religion: A New Approach to the Religious Traditions of Mankind*, repr. ed. (Minneapolis, Minn.: Fortress, 1991 [1963]), 72.

2. See, for example, Shaye J. D. Cohen, *The Beginnings of Jewishness: Boundaries, Varieties, Uncertainties* (Berkeley: University of California Press, 1999), 69–139.

3. See the classic works of Elias Bickerman, *Der Gott der Makkabäer: Untersuchungen über Sinn und Ursprung der makkabäischen Erhebung* (Berlin: Schocken Verlag/Jüdischer Buchverlag, 1937) (English translation by H. R. Moehring, *The God of the Maccabees: Studies on the Meaning and Origin of the Maccabean Revolt* [Leiden: Brill, 1979]); and Victor Tcherikover, *Hellenistic Civilization and the Jews*, repr. ed. (Peabody, Mass.: Hendrickson, 1999 [1959]).

4. These sources are all quite removed from the events they purport to describe, and they are often contradictory. For a close reading of the sources, see Brent Nongbri, "The Motivations of the Maccabees and Judean Rhetoric of Ancestral Tradition," in *Ancient Judaism in Its Hellenistic Context*, ed. Carol Bakhos (Leiden: Brill, 2005), 85–111.

5. For a more detailed account of these family feuds, see ibid., 89–102.

6. 2 Macc. 3:10–11 mentions that "Hyrcanus, the son of Tobias, a very prominent man," was storing a considerable amount of money in the temple in Jerusalem in the time of Onias III (note that the Jerusalem temple was functioning as a bank for wealthy Judeans).

7. *Judean Antiquities* 2.228.

8. *Judean Wars* 1.31.

9. 2 Macc. 4:13.

10. For the burial ground, see 1 Macc. 2:70 and 9:19. The quotation is from Cohen, *The Beginnings of Jewishness*, 89.

11. See 1 Macc. 2:1 and Josephus, *Judean Antiquities* 12.265.

12. See 2 Macc. 5:25–27.

13. For a clear and concise exposition of ancient Greek ethnicity, see David Konstan, "Defining Ancient Greek Ethnicity," *Diaspora* 6 (1997): 97–110.

14. The word *ioudaismos* does not occur in 1 Maccabees. In fact, outside of polemical Christian usage, it is an exceedingly rare term. The author of 1 Maccabees describes Mattathias and Judas as fighting on behalf of "the covenant of our fathers" and "the law and ordinances" (2:20–21). It should be noted that the degree to which the Maccabees actually *preserved* ancestral Judean practices is open to question; 1 Maccabees depicts Judas as undertaking a number of innovations to received practices, including rebuilding the inner court of the temple from scratch and altering the

traditional calendar by adding an annual festival to celebrate the Maccabees' achievements (4:48–59).

15. Steve Mason, "Jews, Judaeans, Judaizing, Judaism: Problems of Categorization in Ancient History," *Journal for the Study of Judaism* 38 (2007): 457–512.

16. See John L. Myres, "Mēdizein: mēdismos," in *Greek Poetry and Life: Essays Presented to Gilbert Murray on his Seventieth Birthday*, ed. C. Bailey et al. (Oxford: Clarendon, 1936), 97–105.

17. See 2 Macc. 4:13 and 8:17.

18. Smith, *The Meaning and End of Religion*, 72.

19. Mary Beard, "Cicero and Divination: The Formation of a Latin Discourse," *Journal of Roman Studies* 76 (1986): 33–46. It is a standard observation that interest in human-divine affairs was renewed in the late republic. See, for example, Arnaldo Momigliano, "The Theological Efforts of the Roman Upper Classes in the First Century B.C.," *Classical Philology* 79 (1984): 199–211. Beard's thesis is distinct, and more intriguing, in that she argues that this period was not simply one of religious change but marked the beginning of an altogether new discursive realm.

20. Beard, "Cicero and Divination," 46. This topic receives further development in Mary Beard, John North, and Simon Price, *Religions of Rome*, 2 vols. (Cambridge: Cambridge University Press, 1998), 1.150–56.

21. *On Divination* 2.33. I cite from the Loeb edition and translation (slightly adapted) of William Armistead Falconer, repr. ed. (Cambridge, Mass.: Harvard University Press, 1971 [1923]).

22. Ibid. 2.72.

23. Beard, "Cicero and Divination," 40.

24. On the intellectual endeavors of Romans in the first century B.C.E., see Elizabeth Rawson, *Intellectual Life in the Late Roman Republic* (London: Duckworth, 1985), esp. 298–316.

25. *On Divination* 2.1. The three pieces mentioned here were all likely written between early 45 B.C.E. and the summer of 44 B.C.E. See Rackham's introduction to the Loeb edition of *De natura deorum*, xii–xiii, and R. W. Sharples's introduction to Cicero: *On Fate and Boethius: The Consolation of Philosophy* IV.5–7, V (Warminster: Aris and Phillips, 1991), 3–5.

26. This treatise survives only in fragmentary form. In the sections we possess, Cicero refutes Stoic and Epicurean views of fate and defends the opinions of the Academic Carneades. Just as he does in *On Divination*

2.1, Cicero links the three dialogues together in the opening fragment of *On Fate*.

27. Fritz Graf has drawn my attention to one other element that might factor into this discussion: the beginning of the differentiation of magic, or, more properly, the activities of magi, from licit interaction with superhuman entities and forces. The term *magus* enters Latin only in the late republican period. See further Fritz Graf, *Magic in the Ancient World*, trans. Franklin Philip (Cambridge, Mass.: Harvard University Press, 1997 [French ed. 1994]), 36–43.

28. *On Divination* 2.1–2. Cicero continues, "The cause of my becoming an expounder of philosophy sprang from the grave condition of the state during the period of the civil war." This point is being emphasized by Celia Schultz in a commentary on Cicero's *On Divination* that is currently under way.

29. Ibid. 2.2.

30. Indeed, it is noteworthy that it is only from our modern perspective that Roman life can be described as an "amalgam" of the political and the religious. On this point, see Timothy Fitzgerald, *Discourse on Civility and Barbarity: A Critical History of Religion and Related Categories* (New York: Oxford University Press, 2007), 16–20.

31. I treat Boyarin's claims in his book *Border Lines: The Partition of Judaeo-Christianity* (Philadelphia: University of Pennsylvania Press, 2004), 202–25. Also relevant are two articles by Boyarin: "Semantic Differences; or, 'Judaism'/'Christianity,'" in *The Ways That Never Parted: Jews and Christians in Late Antiquity and the Early Middle Ages*, ed. Adam H. Becker and Annette Yoshiko Reed (Tübingen: Mohr Siebeck, 2003), 65–85, and "Rethinking Jewish Christianity: An Argument for Dismantling a Dubious Category (to which is appended a correction of my *Border Lines*)," *Jewish Quarterly Review* 99 (2009): 7–36.

32. *Border Lines*, 203.

33. Ibid., 205.

34. For a more thorough engagement with Boyarin's treatment of Gregory of Nazianzus and the emperor Julian, see Brent Nongbri, "Paul without Religion: The Creation of a Category and the Search for an Apostle beyond the New Perspective," Ph.D. diss., Yale University, 2008, 50–66.

35. For Eusebius's works, I rely on the editions of Karl Mras and Édouard Des Places, *Die Praeparatio Evangelica*, 2nd ed. (Berlin: Akademie-Verlag, 1982); and Ivar A. Heikel, *Die Demonstratio Evangelica* (Leipzig:

J. C. Hinrichs'sche Buchhandlung, 1913). Translations of these works are my own.

36. The citation is not from 1.9, as Boyarin suggests in *Border Lines*, 325, n. 24.

37. *Demonstratio* 3.6.31.

38. On the topic of ethnicity and "race" in early Christian rhetoric, see the useful studies of Aaron P. Johnson, *Ethnicity and Argument in Eusebius' Praeparatio Evangelica* (Oxford: Oxford University Press, 2006), and Denise Kimber Buell, *Why This New Race: Ethnic Reasoning in Early Christianity* (New York: Columbia University Press, 2005).

39. *Demonstratio* 1.2.2. The Greek here is *tēn kata ton Mōseōs nomon diatetagmenēn politeian*. For a similar viewpoint, see *Demonstratio* 1.2.5.

40. In Eusebius's view, a distinguishing feature of the Greek ethnicity and way of life is that Greeks borrowed (or perhaps better, "stole") their ancestral customs from other nations. See the passages cited in Johnson, *Ethnicity and Argument*, 128–42.

41. In the preface to *Praeparatio* 13, Eusebius sets out to explain why, if Moses and Plato are so similar, Christians follow Moses and not Plato, who ought to be more "appropriate to us since we are Greeks" (*prosēkōn hēmin genoit' an hellēsin ousin*).

42. Later, Eusebius states that there are three arrangements (*tria tagmata*) into which one can divide the "parties of those who profess to be pious" (*tas tōn theosebein epangellomenōn proaireseis*): that of the idolaters, that of those from the circumcision, and that of "those who have ascended through the gospel teaching" (*Demonstratio* 1.6.62). The single occurrence of the term *hellēnismos* in the *Praeparatio* is paired with *ioudaismos* and again contrasted with *christianismos*, which Eusebius calls instead "a new and genuine knowledge of the divine" (*tis kainē kai alēthēs theosophia*, 1.5.12).

43. See Johnson, *Ethnicity and Argument*, 142–52.

44. There is definitely a tension here, one that is captured in Dale Martin's terminology of Eusebius's idea of "a universal *ethnos*" (*Inventing Superstition: From the Hippocratics to the Christians* [Cambridge, Mass.: Harvard University Press, 2004], 213–25). Martin notes that such a formulation would have struck ancient people as "oxymoronic" and "counterintuitive" (216). As Johnson points out, for Eusebius, "Christian identity is articulated in ethnic terms; its legitimation rests upon its connections to the ancient Hebrew ethnos. Eusebius' Christianity was not merely a 'religion,' nor were its others. Christianity was a nation whose members had been drawn from all other nations" (*Ethnicity and Argument*, 233).

45. I should note that Boyarin's references to the Christian heresiologists (*Border Lines*, 206–14) are also problematic. He reads these authors as describing "heresies" as different "religions" in the modern sense of the term. This formulation is backwards. The heresiologists describe bad groups of Christians, some of whom modern authors would call "different sects" of Christianity but others of whom modern scholars might designate as "other religions." The heresiologists, however, do not differentiate. I elaborate this point in Chapter 4.

46. See, for example, Paul's letter to the Galatians.

47. *Demonstratio* 1.5.2–3.

48. Ibid. 1.5.20–21. The scriptural citation is from Ps. 104:12–15 (according to the Septuagint numbering; in the Hebrew Masoretic Text and most English translations, this is Psalm 105).

49. Bernard Lewis, *The Jews of Islam* (Princeton: Princeton University Press, 1984), 12.

50. A sound, concise treatment of these sources and what we can know from them is available in Michael Cook, *Muhammad* (Oxford: Oxford University Press, 1996).

51. The nominalizing of verbal forms is common in modern translations. A comparison of Dawood's recent English version and Ross's 1649 version helps to show what is at stake in the act of translation: Dawood, Sura 49:14: "The Arabs of the desert declare, 'We are true believers.' Say: 'Believers you are not.' Rather say: 'We profess Islām.'" The last sentence translates a verb, *aslamna*. This is captured in Ross's translation: "Some among the Arabians have said, we believe; Say unto them, Say not we believe, but say, we are obedient" (Ross, p. 323).

52. Arthur J. Arberry, *The Koran Interpreted* (London: Oxford University Press, 1964) (first published in 1955 and reprinted several times).

53. See, for example, the translation of Abdullah Yusuf Ali, which was produced in 1934 but still enjoys wide circulation. I cite from the 1969 edition: *The Holy Qur-an: Text, Translation, and Commentary*, 3 vols. (Lahore: Ashraf, 1969).

54. One thinks in the first instance of the work of John Wansbrough, *Quranic Studies: Sources and Methods of Scriptural Interpretation* (Oxford: Oxford University Press, 1977) (reprinted in 2004 with expanded notes), and Patricia Crone and Michael Cook, *Hagarism: The Making of the Islamic World* (Cambridge: Cambridge University Press, 1977).

55. Donner makes his case in two publications, an article, "From Believers to Muslims: Confessional Self-Identity in the Early Islamic Commu-

nity" *Al-Abhath* 50–51 (2002–2003): 9–53, and more recently a book, *Muhammad and the Believers: At the Origins of Islam* (Cambridge, Mass.: Belknap, 2010). I should note that I do have some misgivings about aspects of Donner's presentation, especially in the latter publication, in which he casts his argument in dichotomous terms: "It is my conviction that Islam began as a religious movement—not as a social, economic, or 'national' one" (xii). As we have seen, the isolation of "the religious" from the worldly (social, economic, national, etc.) is suspect. Moreover, Donner's own characterization stands at odds with his claim that Muslim expansion "was driven by an indissoluble amalgam of religious and material motives" (197). If the amalgam is "indissoluble," then perhaps the descriptor "religious" is best dropped from the discussion.

56. Donner points to Sura 49:14, which clearly distinguishes between "belief" and "submission" (*Muhammad and the Believers*, 57–58).

57. See, for example, Sura 5:73 (in Dawood's translation): "Unbelievers are those that say: 'God is one of three.' There is but one God." Also Sura 112: "Say: 'God is One, the Eternal God. He begot none, nor was He begotten. None is equal to Him.'"

58. See Donner, *Muhammad and the Believers*, 56–68, quotation from p. 63.

59. Ibid., 69.

60. R. B. Serjeant, "The 'Sunnah Jāmi'ah,' Pacts with the Yathrib Jews, and the 'Taḥrīm' of Yathrib: Analysis and Translation of the Documents Comprised in the So-Called 'Constitution of Medina,'" *Bulletin of the School of Oriental and African Studies, University of London* 41 (1978): 1–42, quotation from 8. Serjeant's article provides an Arabic text and translation that divides the work into eight separate documents. Michael Lecker concurs with Serjeant's evaluation of the constitution's importance ("the earliest and most important document from the time of Muḥammad"), but Lecker strongly argues that the constitution is a unified composition. Lecker's edition and translation is available in *The "Constitution of Medina": Muḥammad's First Legal Document* (Princeton, N.J.: Darwin Press, 2004), quotation from 1.

61. Donner, *Muhammad and the Believers*, 72–73. Serjeant's text indicates that one version of the constitution substitutes *mu'minūn* for *muslimūn* in this passage. In either reading the statement that the Jews form one *umma* with the group in question is noteworthy. See Serjeant, "The 'Sunnah Jāmi'ah,'" 27.

62. I have adjusted Dawood's translation in light of Donner's comments (*Muhammad and the Believers*, 71). See also Sura 2:135.

63. Herodotus, *Histories* 8.144. In the fourth century, the orator Isocrates would claim that "the name Greek" (*to tōn hellēnōn onoma*) should be applied to those who have Greek education (*paideia*) rather than simply those who share common Greek descent (*Panegyricus* 50; see the edition and translation of George Norlin in the Loeb series, *Isocrates* [London: W. Heinemann, 1928]).

64. Sura 2:122–31.

4. Christians and "Others" in the Premodern Era

1. The term *manichaismos* is rare in ancient Greek. When it does occur, it is parallel to such formulations as "Manichaean teaching" (*manichaikon dogma*) and "teaching of the Manichaeans" (*manichaiōn dogma*). See Gregory of Nyssa's *Letter against Eunomius* 1.1.504–511. I cite from the edition of Werner Jaeger, *Contra Eunomium libri*, 2 vols. (Leiden: Brill, 1960).

2. Wilfred Cantwell Smith, *The Meaning and End of Religion: A New Approach to the Religious Traditions of Mankind*, repr. ed. (Minneapolis, Minn.: Fortress, 1991 [1963]), 93. Even Jonathan Z. Smith has called Manichaeism "perhaps the first, self-conscious 'world' religion." See his essay, "A Matter of Class: Taxonomies of Religion," *Harvard Theological Review* 89 (1996): 387–403, reprinted in *Relating Religion: Essays in the Study of Religion* (Chicago: University of Chicago Press, 2004), 160–78. The quotation is from the latter at p. 169. Most studies of Mani and religion (or, more usually, "Mani and the religions") since W. C. Smith's work have not been concerned with the category of religion as such. They take it for granted that the concept is native to the ancient world. See, for example, Wolf-Peter Funk, "Mani's Account of Other Religions according to the Coptic *Synaxeis* Codex," in *New Light on Manichaeism: Papers from the Sixth International Congress on Manichaeism*, ed. Jason David BeDuhn (Leiden: Brill, 2009), 115–27. See, however, the critical remarks on the topic by Edwin Judge, "Was Christianity a Religion?," in *The First Christians in the Roman World: Augustan and New Testament Essays*, ed. James R. Harrison (Tübingen: Mohr Siebeck, 2008), 404–9, at 406–7.

3. *Manichaean Texts from the Roman Empire*, ed. Iain Gardner and Samuel N. C. Lieu (Cambridge: Cambridge University Press, 2004), 1.

4. Ibid., 151.

5. See Peter Brown, *Augustine of Hippo: A Biography*, rev. ed. (Berkeley: University of California Press, 2000 [1967]), 29–49, and Jason David

BeDuhn, *Augustine's Manichaean Dilemma, I: Conversion and Apostasy,* 373–388 C.E. (Philadelphia: University of Pennsylvania Press, 2010).

6. For a fuller summary of these discoveries, see Samuel N. C. Lieu, "Manichaean Art and Texts from the Silk Road," in *Studies in Silk Road Coins and Culture, Papers in Honour of Professor Ikuo Hirayama on his 65th Birthday,* ed. Katsumi Tanabe, Joe Cribb, and Helen Wang (Kamakura: Institute of Silk Road Studies, 1997), 261–312, expanded and updated in *Manichaeism in Central Asia and China* (Leiden: Brill, 1998), 1–58.

7. See James M. Robinson, "The Fate of the Manichaean Codices of Medinet Madi 1929–1989," in *Studia Manichaica: II. Internationaler Kongreß zum Manichäismus,* ed. Gernot Wießner and Hans-Joachim Klimkeit (Wiesbaden: Otto Harrassowitz, 1992), 19–62.

8. See Albert Henrichs and Ludwig Koenen, "Ein griechischer Mani-Codex (P. Colon. Inv. nr. 4780)," *Zeitschrift für Papyrologie und Epigraphik* 5 (1970): 97–216, and Ludwig Koenen and Cornelia Römer, *Der Kölner Mani-Kodex: Abbildungen und diplomatischer Text* (Bonn: Habelt, 1985).

9. The texts have been published in a variety of venues. For a short summary of the find and its significance, see *Manichaean Texts from the Roman Empire,* 43–45. For the Manichaean materials in particular, see Iain Gardner, *Kellis Literary Texts,* 2 vols. (Oxford: Oxbow, 1996 and 2007).

10. For a succinct modern summary of Mani's teachings, see *Manichaean Texts from the Roman Empire,* 8–21. For an ancient perspective, see the fourth-century (or perhaps third-century) account of Alexander of Lycopolis, provided in translation in Pieter Willem van der Horst and Jaap Mansfeld, *An Alexandrian Platonist against Dualism: Alexander of Lycopolis' Treatise 'Critique of the Doctrines of Manichaeus'* (Leiden: Brill, 1974).

11. For the Middle Persian text, see F. C. Andreas and Walter Henning, *Mitteliranische Manichaica aus Chinesisch-Turkestan II* (Berlin: Verlag der Akademie der Wissenschaften, 1933), 295–96, and Werner Sundermann, *Mitteliranische manichäische Texte kirchengeschichtlichen Inhalts* (Berlin: Akademie-Verlag, 1981), 131–33. The English translation provided here is from *Manichaean Texts from the Roman Empire,* 109. For further discussion of this passage, see Samuel N. C. Lieu, "'My Church Is Superior . . .': Mani's Missionary Statement in Coptic and Middle Persian," in *Coptica Gnostica Manichaica: Mélanges offerts à Wolf-Peter Funk,* ed. Louis Painchaud and Paul-Hubert Poirier (Louvain: Peeters, 2006), 519–27.

12. See E. W. West, *Pahlavi Texts Part I: The Bundahis, Bahman Yast, and Shâyast Lâ-Shâyast* (Oxford: Clarendon, 1880), lxxiii; R. C. Zaehner,

Zurvan: A Zoroastrian Dilemma (Oxford: Clarendon, 1955), 207–8, 481; Mary Boyce, *A Word-List of Manichaean Middle Persian and Parthian* (Leiden: Brill, 1977), 38; and Mansour Shaki's entry for *dēn* in *Encyclopaedia Iranica*, Vol. 7, ed. Ehsan Yarshater (Costa Mesa, Calif.: Mazda, 1996), 279–81.

13. See Philippe Gignoux's entry for *Dēnkard* in *Encyclopaedia Iranica*, Vol. 7, 284–89.

14. For the Coptic text, see Wolf-Peter Funk, *Kephalaia I, Zweite Hälfte* (Stuttgart: Kohlhammer, 1999–2000), 370–75. The translation is by Iain Gardner in *Manichaean Texts from the Roman Empire*, 265.

15. For the Arabic text, see C. Eduard Sachau, *Chronologie orientalischer Völker von Alberuni* (Leipzig: F. A. Brockhaus, 1878), 207. The translation is also by Sachau, *The Chronology of Ancient Nations: An English Version of the Arabic Text of the Athar-ul-bakiya of Albiruni* (London: William H. Allen, 1879), 190.

16. My account here draws upon the insights of J. Kevin Coyle in "Foreign and Insane: Labelling Manichaeism in the Roman Empire," *Studies in Religion/Sciences Religieuses* 33 (2004): 217–34, reprinted in J. Kevin Coyle, *Manichaeism and Its Legacy* (Leiden: Brill, 2009), 3–23.

17. For the Latin text, see M. Hyamson, *Mosaicarum et Romanarum Legum Collatio* (London: Oxford University Press, 1913), 130–32. The translation is my own.

18. *Church History* 7.31. I cite from the edition of Eduard Schwartz, *Eusebius Werke Zweiter Band: Die Kirchengeschichte*, 3 vols. (Leipzig: J. C. Hinrichs'sche, 1903–1908). The translation is adapted from the Loeb translation of J. E. L. Oulton, *Eusebius: The Ecclesiastical History*, 2 vols. (London: William Heinemann, 1926–1932).

19. Augustine, *Against the Epistle of Manichaeus* 5, and Evodius, *De fide contra Manichaeos* 5; I cite the editions of Joseph Zycha, *Sancti Aureli Augustini: De utilitate credendi, De duabus animabus, Contra Fortunatum, Contra Adimantum, Contra epistulam fundamenti, Contra Faustum* (Vienna: F. Tempsky, 1891) and *Sancti Aureli Augustini: Contra Felicem de natura boni, Epistula secundini contra Secundinum, accedunt Euodii De Fide Contra Manichaeos* (Vienna: F. Tempsky, 1892). For an English translation of the fragments of Mani's "Fundamental Epistle," see *Manichaean Texts from the Roman Empire*, 168–72.

20. The assertion is at *Acts of Archelaus* 15 (13).1: "*Ego, viri fratres, Christi quidem sum discipulus, apostolus vero Iesu.*" I cite from Charles Henry Beeson, ed., *Hegemonius: Acta Archelai* (Leipzig: J. C. Hinrichs'sche, 1906).

21. The quotation is from the Cologne Mani Codex (66.4–7: *egō Mannichaios Ihu Chru apostolos*), cited in Koenen and Römer, *Der Kölner Mani-Kodex*, 130–31.

22. See P.Kell.Copt. 32 in Iain Gardner, Anthony Alcock, and Wolf-Peter Funk, *Coptic Documentary Texts from Kellis*, Vol. 1 (Oxford: Oxbow, 1999). An English translation can also be found in *Manichaean Texts from the Roman Empire*, 277.

23. Samuel N. C. Lieu, "The Self-Identity of the Manichaeans in the Roman East," *Mediterranean Archaeology* 11 (1998), 205–27, quotation from 224, emphasis in original.

24. *Against Faustus* 1.2, cited from Zycha's edition (see note 19 above).

25. The most accessible and thorough account of Chinese Manichaeans in English is Samuel N. C. Lieu, *Manichaeism in the Later Roman Empire and Medieval China*, 2nd rev. ed. (Tübingen: Mohr Siebeck, 1992), 219–304.

26. See, for example, G. Haloun and W. B. Henning, "The Compendium of the Doctrines and Styles of the Teaching of Mani, the Buddha of Light," *Asia Minor, N.S.* 3 (1952): 184–212, and the *Scripture on Laozi's Conversion of the Barbarians*, portions of which are translated in Lieu, *Manichaeism*, 257–61.

27. See the hymn mentioning Jesus-Buddha translated in Tsui Chi, "Mo Ni Chiao Hsia Pu Tsan 'The Lower (Second?) Section of the Manichaean Hymns,'" *Bulletin of the School of Oriental and African Studies* 11 (1943): 174–219. I owe this reference to Gunner B. Mikkelsen, *Dictionary of Manichaean Texts, Vol. 3: Texts from Central Asia and China, Part 4: Dictionary of Manichaean Texts in Chinese* (Turnhout: Brepols, 2006), 109.

28. Leonardo Olschki, "Manichaeism, Buddhism, and Christianity in Marco Polo's China," *Asiatische Studien* 5 (1951): 1–21. Olschki is reasonably certain that the people in question were Manichaeans, but he regards their self-identification as Christians as disingenuous, most likely because he (mistakenly) thinks of "Manichaeism" and "Christianity" as mutually exclusive.

29. Unfortunately, we rely on later hagiographical summaries for the details of John's life. For a sober assessment of the life and works of John of Damascus, see Andrew Louth, *St. John Damascene: Tradition and Originality in Byzantine Theology* (Oxford: Oxford University Press, 2002). On the question of John's relations with Islam, see Daniel J. Sahas, *John of Damascus on Islam: The "Heresy of the Ishmaelites"* (Leiden: Brill, 1972), and Raymond Le Coz, *Jean Damascène: Écrits sur l'Islam* (Paris: Éditions du Cerf, 1992).

30. For Christian thoughts on followers of Muhammad before the time of John, see the sources collected in Robert G. Hoyland, *Seeing Islam as Others Saw It: A Survey and Evaluation of Christian, Jewish, and Zoroastrian Writings on Early Islam* (Princeton, N.J.: Darwin Press, 1997).

31. Louth, *St. John Damascene*, 60.

32. Although some scholars in the middle of the twentieth century challenged the attribution of this chapter to John of Damascus, the current consensus opinion regards it as the work of John. For a presentation of the arguments, see Sahas, *John of Damascus on Islam*, 60–66.

33. The translation is my own and is based on the edition of P. Bonifatius Kotter, *Die Schriften des Johannes von Damaskos IV: Liber de haeresibus. Opera polemica* (Berlin: de Gruyter, 1981).

34. See John E. Merrill, "Of the Tractate of John of Damascus on Islam," *Moslem World* 41 (1951): 88–97.

35. John's use of the phrase "precursor of the Antichrist" should not be overblown. John uses the term to refer to anyone who does not confess the divinity of Jesus. See, for example, the chapter on the Antichrist in *On the Orthodox Faith*, 4.26. For a critical text, see the second volume of Kotter, *Die Schriften des Johannes von Damaskos.*

36. The idea that Muhammad was taught by a Christian heretic of some sort is found in a number of subsequent forms. See, for example, Barbara Roggema, "The Legend of Sergius-Baḥīrā: Some Remarks on Its Origin in the East and Its Traces in the West," in *East and West in the Crusader States: Contexts, Contacts, Confrontations III: Acta of the Congress Held at Hernen Castle in September 2000*, ed. Krijnie Ciggaar and Herman Teule (Leuven: Peeters, 2003), 107–23.

37. Earlier editions of the works of John of Damascus (including Migne's *Patralogiae Graecae*) read *skeia* for *thrēskeia* here. The former was understood (for example, by Sahas) as a corruption of the Greek *skia* ("shadow"), but more recent editors (Kotter and Le Coz) have opted for *thrēskeia.*

38. Hoyland, *Seeing Islam*, 484.

39. For a host of examples, see the overview and rich endnotes of Norman Daniel, *Islam and the West: The Making of an Image*, rev. ed. (Oxford: Oneworld, 2009 [1960]), 209–13. See also the discussion in R. W. Southern, *Western Views of Islam in the Middle Ages* (Cambridge, Mass.: Harvard University Press, 1962).

40. My source for this example is Kenneth Baxter Wolf, "The Earliest Spanish Christian Views of Islam," *Church History* 55 (1986): 281–93, and by the same author, "Christian Views of Islam in Early Medieval

Spain," in *Medieval Christian Perceptions of Islam*, ed. John V. Tolan (New York: Routledge, 2000), 85–108.

41. I quote the text and translation of this section from Wolf, "The Earliest Spanish Christian Views," 291.

42. See Thomas E. Burman, *Reading the Qur'ān in Latin Christendom, 1140–1560* (Philadelphia: University of Pennsylvania Press, 2007).

43. The point is well made by John Tolan: "For Peter, the point is not to 'study' a 'religion' but to refute a particularly vile form of heresy" ("Peter the Venerable on the 'Diabolical Heresy of the Saracens,'" in *The Devil, Heresy, and Witchcraft in the Middle Ages: Essays in Honor of Jeffrey B. Russell*, ed. Alberto Ferreiro [Leiden: Brill, 1998], 345–67, quotation from 346).

44. See John V. Tolan, *Saracens: Islam in the Medieval European Imagination* (New York: Columbia University Press, 2002), esp. 105–34.

45. "*Sed utrum Mahumeticus error haeresis dici debeat, et ejus sectatores haeretici, vel ethnici vocari, non satis discerno*" (*Against the Sect or Heresy of the Saracens*, Prologue 13; cited from Migne's *Patrologia Latina*, Vol. 189, cols. 669–70).

46. The story is related most famously by Thomas William Rhys Davids in *Buddhist Birth Stories; or, Jātaka Tales*, ed. V. Fausböll, trans. T. W. Rhys Davids (London: Trübner, 1880), xxxvi–xli, although Davids incorrectly attributes the impetus for the new *Martyrology* to Pope Sixtus V. See Cyriac K. Pullapilly, *Caesar Baronius: Counter-Reformation Historian* (Notre Dame, Ind.: University of Notre Dame Press, 1975), 37–42.

47. *Martyrologium Romanum. Ad novam Kalendarii rationem, & Ecclesiasticae historiae vertitatem restitutum. Gregorii XIII. Pont. Max. iussu editum* (Salamanca: Apud Lucam Iuntam, 1584), 353. Later editions include Baronius's learned notes and credit him as author; for example, Caesar Baronius, *Martyrologium Romanum. Ad novam Kalendarii rationem, & Ecclesiasticae historiae vertitatem restitutum. Gregorii XIII. Pont. Max. iussu editum* (Venice: Apud Marcum Antonium Zalterium , 1597), 534.

48. The most readily available English translation of *Barlaam and Ioasaph* is Woodward and Mattingly's rendering of the Greek text in the Loeb Classical Library, which first appeared in 1914 and has been updated and reprinted numerous times (*St. John Damascene: Barlaam and Ioasaph* [London: William Heinemann, 1967]). The Greek text is later than (and derives from) versions in other languages. See now the much improved Greek text and learned introduction by Robert Volk, *Die Schriften des*

Johannes von Damaskos: Historia animae utilis de Barlaam et Ioasaph (spuria), 2 vols. (Berlin: Walter de Gruyter, 2006–2009).

49. See *Buddhist Birth Stories*, xl. In the Eastern church calendar, only Ioasaph is celebrated (on 26 August).

50. This summary reflects the contents of the Greek version.

51. Clement, *Stromateis* 1.15.71, my translation, based on the edition of Claude Mondésert and Marcel Caster, *Clément d'Alexandrie: Les Stromates* (Paris: Éditions du Cerf, 1951).

52. See R. C. Majamdar, *The Classical Accounts of India* (Calcutta: Mukhopadhyay, 1960), 439–48.

53. On this topic, see Philip C. Almond, "The Buddha in the West, 1800–1860," in *Perspectives on Language and Text: Essays and Poems in Honor of Francis I. Andersen's Sixtieth Birthday*, ed. Edgar W. Conrad and Edward G. Newing (Winona Lake, Ind.: Eisenbrauns, 1987), 381–92.

54. The credit for the discovery is generally given to Édouard Laboulaye, who, in a review of Stanislaus Julien's *Les Avadānas* in the *Journal des Débats* (26 July 1859): 2–3, made the connection. After listing several similarities between *Barlaam and Ioasaph* and the lives of Buddha, Laboulaye concluded "chance cannot bring about such similarities; one must acknowledge the agency of the East [Ce n'est pas le hasard qui peut amener de telles ressemblances, il y faut reconnaître l'action de l'Orient]" (3).

55. *Buddhacarita* 3.4–63. I cite the edition and translation of E. H. Johnston, *Aśvaghoṣa's Buddhacarita or Acts of the Buddha*, repr. ed. (Delhi: Motilal Banarsidass, 1992).

56. Ibid. 3.58.

57. I cite from an English translation of the longer Georgian version: David M. Lang, *The Balavariani (Barlaam and Josaphat): A Tale from the Christian East Translated from the Old Georgian* (London: George Allen and Unwin, 1966), 68.

58. The citation is from Lang's translation of the longer Georgian version, *The Balavariani*, 70.

59. *Buddhacarita* 27.32.

60. I should point out that the most obvious difference between the lives of the Buddha and *Barlaam and Ioasaph* is the prominent role of the teacher Barlaam. There is no such figure to aid the Buddha in reaching enlightenment, but the Buddhist lives do seem to contain the seeds of this figure. In the *Buddhacarita*, the young prince has a brief encounter with "a man in mendicant's clothes" who speaks thus to him: "Since the

world is subject to destruction, I desire salvation and seek the blessed incorruptible stage. I look with equal mind on kinsman and stranger, and longing for and hatred of the objects of sense have passed from me. . . . I wander without ties or expectations in search of the highest good." After saying this, the man disappeared into heaven, and the young prince "was thrilled and amazed. And then he gained awareness of *dharma*." Lang draws attention to a similar story recorded in the *Mahavastu* (*The Wisdom of Balahvar: A Christian Legend of the Buddha* [London: George Allen and Unwin, 1957], 14–15).

61. A fuller account of the legend, its influence in medieval Christianity, and the eventual identification of its Buddhist origins can be found in Philip C. Almond, "The Buddha of Christendom: A Review of the Legend of Barlaam and Josaphat," *Religious Studies* 23 (1987): 391–406.

62. Max Müller, *Chips from a German Workshop*, 4 vols. (London: Longmans, Green, 1867–1875), 4.188–89.

63. See, for example, the use of the story in the introductory textbook *World Religions Today*, by John L. Esposito, Darrell J. Fasching, and Todd Lewis (3rd ed. [New York: Oxford University Press, 2009]), 589–90.

64. *Chips from a German Workshop*, 1.223.

65. My account here is dependent upon that of Robert Lee Wolff, "Barlaam and Ioasaph," *Harvard Theological Review* 32 (1939): 131–39, and David M. Lang's introduction to the more recent printings of the Loeb edition of *Barlaam and Ioasaph*, ix–xxxv, as well as Lang's *The Wisdom of Balahvar*, 11–65.

66. David M. Lang, "Bilawhar wa-Yūdāsaf," in *The Encyclopaedia of Islam*, Vol. 1, ed. B. Lewis et al. (Leiden: Brill, 1960), 1215–17.

67. There is a Christian Arabic version of the story, but it is later and dependent upon the Greek version. See ibid.

68. See, for example, John C. Hirsh, *Barlam and Iosaphat: A Middle English Life of Buddha* (London: Oxford University Press, 1986), xxiii–xxviii. See also Lang's introduction to the revised Loeb edition and Almond, "The Buddha of Christendom," 404–6.

69. W. B. Henning, "Persian Poetical Manuscripts from the Time of Rūdakī," in *A Locust's Leg: Studies in Honor of S. H. Taqizadeh* (London: Percy Lund, Humphries, 1962), 89–104, reprinted in W. B. Henning, *Selected Papers*, 2 vols. (Leiden: Brill, 1977), 2.559–74.

70. See François de Blois, "On the Sources of the Barlaam Romance, or: How the Buddha Became a Christian Saint," in *Literarische Stoffe und*

ihre Gestaltung in mitteliranischer Zeit: Kolloquium anlässlich des 70. Geburtstages von Werner Sundermann, ed. Desmond Durkin-Meisterernst, Christiane Reck, and Dieter Weber (Wiesbaden: Dr. Ludwig Reichert, 2009), 7–26. See also Lang, *The Wisdom of Balahvar*, 36–37.

71. Blois, "On the Sources of the Barlaam Romance," 24. Another scholar of the Silk Road goes as far as describing the story of *Bilawhar wa-Yudasaf* as "simply part of the Muslim cultural repertoire." See Johan Elverskog, *Buddhism and Islam on the Silk Road* (Philadelphia: University of Pennsylvania Press, 2010), 73.

5. Renaissance, Reformation, and Religion in the Sixteenth and Seventeenth Centuries

1. These multiple different systems emerged alongside the idea of religion as a generic category. As Jonathan Z. Smith has put it, "It is the question of the plural *religions* (both Christian and non-Christian) that forced a new interest in the singular, generic *religion*" ("Religion, Religions, Religious," in *Relating Religion: Essays in the Study of Religion* [Chicago: University of Chicago Press, 2004], 182).

2. Peter Harrison, *"Religion" and the Religions in the English Enlightenment* (Cambridge: Cambridge University Press, 1990), 174.

3. See, for example, Mark Lilla, *The Stillborn God: Religion, Politics, and the Modern West* (New York: Alfred A. Knopf, 2007). Lilla tells his story not in terms of the emergence of religion, but rather in terms of the demise of medieval Christian political theology in the seventeenth century and the rise of various alternatives from the eighteenth century to the twentieth century. He focuses on the role of such figures as Thomas Hobbes, Jean-Jacques Rousseau, and Immanuel Kant, and the issue of the development of religion as a distinct category is a latent theme throughout the early portion of the book. For example, he writes: "Hobbes found a new way to discuss religion and the common good without making reference to the nexus between God, man, and world. The very fact that we think and speak in terms of 'religion,' rather than of the true faith, the law, or the revealed way, is owing in large measure to Hobbes" (88). For a treatment that focuses more on the philological enterprises of the seventeenth century, see Guy G. Stroumsa, *A New Science: The Discovery of Religion in the Age of Reason* (Cambridge, Mass.: Harvard University Press, 2010).

4. *Retractationes* 1.13.3. The translation is modified from that of John H. S. Burleigh in *Augustine: Earlier Writings* (Philadelphia: Westminster, 1953).

5. See, for example, *Divine Institutes* 4.6, in which Lactantius enlists both Hermes and the Sibylline Oracles as witnesses to Christian truth. In late antiquity, assessments of the age of writings such as the Hermetic literature varied. Augustine located Hermes Trismegistus three generations after the time of Moses (*City of God* 18.39). Some of the later Italian Neo-Platonists placed figures like Hermes well before the time of the Hebrews (see Frances A. Yates, *Giordano Bruno and the Hermetic Tradition* [Chicago: University of Chicago Press, 1964], 223). It was not until 1614 that Isaac Casaubon definitively redated the Hermetic literature to the Christian era (*De rebus sacris et ecclesiasticis exercitationes XVI* [London: Nortoniana apud Jo. Billium, 1614]; for the significance of this adjusted dating, see Yates, *Giordano Bruno*, 398–402). Even after Casaubon's work, claims of the antiquity of the Hermetic material persisted into the late seventeenth century. Most scholars now date the texts to the early centuries of the Christian era. For a general introduction to the Hermetic literature, see Brian P. Copenhaver, *Hermetica: The Greek Corpus Hermeticum and the Latin Asclepius in a New English Translation* (Cambridge: Cambridge University Press, 1992).

6. Photius, *Bibliotheca* 170.

7. For a general overview of the renewed interest in Plato in Renaissance Italy, see James Hankins, *Plato in the Italian Renaissance*, 2 vols. (Leiden: Brill, 1990).

8. See Daniel Pickering Walker, *The Ancient Theology: Studies in Christian Platonism from the Fifteenth to the Eighteenth Century* (Ithaca, N.Y.: Cornell University Press, 1972).

9. Ficino's *Theologia Platonica* was first published in 1482 (Florence: Antonio Miscomini). See now the edition and English translation of Michael J. B. Allen et al., *Platonic Theology*, 6 vols. (Cambridge, Mass.: Harvard University Press, 2001–2006).

10. See Michael J. B. Allen, "Marsilio Ficino, Hermes Trismegistus and the Corpus Hermeticum," in *New Perspectives on Renaissance Thought. Essays in the History of Science, Education and Philosophy: In Memory of Charles B. Schmitt*, ed. John Henry and Sarah Hutton (London: Duckworth, 1990), 38–47; reprinted as chapter 12 with added notes in *Plato's Third Eye: Studies in Marsilio Ficino's Metaphysics and Its Sources* (Aldershot: Variorum, 1995). Also see Yates, *Giordano Bruno*, 12.

11. The tracts were published under the title of the first piece, *Mercurii Trismegisti, Liber de potestate et sapientia Dei: Pimander* (Treviso: Gerardus de

Lisa, 1471); I have consulted a facsimile edition produced in 1989 (Florence: S.P.E.S., 1989).

12. See Yates, *Giordano Bruno*, 17. Several translations based on Ficino's Latin into the modern vernaculars also appeared (Allen, "Marsilio Ficino," 39).

13. Ficino, "Argumentum" to the *Mercurii Trismegisti*, 2–3.

14. For Ficino's changing attitude toward the *prisca theologia*, see Hankins, *Plato in the Italian Renaissance*, 460–64. For a summary of the Platonic thinkers between Proclus and the Renaissance, see Paul Oskar Kristeller, *The Philosophy of Marsilio Ficino*, trans. Virginia Conant (New York: Columbia University Press, 1943), 25–29. The idea that Greeks had some inkling of the revelation given to Moses can claim considerable antiquity. Eusebius attributes to Artapanus (who wrote no later than the first century B.C.E.) the view that Moses was himself "called Hermes" (*prosagoreuthēnai Hermēn*) and was the "teacher of Orpheus" (*Orpheōs didaskalon*). See Eusebius, *Praeparatio* 9.27.1–37.

15. *Marsilio Ficino: Opera Omnia*, repr. ed. (Turin: Bottega d'Erasmo, 1959 [1576]), 4. The translation is that of Kristeller in *The Philosophy of Marsilio Ficino*, 317. Ficino composed *De christiana religione* in the early 1470s, and it was published in both Latin and Italian. For details, see Kristeller, *Supplementum Ficinianum*, 2 vols. (Florence: Leonis S. Olschki, 1937), 1.lxxvii–1.lxxix. A translation in modern Italian appeared in 2005 (Roberto Zanzarri, *La religione Cristiana* [Rome: Città Nuova, 2005]).

16. On Ficino and the principle of the *primum in aliquo genere*, see Kristeller, *The Philosophy of Marsilio Ficino*, 146–47; and more recently Hankins, *Plato in the Italian Renaissance*, 1.285–87.

17. Kristeller, *The Philosophy of Marsilio Ficino*, 147. There is a sense in which I overstate the case when I stress the difference between Ficino's thinking and more "modern" concepts of religion. For in fact, in many modern models of "the religions," there is a definite (though usually unstated) hierarchy that designates Christianity as the outstanding and best example of the genus "religion." To take but one very important example, consider C. P. Tiele's entry for "Religions" in the ninth edition of the *Encyclopaedia Britannica* (Boston: Little, Brown, 1886), 20.358–71. Tiele claims to write an impartial, objective description of the various religions ("we are giving here nether a confession of faith nor an apology, but . . . we have here to treat Christianity simply as a subject of comparative study," 369, n. 1). Yet he concludes (scientifically, of course) that "Christianity ranks incommensurably high above . . . its

rivals" (369). What separates a schema like Ficino's from one like Tiele's is not so much a difference in the evaluation of how much better Christianity is than all other religions, but rather it is Tiele's claim to objectivity.

18. The Latin reads *Omnis religio boni habet nonnihil, modo ad deum ipsum creatorem omnium dirigatur, Christiana syncera est* (*Marsilio Ficino: Opera Omnia*, 4).

19. Kristeller, *The Philosophy of Marsilio Ficino*, 317.

20. On Bruno's life and travels, see Dorthea Waley Singer, *Giordano Bruno: His Life and Thought*, repr. ed. (New York: Greenwood, 1968 [1950]).

21. See Yates, *Giordano Bruno*, 11, and Walker, *The Ancient Theology*, 175. Hilary Gatti writes that Bruno "was taking over an already familiar theme . . . [but] was also bending and modifying it in important ways. . . . For example, Bruno was far from sharing Ficino's interest in the *prisca theologia* as an anticipation of the future coming of Christ. Rather he expounded it as an alternative form of morality and religion. He was also considerably more radical than most of his contemporaries in using the eloquent praise of unsullied origins as a critical weapon to castigate the modern world" (*Giordano Bruno and Renaissance Science* [Ithaca, N.Y.: Cornell University Press, 1999], 14–15). On Bruno's distaste for aspects of Christianity, see Alfonso Ingegno, *La Sommersa nave della religione: studio sulla polemica anticristiana del Bruno* (Naples: Bibliopolis, 1985).

22. Bruno is famously dismissive of Jews (in one of his dialogues, they receive the title "the excrements of Egypt"; see Yates, *Giordano Bruno*, 223), but his relationship to cabbalistic thought has been a matter of some speculation recently. Karen Silvia de León-Jones presents an intriguing argument to the effect that some of Bruno's work is best read as an enactment of Jewish cabbalistic practices. See her *Giordano Bruno and the Kabbalah: Prophets, Magicians, and Rabbis* (New Haven, Conn.: Yale University Press, 1997), 18–20. For more general reflections on the relationship between Kabbalah and the Ancient Theology, see Moshe Idel, "Kabbalah, Platonism, and Prisca Theologia: The Case of R. Menasseh ben Israel," in *Menasseh ben Israel and His World*, ed. Yosef Kaplan et al. (Leiden: Brill, 1989), 207–19. My thanks to Dylan Burns for drawing this work to my attention.

23. *La Cena de le Ceneri Descritta in cinque dialogi* (1584). The Italian works Bruno produced in England either lacked place and publisher identification or were falsely identified. There is now agreement that the books

were printed in London, and the most likely publisher was John Char-lewood. See Singer, *Giordano Bruno*, 215–16. I cite the translation of Edward A. Gosselin and Lawrence S. Lerne, *The Ash Wednesday Supper: La cena de le ceneri*, repr. ed. (Toronto: University of Toronto Press, 1995), 96. Also see Yates, *Giordano Bruno*, 11 and 223.

24. Although Bruno was hardly orthodox, he does seem to have wanted to reform Christianity into agreement with the true Ancient Theology. Giovanni Aquilecchia attributes to Bruno "an advocacy of reciprocal tolerance between different Christian denominations [that] often as-sumed the tone of an extreme polemical attitude." He argues that Bruno valued religion "entirely for pragmatic purposes of a civil and social na-ture" ("Giordano Bruno as Philosopher of the Renaissance," in *Giordano Bruno: Philosopher of the Renaissance*, ed. Hillary Gatti [Aldershot: Ash-gate, 2002], 3–14, quotation from 10). Although I think this reading of Bruno underplays some of the mystical aspects of his thought, it does illustrate how later political thinkers and theorists of "tolerance" could arise from this Neo-Platonic milieu (see, for instance, the material on Jean Bodin below).

25. *Spaccio de la bestia trionfante, proposto da Giove, effettuato dal conseglo, Revelato da Mercurio, Recitato da Sophia, Udito da Saulino, Registrato dal Nolano* (1584). The imprint of the 1584 edition claims to be from Paris, but there is agreement that the book was printed in London by John Charlewood. See Singer, *Giordano Bruno*, 215–16. I cite the anonymous translation *Spaccio della bestia trionfante, Or the Expulsion of the Trium-phant Beast* (London: n.p., 1713), 97–98. I have also consulted the trans-lation of Arthur D. Imerti, *The Expulsion of the Triumphant Beast* (New Brunswick, N.J.: Rutgers University Press, 1964). The speaker in this passage is Sophia, who is passing along to humans wisdom gained from Mercury.

26. Harrison, *"Religion" and the Religions*, 63.

27. Harrison lists several similar pamphlets ranging in date from the late sixteenth to the late seventeenth centuries (ibid., 183, n. 2).

28. In Harrison's words, "Salvation was intimately linked to teaching, knowing, and believing" (ibid., 20).

29. Joshua Stopford employed a similar title in 1675: *Pagano-papismus, Or, An Exact Parallel between Rome-pagan, and Rome-Christian, in their Doctrines and Ceremonies* (London: Printed by A. Maxwell for R. Clavel, 1675).

30. David A. Pailin, *Attitudes to Other Religions: Comparative Religion in Seventeenth- and Eighteenth-Century Britain* (Manchester: Manchester

University Press, 1984). See especially the chapter titled "The Uses of 'Other Religions' in Controversy," 121–36.

31. John Edwards, *The Socinian Creed: Or, A Brief Account of the Professed Tenets and Doctrines of the Foreign and English Socinians* (London: Printed for J. Robinson and J. Wyat, 1697), 221. Later Edwards charges that the Socinians returned the favor: "To conclude, if what I have said sound harsh in these Gentlemens ears, I request them to call to mind how severe they have been in censuring the *Trinitarians*. . . . They speak it without any mincing that the *Trinitarians are Idolaters, and Pagans, and much worse,* and this they often inculcate" (231–32).

32. England in the seventeenth century was in many ways heir to the Italian Neo-Platonic thought of the preceding centuries. Ficino's works circulated widely in England, and Bruno's travels in Oxford and London created a stir in those areas. The most important center for Platonic thought in seventeenth-century England was Cambridge. For an overview, see Ernst Cassirer, *The Platonic Renaissance in England*, trans. James P. Pettegrove (Austin: University of Texas Press, 1953). For Herbert's relationship to the Cambridge Platonists, see Harrison, *"Religion" and the Religions*, 62–63, and for how Herbert fits into the history of the *prisca theologia*, see Walker, *The Ancient Theology*, 191–93.

33. See the evidence cited in Walker, *The Ancient Theology*, 164–65. Herbert's reputation as a deist stems in large part from the positions he espoused in the posthumously published *De religione gentilium*, which I discuss below.

34. Meyrick H. Carré, introduction to *De Veritate by Edward, Lord Herbert of Cherbury*, trans. Meyrick H. Carré (Bristol: J. W. Arrowsmith, 1937), 10.

35. For the details of Herbert's life, see Mario M. Rossi, *La vita, le opere, i tempi di Edoardo Herbert di Chirbury*, 3 vols. (Florence: G. C. Sansoni, 1947). A concise treatment in English is Sidney Lee's introduction to his edition of Herbert's autobiography, *The Autobiography of Edward, Lord Herbert of Cherbury*, repr. ed. (Westport, Conn.: Greenwood, 1970). Lee also continues the biographical sketch where Herbert himself leaves off.

36. *De Veritate* appeared in subsequent editions in 1633, 1645, and 1649, but it was not translated into English until the twentieth century (Carré's translation of 1937). I cite the 1633 edition of the Latin (London: Augustinum Matthaeum) and Carré's translation.

37. As Basil Willey summarizes, "Whatsoever is vouched for by the notions commonly inscribed upon the minds of men as such, whatsoever is received by universal consent, that, and that only, is Truth" (*The*

Seventeenth Century Background: Studies in the Thought of the Age in Relation to Poetry and Religion, repr. ed. [New York: Columbia University Press, 1977 (1934)], 123).

38. Herbert, *De Veritate*, 43 (Carré, trans., *De Veritate*, 121).

39. Ibid., 208–23 (289–307).

40. Ibid., 209–10 (291).

41. Although the text of *De religione gentilium* was sent to the publisher in 1645, it was not published until fifteen years after Herbert's death (*De religione gentilium, errorumque apud eos causis* [Amsterdam: Typis Blaeviorum, 1663]). He likely wrote the work in the early 1640s; for a discussion of the circumstances of composition, see Rossi, *La vita*, 3.506–7. I have cited the translation of William Lewis, *The Antient Religion of the Gentiles, and Causes of their Errors Consider'd* (London: William Taylor, 1711 [reissue of the 1705 ed.]), 3–4. I have also consulted the translation and notes of John Anthony Butler, *Pagan Religion: A Translation of De religione gentilium* (Ottawa: Dovehouse, 1996).

42. *The Antient Religion*, 3. Herbert goes on: "I suppose none will deny but that Priests have introduced Superstition and Idolatry, as well as sown Quarrels and Dissentions where-ever they came." There is a good deal of fulminating against priests in *De religione gentilium*. For further discussion of such attacks on the priesthood, see Harrison, *"Religion" and the Religions*, 77–85.

43. *The Antient Religion*, 33.

44. Ibid., 270–71.

45. See Willey, *The Seventeenth Century Background*, 122–32; and Walker, *The Ancient Theology*, 165. Walker observes that this book reveals "Herbert's strong tendencies towards a Brunonian kind of Religion" (171). I hesitate to describe Herbert's theory as "natural religion" since that phrase has so many meanings. Peter Byrne describes four broad uses of the term (*Natural Religion and the Nature of Religion: The Legacy of Deism* [London: Routledge, 1989]), and more recently, David A. Pailin has identified eleven different uses ("The Confused and Confusing Story of Natural Religion," *Religion* 24 [1994]: 199–212). Later deist writers would make the connection between Christianity and "natural religion" explicit. See, for example, Matthew Tindal, *Christianity as Old as the Creation: Or, the Gospel, a Republication of the Religion of Nature* (London: n.p., 1730).

46. Hume's history, though, would lack the happy monotheistic starting point of Herbert, instead placing the worship of many gods at the root

of religion. See Hume's *The Natural History of Religion*, first published in *Four Dissertations* (London: Printed for A. Millar, 1757).

47. Walker writes: "What had begun as just one element in Christian apologia, namely, the *consensus gentium* argument to prove the fundamental truths of Christianity, has begun to grow lushly and, like a parasitic plant, to swamp and eventually kill its host. The Ancient Theology has started to turn into the comparative study of religions, with Christianity as only one member of a very large class" (*The Ancient Theology*, 215; Walker makes this remark in reference to the work of Pierre-Daniel Huet [1630–1721], but I think it is equally valid for Herbert).

48. On this point, see Harrison, *"Religion" and the Religions*, 64.

49. For a biographical overview of Toland, see Robert E. Sullivan, *John Toland and the Deist Controversy* (Cambridge, Mass.: Harvard University Press, 1982), 1–50.

50. On Jewish integration, *The Reasons for Naturalising the Jews in Great Britain and Ireland: On the Same Foot with All Other Nations: Containing also a Defence of the Jews against all Vulgar Prejudices in all Countries* (London: Printed for J. Roberts, 1714). See Justin Champion, *Republican Learning: John Toland and the Crisis of Christian Culture, 1696–1722* (New York: Palgrave, 2003), 142–44; and his "Toleration and Citizenship in Enlightenment England: John Toland and the Naturalization of the Jews, 1714–1753," in *Toleration in Enlightenment Europe*, ed. Ole Peter Grell and Roy Porter (Cambridge: Cambridge University Press, 2000), 133–56.

51. *Nazarenus: Or, Jewish, Gentile and Mahometan Christianity. Containing the history of the antient Gospel of Barnabas, and the modern Gospel of the Mahometans, attributed to the same Apostle: this last Gospel being now first made known among Christians*, 2nd rev. ed. (London: J. Brotherton, J. Roberts, and A. Dodd, 1718). Current opinion is that the Gospel of Barnabas, now known from two manuscripts not earlier than the fifteenth century, is a modern composition. See the bibliography in Jan Joosten, "The *Gospel of Barnabas* and the Diatessaron," *Harvard Theological Review* 95 (2002): 73–96. An edition and English translation is available in Lonsdale and Laura Ragg, *The Gospel of Barnabas: Edited and Translated from the Italian Ms. in the Imperial Library at Vienna* (Oxford: Clarendon, 1907).

52. *Nazarenus*, iii. Toland expected his claim to be controversial: "The very title of *Mahometan Christianity* may be apt to startle you (for *Jewish* or *Gentile Christianity* shou'd not sound quite so strange) yet I flatter my self, that, by perusing the following *Dissertation*, you'll be fully convinc'd there is a sense, wherin the Mahometans may not improperly be reckon'd

and call'd a sort or sect of Christians, as Christianity was at first esteem'd a branch of Judaism" (*Nazarenus*, 4–5).

53. It is interesting that the notion of Nazarenes (or, as they are now called, "Jewish Christians") has become a mainstay of scholarship on early Christianity, while the idea of Mahometan Christians ("Muslim Christians") is almost unheard of (though see my discussion of Donner's work in Chapter 4). The present flourishing of the idea of ancient "Jewish Christians" probably owes something to the currency of the idea of a "Judeo-Christian tradition" in the modern world. This hyphenated phrase seems to be a late-nineteenth-century coinage that has changed its meaning considerably since its inception. In its early uses, the term referred to a strictly ancient phenomenon, what is now usually termed "Jewish Christianity," that is, groups of Jews in antiquity who were also followers of Jesus (see, for example, J. Rendel Harris's review of several books on the Didache in the *American Journal of Philology* 6 [1885]: 102–5; and W. F. Albright, "The Goddess of Life and Wisdom," *American Journal of Semitic Languages and Literatures* 36 [1920]: 258–94, at 288). In the 1930s, one begins to see the modern usage that isolates the shared ethical and cultural values of Judaism and Christianity (see André Lalande, "Philosophy in France, 1934–1935," *Philosophical Review* 45 [1936]: 1–25, at 22).

54. A good general account of this period in European history is Richard S. Dunn, *The Age of Religious Wars: 1559–1715*, 2nd ed. (New York: Norton, 1979). For a treatment more directly concerned with the formation of the modern state, see Martin van Creveld, *The Rise and Decline of the State* (Cambridge: Cambridge University Press, 1999), 59–184. For a more in-depth discussion of the Wars of Religion in relation to the development of the concept of religion, see William T. Cavanaugh, *The Myth of Religious Violence* (New York: Oxford University Press, 2009), 142–77.

55. See the essays collected in Peter Diehl and Scott L. Waugh, eds., *Christendom and Its Discontents: Exclusion, Persecution, and Rebellion, 1000–1500* (Cambridge: Cambridge University Press, 1996).

56. Successful resistance to the Catholic Church by local "temporal" leaders had taken place before the time of the reformers but never on so large a scale. See William T. Cavanaugh, "'A Fire Strong Enough to Consume the House': The Wars of Religion and the Rise of the State," *Modern Theology* 11 (1995): 397–420. He cites the Pragmatic Sanction of Bourges (1438) and the Concordat of Bologna (1516) as early examples of concessions of papal power.

57. For Luther's firm separation of civil and ecclesiastical authorities (and the full subjugation of the latter to the former), see his *Open Letter to the Christian Nobility of the German Nation Concerning the Reform of the Christian Estate* (1520) and *Temporal Authority: To What Extent it Should be Obeyed* (1523). On the growth of Luther's popularity, see A. G. Dickens, *Reformation and Society in Sixteenth-Century Europe* (London: Thames and Hudson, 1966), 74–79; and Quentin Skinner, *The Foundations of Modern Political Thought*, 2 vols. (Cambridge: Cambridge University Press, 1978), 2.3–19.

58. Introduction to *Six Books of the Commonwealth: Abridged and Translated by M. J. Tooley* (Oxford: Blackwell, 1955), xv.

59. Richard S. Dunn observes that in the sixteenth century "the German Catholic princes, the Hapsburgs in Spain, and the Valois in France all had exerted papal concessions which tightened their hold over their territorial churches. . . . In refusing to cooperate with Rome, the Catholic princes checked papal ambitions to restore the Church's medieval political power" (*The Age of Religious Wars*, 13). During the Thirty Years War (1618–1648), one finds Catholics such as Cardinal Richelieu allying themselves with Protestants such as Gustavus Adolphus when it suited their purposes (ibid., 82–92).

60. "'A Fire Strong Enough to Consume the House,'" 402–3.

61. Ibid., 398. Cavanaugh also points out that these wars were not purely the result of religious fanaticism: "It is important therefore to see that the principal promoters of the wars in France and Germany were in fact not pastors and peasants, but kings and nobles with a stake in the outcome of the movement toward the centralized, hegemonic State" (403).

62. For Bodin's intellectual milieu, see the exchange between Frances A. Yates ("The Mystery of Jean Bodin") and Marion L. Kuntz ("Bodin's Demons") in the *New York Review of Books* (vols. 23 and 24, 1976–1977, http://www.nybooks.com/articles/8723, accessed 23 October 2011).

63. On the complexity of Bodin's political leanings, especially in his later years, see Paul Lawrence Rose, "The *Politique* and the Prophet: Bodin and the Catholic League, 1589–1594," *Historical Journal* 21 (1978): 783–808.

64. The first French edition was *Les six livres de la republique* (Paris: Chez Jacques du Puys, 1576). Successive revised French editions appeared over the next decade. In 1586, Bodin produced a new Latin rewriting of the book (*De Republica libri sex* [Paris: Jacobum Du-puys, 1586]). In

1606 Richard Knolles published the first (and only complete) English translation, which was based on both the French and the Latin versions. I cite from the annotated facsimile edition of the 1606 English translation prepared by Kenneth Douglas McRae, *The Six Bookes of a Commonweale: A Facsimile Reprint of the English Translation of 1606* (Cambridge, Mass.: Harvard University Press, 1962). For a thorough discussion of the publication history of *The Six Books*, see McRae's introduction to this edition.

65. *The Six Bookes of a Commonweale*, 535 (Book 4, chapter 7).

66. Ibid., 536.

67. Ibid., 537.

68. I cite the translation of Marion L. Kuntz, *Colloquium of the Seven about Secrets of the Sublime* (Princeton, N.J.: Princeton University Press, 1975). Attribution of this work to Bodin has been challenged. Bodin himself never mentions the work, and it was not published until 1857 (*Colloquium heptaplomeres de rerum sublimium arcanis abditis*, ed. Ludovicus Noack (Schwerin: F. G. Baerensprung, 1857]; a facsimile of this edition was produced in 1966 [Stuttgart: Friedrich Frommann Verlag]). No autograph exists, and David Wootton has questioned the dating of the earliest manuscripts; see Wootton, "Pseudo-Bodin's *Colloquium heptaplomeres* and Bodin's *Démonomanie*," in *Magie, Religion und Wissenschaften im* Colloquium heptaplomeres: *Ergebnisse der Tagungen in Paris 1994 und in der Villa Vigoni 1999*, ed. Karl Friedrich Faltenbacher (Darmstadt: Wissenschaftliche Buchgesellschaft, 2002), 175–225. For my purposes, actual authorship is not especially important; what matters is that the piece enjoyed wide popularity under Bodin's name even before its official publication so that by "the beginning of the eighteenth century almost every scholar of importance had his copy" (Kuntz, *Colloquium*, lxix).

69. *Colloquium*, 462. The Latin reads *simplicissimam illam et antiquissimam eandemque verissimam naturae religionem, uniuscuiusque mentibus ab immortali Deo insitam, a qua dissidendum non erat* (Noack, 351–52). On the slippery notion of "natural religion" or "the religion of nature," see note 45 above.

70. Ibid., 471. The phrase echoes a passage from Lactantius, *Epitome of the Divine Institutes* 54, with a key change. Whereas Lactantius had asserted that due to the freedom (*libertas*) present in *religio*, it was impossible to force worship (*ut colat*), the agreement among Bodin's characters concerns belief (*ut credat*).

71. *Colloquium*, 471.
72. J. Samuel Preus makes this point in his discussion of Bodin in *Explaining Religion: Criticism and Theory from Bodin to Freud* (New Haven, Conn.: Yale University Press, 1987), 3–20.
73. Ingrid Creppell, *Toleration and Identity: Foundations in Early Modern Thought* (London: Routledge, 2003), 39.
74. I choose Locke here as the most articulate spokesperson for a number of political thinkers delineating the realm of religion in the seventeenth century. For further details on these figures, see John Marshall, *John Locke, Toleration and Early Enlightenment Culture: Religious Intolerance and Arguments for Religious Toleration in Early Modern and 'Early Enlightenment' Europe* (Cambridge: Cambridge University Press, 2006).
75. See Wayne Glausser, "Three Approaches to Locke and the Slave Trade," *Journal of the History of Ideas* 51 (1990): 199–216.
76. See John C. Biddle, "Locke's Critique of Innate Principles and Toland's Deism," *Journal of the History of Ideas* 37 (1976): 411–22, esp. 418.
77. I cite from the translation attributed to William Popple, *A Letter Concerning Toleration: Humbly Submitted &c.* (London: Printed for Awnsham Churchill, 1689). The first Latin edition had been published earlier in the same year in Holland, where Locke had composed it (*Epistola de tolerantia ad clarissimum Virum* [Gouda: Justus van der Hoeve, 1689]). See the introductory material in Raymond Klibansky and J. W. Gough's edition of the Latin text, *Epistola de Tolerantia: A Letter on Toleration* (Oxford: Clarendon, 1968).
78. Locke, *A Letter Concerning Toleration*, 6.
79. Ibid., 7. The placement of "belief" outside the realm of bodily persuasion is central for Locke's argument. For an assessment of Locke's logic, see Jeremy Waldron, "Locke: Toleration and the Rationality of Persecution," in *Justifying Toleration: Conceptual and Historical Perspectives*, ed. Susan Mendus (Cambridge: Cambridge University Press, 1988), 61–86.
80. The quotation comes from Peter Brown's description of Ambrose of Milan's outlook on the church, but I find that it quite appropriately captures later medieval thinking as well. See Brown, *The Body and Society: Men, Women, and Sexual Renunciation in Early Christianity* (New York: Columbia University Press, 1988), 346. R. W. Southern's description is more temporally accurate, if a bit more prosaic: The medieval church was ideally "a society of disciplined and organized clergy directing the thoughts and activities of an obedient and receptive laity—kings,

magnates, and peasants alike" (*Western Society and the Church in the Middle Ages* [New York: Penguin, 1978], 38).

81. *A Letter Concerning Toleration*, 9–10.

82. Ibid., 6.

83. Ibid., 12–13.

84. In the standard reading of the *Letter*, Locke does not extend tolerance to Catholics or Muslims. For a dissenting view, see Jeremy Waldron, *God, Locke, and Equality: Christian Foundations in Locke's Political Thought* (Cambridge: Cambridge University Press, 2002), 217–23. Whatever Locke's opinion on the matter, it was the civil authorities who would decide just what could be tolerated. The Toleration Act of 1689 (passed in May of that year) "granted toleration of worship to Protestant trinitarians. It excluded unitarians, Roman Catholics and atheists . . . There was no recognition, in other words, that the community did not have the right to abridge peaceful forms of worship" (John Marshall, *John Locke: Resistance, Religion and Responsibility* [Cambridge: Cambridge University Press, 1994], 370).

85. *A Letter Concerning Toleration*, 57–58.

86. The Latin here (*habent fidei et cultus divini regulam*) is useful in clearing up an ambiguity in Popple's translation. The two genitives make it clear that what is meant is "Rule of both Faith and Worship," that is, scriptures.

87. On this point, see the recent work of Craig Martin, especially *Masking Hegemony: A Genealogy of Liberalism, Religion, and the Private Sphere* (London: Equinox, 2010), 58–108. Martin's argument that "the religion/state distinction did not . . . separate, segregate, or insulate the state from religion . . . but rather . . . it had the effect of masking the circulation of power from one to the other" (35) is well taken. My interest is more in the rhetoric of the religion/state divide than the "reality" of power circulation.

88. Maurice Cranston, *John Locke: A Biography*, repr. ed. (London: Longmans, 1966 [1957]), 107. Cranston would attribute Locke's own views on toleration to "religious" motives (209–10), but it is unclear what he means by the term "religious."

6. New Worlds, New Religions, World Religions

1. Again, I emphasize that I am not arguing that "secularism" imposed itself on what was previously a uniformly "religious" world. Rather, this period saw the introduction of the distinction between a "religious sphere" and a "secular sphere."

2. Giuliano Dati, *Lettera delle isole che ha trovato il re di Spagna* (Florence: Lorenzo Morgiani and Johannes Petri, 1493). For facsimiles and translations of the Latin and Italian versions of Columbus's letter, see Martin Davies, *Columbus in Italy: An Italian Versification of the Letter on the Discovery of the New World* (London: British Library, 1991).

3. Peter Jackson, *The Mongols and the West, 1221–1410* (New York: Pearson Longman, 2005), esp. 135–64.

4. J. H. Elliott, *The Old World and the New: 1492–1650* (Cambridge: Cambridge University Press, 1970), 8.

5. This point is one of the many insights packed into Jonathan Z. Smith's dense essay, "Religion, Religions, Religious," in *Relating Religion: Essays in the Study of Religion* (Chicago: University of Chicago Press, 2004), 179–96.

6. The Dutch verse version was published in 1622, and the first Latin edition appeared in 1627. See Jan-Paul Heering, "Hugo Grotius' *De Veritate Religionis Christianae*," in *Hugo Grotius: Theologian: Essays in Honour of G. H. M. Posthumus Meyjes*, ed. Henk J. M. Nellen and Edwin Rabbie (Leiden: Brill, 1994), 41–52, and by the same author, *Hugo Grotius as Apologist for the Christian Religion: A Study of His Work De Veritate Religionis Christianae*, trans. J. C. Grayson (Leiden: Brill, 2004 [Dutch ed. 1992]). The book was extremely popular long after its initial publication. In 1925, W. S. M. Knight summarized its reception: "At least thirty-three editions of the original Latin may be identified, from the first in 1627 to the last in 1836, these appearing in various places—for instance in Paris, Oxford, and London. . . . Of translations we can count six editions in Dutch, from 1653 to 1728; six in German from 1631 to 1768; five in French, from 1688 to 1754; two in Arabic, 1660 and 1735; two in Scandinavian languages, from 1678 to 1737, and one each in Hungarian (1723) and Urdu. But judging from translations, as well as from the many English reprints of the original, England must have been the country where this work was best received and most appreciated. We can trace fourteen English editions of translations, the first in 1632 and the last in 1860. . . . In the Welsh we notice three editions of translations of the years 1716, 1820, and 1854" (*The Life and Works of Hugo Grotius* [London: Sweet and Maxwell, 1925], 178–79). New editions and translations of *De veritate* ceased appearing after the middle of the nineteenth century.

7. The English translation is that of Spencer Madan, *Hugo Grotius: On the Truth of Christianity* (London: J. Dodsley, 1782), 4–5. The translator remarks that this version of the text was specifically designed for "the lower ranks of people" (iv).

8. "First Report from the Select Committee on Indian Territories; Together with the Minutes of Evidence," in *Reports from Committees* (London: House of Commons, 1853), 281–82.

9. See Robert Eric Frykenberg, "The Emergence of Modern 'Hinduism' as a Concept and as an Institution: A Reappraisal with Special Reference to South India," in *Hinduism Reconsidered*, rev. ed., ed. Günther-Dietz Sontheimer and Hermann Kulke (New Delhi: Manohar, 2005), 82–107.

10. The earliest usage of the term known to me occurs in a letter by Charles Grant, an employee of the British East India Company, written in 1787. The letter is cited and discussed in Geoffrey A. Oddie, *Imagined Hinduism: British Protestant Missionary Constructions of Hinduism, 1793–1900* (New Delhi: Sage, 2006), 68–71.

11. The name "Banian" most likely derives (by way of Portuguese and Arabic) from the Gujarati word *vāṇiyo*, a person of the merchant or trading class. See the entry for "banian" in the *Oxford English Dictionary*.

12. The publication was actually two short titles by Lord bound in a single volume called *A Display of Two Forraigne Sects in the East Indes* (London: T. and R. Cotes for Francis Constable, 1630). I cite from this edition. The title of the second part of the work was *The Religion of the Persees. As it was Compiled from a Booke of theirs, containing the Forme of their Worshippe, written in the Persian Character, and by them called their Zundavastaw. Wherein is shewed the Superstitious Ceremonies used amongst them.* An edition of the whole, newly typeset with an introduction, has been produced by Will Sweetman, *A Discovery of the Banian Religion and the Religion of the Persees: A Critical Edition of Two Early Works on Indian Religions* (Lewiston, N.Y.: Edwin Mellen, 1999).

13. *A Discoverie of the Sect of the Banians*, 93.

14. Ibid., from the introduction, n.p.

15. Ibid. "Shaster" in all likelihood refers to the Sanskrit term *śāstra*, which is a general term for a rulebook rather than the name of a specific text.

16. Ibid., 71.

17. Sweetman's introduction to the critical edition attempts to deemphasize this aspect of Lord's work.

18. Although Müller is celebrated by some as the founder of a "scientific" approach to the study of religion, I do not think it inappropriate to place his work on a continuum with the works of people like Henry Lord. To be sure, Müller was no cleric; he was a philologist of the highest skill, but it is worth recalling that he was not without Christian missionary interests. In the preface to the first volume of *Chips from a*

German Workshop (4 vols. [London: Longmans, Green, 1867–1875]), Müller writes, "To the missionary, more particularly, a comparative study of the religions of mankind will be, I believe of greatest assistance. . . . missionaries, instead of looking only for points of difference, will look out more anxiously for any common ground, any spark of the true light that may still be revived, any altar that may be dedicated afresh to the true God" (1.xxi–xxii).

19. See the account in Gandhi's autobiography, *An Autobiography or the Story of My Experiments with Truth*, repr. ed. (Ahmedabad: Navajivan, 1996 [1927]), 57–59. When Gandhi wrote of his "enhanced . . . regard for Hinduism," he mentioned as causes his reading of both "the translation of the *Upanishads* published by the Theosophical Society" and "Max Muller's book, *India—What can it teach us?*" (132–33).

20. *Chips from a German Workshop*, 1.170–71. Earlier in the same essay, Müller makes the following observation: "Though every religion is of real and vital interest in its earliest state only, yet its later development too, with all its misunderstandings, faults, and corruptions, offers many an instructive lesson to the thoughtful student of history" (1.163).

21. For example, in a dense survey of "the religions of India" published in 1895, Edward Washburn Hopkins (who would become Salisbury Professor of Sanskrit and Comparative Philology at Yale later in that year), recommended that missionaries leave alone "the Hindu doctors" (Brahmins who actually could read ancient texts) on account of their cleverness, but "among the uneducated and 'depressed' classes there is plenty for the missionary to do" (*The Religions of India* [Boston: Ginn and Company, 1895], 568). For details on Hopkins's career, see Franklin Edgerton, "Edward Washburn Hopkins, 1857–1932," *Journal of the American Oriental Society* 52 (1932): 311–15.

22. See, for example, Richard King, *Orientalism and Religion: Post-colonial Theory, India and "the Mystic East"* (New York: Routledge, 1999); Philip C. Almond, *The British Discovery of Buddhism* (Cambridge: Cambridge University Press, 1988); *Curators of the Buddha: The Study of Buddhism under Colonialism*, ed. Donald S. Lopez, Jr. (Chicago: University of Chicago Press, 1995); and Arvind-pal S. Mandair, *Religion and the Specter of the West: Sikhism, India, Postcoloniality, and the Politics of Translation* (New York: Columbia University Press, 2009).

23. The debates are contentious. A good place to start to get a sense of the variety and complexity of positions in these discussions is the collection

of essays edited by J. E. Llewellyn, *Defining Hinduism: A Reader* (New York: Routledge, 2005).

24. Knut A. Jacobsen, "Introduction," in *Brill's Encyclopedia of Hinduism* (Leiden: Brill, 2009), xxxiii–xliii, quotation from xli.

25. David Chidester, *Savage Systems: Colonialism and Comparative Religion in Southern Africa* (Charlottesville: University Press of Virginia, 1996).

26. See Nigel Penn, "The Voyage Out: Peter Kolb and the VOC Voyages to the Cape," in *Many Middle Passages: Forced Migration and the Making of the Modern World*, ed. Emma Christopher, Cassandra Pybus, and Marcus Rediker (Berkeley: University of California Press, 2007), 72–91.

27. Chidester, *Savage Systems*, 47–48.

28. Peter Kolb, *Caput Bonae Spei hodiernum. Das ist, vollständige Beschreibung des afrikanischen Vorgebürges der Guten Hofnung* (Nürnberg: Peter Conrad Monath, 1719). The book was quite popular; it was translated into Dutch (1727) and later into English, as *The Present State of the Cape of Good Hope: Or, A Particular Account of the Several Nations of the Hottentots: Their Religion, Government, Laws, Customs, Ceremonies, and Opinions: Their Art of War, Professions, Language, Genesis, &c.*, trans. Mr. Medley (London: W. Innys, 1731). My citations are drawn from the second edition of the English version, which appeared in 1738. A French translation was published in 1741. For details of the influence of Kolb's work, see Anne Good, "The Construction of an Authoritative Text: Peter Kolb's Description of the Khoikhoi at the Cape of Good Hope in the Eighteenth Century," *Journal of Early Modern History* 10 (2006): 61–94, esp. 89–94.

29. *The Present State of the Cape of Good Hope*, 56.

30. Kolb described his method of inquiry as follows: "If you find 'em at this Devotion, and ask the Meaning of it, they only laugh, with an Air that informs you, You are to guess it, and not to ask them. And if you urge them to an Explanation, they grow angry, and answer very short, 'Why, this is the custom of the *Hottentots*.' But for a Pipe of Tobacco, or a Dram of Brandy, you will now and then find One who will give you an Account of the Matter, and tell you a long Story of the Virtues and Achievements of those Ancestors of the *Hottentots* to whom those Dedications are made" (ibid., 103).

31. Ibid., 91. For assertions from several other authors that the Hottentots lacked religion, see Chidester, *Savage Systems*, 34–46.

32. *The Present State of the Cape of Good Hope*, 30.

33. Ibid.

34. Ibid., 99.
35. Ibid., 102.
36. Ibid., 99-101.
37. Ibid., 105.
38. Chidester, *Savage Systems*, 56. As Chidester points out, this kind of comparative enterprise was a double-edged sword in terms of producing knowledge; both sides of the analogy were affected: "This comparison also required a redefinition of Judaism as a religious tradition that resembled the practices of the Hottentots" (52).
39. Ibid., 56-72.
40. My account here is especially indebted to Sarah Thal, "A Religion That Was Not a Religion: The Creation of Modern Shinto in Nineteenth-Century Japan," in *The Invention of Religion: Rethinking Belief in Politics and History*, ed. Derek R. Petersen and Darren R. Walhof (New Brunswick, N.J.: Rutgers University Press, 2002), 100-14.
41. Hirai Naofusa (trans. Helen Hardacre), "Shinto," in *The Encyclopedia of Religion*, ed. Mircea Eliade (New York: Macmillan, 1987), 13.280-94. This view is repeated in typical World Religions textbooks: Shinto is "the indigenous religion of Japan" (see John L. Esposito, Darrell J. Fasching, and Todd Lewis, *World Religions Today*, 3rd ed [New York: Oxford University Press, 2009], G-16).
42. For key studies of the history of the term, see Kuroda Toshio, "Shinto in the History of Japanese Religion" (trans. James C. Dobbins and Suzanne Gay), *Journal of Japanese Studies* 7 (1981): 1-21, and Mark Teeuwen, "From *Jindō* to Shinto: A Concept Takes Shape," *Japanese Journal of Religious Studies* 29 (2002): 233-63.
43. This point is demonstrated at length in the studies collected in *Buddhas and Kami in Japan: honji suijaku as a Combinatory Paradigm*, ed. Mark Teeuwen and Fabio Rambelli (London: RoutledgeCurzon, 2003).
44. Thal, "A Religion That Was Not a Religion," 101.
45. On this phenomenon, see Helen Hardacre, *Shintō and the State, 1868-1988* (Princeton: Princeton University Press, 1989), 27-28, and Allan G. Grapard, "Japan's Ignored Cultural Revolution: The Separation of Shinto and Buddhist Divinities in Meiji (*shimbutsu bunri*) and a Case Study: Tōnomine," *History of Religions* 23 (1984): 240-65.
46. For a fuller account, see Hardacre, *Shintō and the State*, 1-36.
47. Mori Arinori, *Religious Freedom in Japan: A Memorial and Draft of Charter* (Washington, D.C.: privately published, 1872), reprinted as an appendix in John E. Van Sant, *Mori Arinori's Life and Resources in America*

(Lanham, Md.: Lexington Books, 2004), 143–49; quotation from 144. I owe the reference to Mori to Thal, "A Religion That Was Not a Religion," 104.

48. Cited in Thal, "A Religion That Was Not a Religion," 107.

49. Supreme Commander for the Allied Powers Instructions (SCAPIN) 448, 15 December 1945, "Abolition of Governmental Sponsorship, Support, Perpetuation, Control, and Dissemination of State Shinto," reprinted in William P. Woodard, *The Allied Occupation of Japan 1945–1952 and Japanese Religions* (Leiden: Brill, 1972), 295–99, quotation from 297. For the text of the background study that justified the directive, see pp. 322–41.

50. Thal, "A Religion That Was Not a Religion," 100.

51. A point well made in Smith, "Religion, Religions, Religious." In what follows, I treat a selection of works in English. See Smith's chapter for a fuller bibliography of relevant French and German works.

52. The full title runs as follows: *Purchas his Pilgrimage: Or Relations of the World and the Religions Observed in all Ages and Places discovered, from Creation unto this Present: In Foure Partes. This first containeth a theologicall and geographicall historie of Asia, Africa, and America, with the ilands adjacent. Declaring the ancient religions before the Floud, the Heathnish, Jewish, and Saracenicall in all Ages since, in those parts professed, with their severall Opinions, Idols, Oracles, Temples, Priests, Fasts, Feasts, Sacrifices, and Rites Religious: Their beginnings, Proceedings, Alterations, Sects, Orders and Successions. With briefe descriptions of the countries, nations, states, discoveries, private and publike customes, and the most remarkable rarities of nature, or humane industrie, in the same* (London: William Stansby for Henrie Fetherstone, 1613). A second and much enlarged edition appeared in 1614, followed by several subsequent editions. For a rich treatment of the context of Purchas's life and works as well as a thorough bibliography, see *The Purchas Handbook: Studies in the Life, Times and Writings of Samuel Purchas 1577–1626*, 2 vols., ed. L. E. Pennington (London: Hakluyt Society, 1997).

53. Purchas, *Purchas his Pilgrimage*, 15 and 27.

54. Ibid., 26.

55. Ibid., 15. For a much more extended treatment of Purchas, with special attention to his use of "religion," see Timothy Fitzgerald, *Discourse on Civility and Barbarity: A Critical History of Religion and Related Categories* (New York: Oxford University Press, 2007), 193–230.

56. *Purchas his Pilgrimage*, 16.

57. For biographical details on Ross, see David Allan, "'An Ancient Sage Philosopher': Alexander Ross and the Defence of Philosophy," *Seventeenth Century* 16 (2001): 68–94.

58. I have seen reference made to an edition of 1652, but I have been unable to locate such an edition myself. I cite from the 1653 edition published in London by James Young and John Saywell. The title page carries no indication of edition. The 1655 printing by Saywell is labeled as "The Second Edition, Enlarged and Perfected, By Alexander Ross." The work appears to have been quite popular. It went through six editions and several printings before the close of the seventeenth century.

59. Ross, *Pansebeia*, preface to the reader, n.p.

60. Ibid., dedicatory epistle, n.p.

61. Ibid., 518–25.

62. Ibid., 527–29.

63. Ibid., 537.

64. The name David Hume looms large in this regard. See Peter Harrison, *"Religion" and the Religions in the English Enlightenment* (Cambridge: Cambridge University Press, 1990), esp. 167–72.

65. For a recent treatment of the widespread influence of this work, see Lynn Hunt, Margaret C. Jacob, and Wijnand Mijnhardt, *The Book That Changed Europe: Picart and Bernard's Religious Ceremonies of the World* (Cambridge, Mass.: Belknap, 2010).

66. There were also translations into Dutch and German.

67. Bernard Picart, *The Ceremonies and Religious Customs of the Various Nations of the Known World Together with Historical Annotations and several Curious Discourses Equally Informative and Entertaining*, 7 vols. (London: William Jackson for Claude du Bosc, 1733–1739), quotation from 5.288.

68. Ibid., 1.5.

69. A fuller version of the title runs as follows: *An Historical Dictionary of All Religions from the Creation of the World to this Present Time. Containing, I. A Display of all the Pagan Systems of Theology, their Origin, their superstitious Customs, Ceremonies, and Doctrines. II. The Jewish, Christian, and Mohammedan Institutions, with the Ecclesiastical Laws, and History respecting each Denomination. III. The Rise and Progress of the various Sects, Heresies, and Opinions, which have sprung up in different Ages and Countries; with an Account of the Founders and Propagators thereof. IV. A Survey of the several Objects of Adoration; Deities and Idols. Of Persons dedicated to the sacred Function; Priests and Religious Orders. Times, and Places of Divine*

Worship; Fasts, Festivals, Temples, Churches, and Mosques. V. Of Sacred Books and Writings, the Vestments of Religious Orders, and a Description of all the Utensils employed in Divine Offices. VI. The Changes and Alterations, which Religion has undergone both in ancient and modern Times, 2 vols. (London: C. Davis and T. Harris, on London-Bridge, 1742). The work had been printed before under the title *Bibliotheca historico-sacra* (1737–1739). It was reprinted in 1756, at which time a German edition in a single volume also appeared.

70. Ibid., iii.

71. Ibid., iv.

72. These are the printings known to me; there may be others. I cite from the 1799 edition printed by J. Hemmingway at Blackburn.

73. Hurd, *A New Universal History,* 481–91.

74. See ibid., 815–16 (on the Muggletonians) and 823–25 (on the Hutchinsonians).

75. Ibid., 116.

76. For a history of the academic field of religious studies, with a focus on the nineteenth century, see Eric J. Sharpe, *Comparative Religion: A History,* 2nd ed. (La Salle, Ill.: Open Court, 1986 [1975]). Guy Stroumsa has made a case for seeing the philological efforts of the seventeenth century as an earlier beginning to the field of religious studies proper (*A New Science: The Discovery of Religion in the Age of Reason* [Cambridge, Mass.: Harvard University Press, 2010]).

77. Tomoko Masuzawa, *The Invention of World Religions: Or, How European Universalism Was Preserved in the Language of Pluralism* (Chicago: University of Chicago Press, 2005). See also the sets of essays reviewing the book and Masuzawa's responses in *The Bulletin of the Council of Societies for the Study of Religion* 35 (2006): 6–16, and in *Method and Theory in the Study of Religion* 20 (2008): 111–49.

78. Masuzawa, *The Invention of World Religions,* xii.

79. Ibid., 64. In the formulation of Peter Harrison (writing of the seventeenth and eighteenth centuries), "Paradoxical though it may sound, it is evident from the philosophy of science that objects of study are shaped to a large degree by the techniques which are used to investigate them. If we apply this principle to the history of 'religion,' it can be said that the very methods of the embryonic science of religion determined to a large extent what 'religion' was to be" (*"Religion" and the Religions,* 2).

80. I owe the reference to Jan N. Bremmer, "Methodologische en terminologische notities bij de opkomst van de godsdienstgeschiedenis in de achttiende en negentiende eeuw," *Nederlands Theologisch Tijdschrift* 57 (2003): 308–20.

81. "De hoogste klasse omvat slechts een drietal, de bekende trits van godsdiensten namelijk, waaraan men den naam van universalistische of wereld-godsdiensten zou kunnen geven: het Buddhisme, het Christendom en het Mohammedanisme" (Cornelis P. Tiele, *De godsdienst van Zarathustra van haar ontstaan in Baktrië tot den val van het Oud-Perzische Rijk* [Haarlem: A. C. Kruseman, 1864], 275).

82. William D. Whitney, "On the So-Called Science of Religion," *Princeton Review* 57 (1881): 429–52, quotation from 429.

83. Ibid., 436. In his thinking about changes in religion over time, Whitney was heir to the "priestcraft" theorists of the seventeenth century: "a most important item in the history of development of a religion, giving enhanced efficiency to all its bad tendencies, is the uprisal of a priestly caste or guild" (449).

84. Ibid., 451.

85. Ibid., 450–51.

86. Abraham Kuenen, *National Religions and Universal Religions* (New York: C. Scribner's Sons, 1882). The title of the later German translation was *Volksreligion und Weltreligion: Fünf Hibbert-Vorlesungen* (Berlin: G. Reimer, 1883).

87. Ibid., 5.

88. Ibid., 6.

89. Ibid., 58. In a remarkable passage, Kuenen elaborates on the situation of Islam in relation to Christianity: "Dante, long ago, sketched the character of the historical Islam in nearer accordance with the truth, when he assigned a place to Mohammed, the arch-heretic, in one of the lowest circles of the Inferno. For it was thus that he expressed, under current forms, the fact that Islam is a side branch of Christianity, or better still, as we should now say, of Judaism: a selection as it were from Law and Gospel, made by an Arab for Arabs, levelled to their capacity, and further supplemented—or must we say adulterated?—by national elements calculated to facilitate their reception of it" (57).

90. Ibid., 311–12.

91. On the publication history of the book, see Jonathan Z. Smith, "A Matter of Class," in *Relating Religion*, 167.

92. Cornelis P. Tiele, "Religions," in *The Encyclopaedia Britannica*, 9th ed. (Boston: Little, Brown, 1886).
93. Tiele used "Islâm" and "Mohammedanism" interchangeably. The latter term fell out of use in the early twentieth century.
94. Tiele, "Religions," 369.
95. On this point, see Masuzawa's chapter "Islam, a Semitic Religion," in *The Invention of World Religions*, 179–206.
96. Jonathan Z. Smith has described Judaism's eventual inclusion among the World Religions as the result of "a sort of pluralistic etiquette. If Christianity and Islam count as 'world' religions, it would be rude to exclude Judaism (the original model for the opposite type, 'ethnic' or 'national' religion)" ("A Matter of Class," in *Relating Religion*, 169).
97. Huston Smith, *The World's Religions: Our Great Wisdom Traditions* (San Francisco: Harper SanFrancisco, 1991). Earlier editions went under the name *The Religions of Man* (New York: Harper, 1958).
98. Esposito et al., *World Religions Today*.
99. See the lists in *A Concise Introduction to World Religions*, ed. Willard G. Oxtoby and Alan F. Segal (Oxford: Oxford University Press, 2007): Indigenous Religious Traditions, The Jewish Tradition, The Christian Tradition, The Islamic Tradition, The Hindu Tradition, The Sikh Tradition, The Jain Tradition, The Buddhist Tradition, Chinese Religions (Confucianism and Daoism), and Korean and Japanese Religions; and in Brandon Toropov and Luke Buckles, *The Complete Idiot's Guide to World Religions*, 3rd ed. (Indianapolis, Ind.: Alpha, 2002): Judaism, Christianity, Islam, Hinduism, Buddhism, and "Nature, Man, and Society in Asia" (which includes Confucianism, Taoism, and Shinto).
100. On the idea of "living religions," see Katherine K. Young, "World Religions: A Category in the Making?," in *Religion in History: The Word, the Idea, the Reality*, ed. Michel Despland and Gérard Vallée (Waterloo, Ontario: Wilfred Laurier University Press, 1992), 111–30. This piece can be viewed as a kind of supplement to Masuzawa's account in *The Invention of World Religions*, which leaves off in the mid-twentieth century.
101. Smith, "Religion, Religions, Religious," 191–92.
102. The foremost exception is Masuzawa, *The Invention of World Religions*. For further reflections on the political implications of the pluralistic World Religions model, see *Religious Studies Review* 31 (2005), an issue dedicated to critiques of World Religions textbooks from a number of perspectives. See especially Russell T. McCutcheon's response, "The

Perils of Having One's Cake and Eating It Too: Some Thoughts in Response," 32–36.

103. William James, *The Varieties of Religious Experience: A Study in Human Nature* (London: Longmans, Green, 1902), 31, emphasis in the original. The work remains highly influential. It has been reprinted dozens of times, most recently in 2009 (Library of America Press).

104. Rudolf Otto, *The Idea of the Holy: An Inquiry into the Non-rational Factor in the Idea of the Divine and Its Relation to the Rational*, 2nd ed., trans. John W. Harvey (New York: Oxford University Press, 1958), 6–7, 1–13, and 140. The work has been reprinted numerous times since its original publication in 1917 as *Das Heilige. Über das Irationalein der Idee des Göttlichen und sein Verhältnis zum Rationalen* (Breslau: Trewendt und Granier).

105. John Hick, *An Interpretation of Religion: Human Responses to the Transcendent*, 2nd ed. (New Haven, Conn.: Yale University Press, 2004 [1989]), 13 and 380 and throughout. Hick's characterization of religions as "part of a universal soteriological process" suggests that in some ways the legacy of the deists lives on in modern discussions of religious pluralism. The idea of a universal religion that unites all religions was, ironically, a driving force in the religious pluralism movement. In his speech at the dedication ceremony for Harvard's Center for the Study of World Religions in 1960, Sarvepalli Radhakrishnan, the philosopher and first vice president of India, warned against the development of "any religious Esperanto" but ended his speech with the following passionate call: "The different religions are to be used as building stones for the development of a human culture in which the adherents of the different religions may be fraternally united as the children of the one Supreme. All religions convey to their followers a message of abiding hope. The world will give birth to a new faith which will be but the old faith in another form, the faith of all ages, the potential divinity of man which will work for the supreme purpose written in our hearts and souls, the unity of mankind. It is my hope and prayer that unbelief shall disappear and superstition shall not enslave the mind and we shall recognise that we are brothers, one in spirit and one in fellowship" (portions of this speech are reprinted as "Fellowship of the Spirit," in *Philosophy, Religion, and the Coming World Civilization: Essays in Honor of William Ernest Hocking*, ed. Leroy S. Rouner [The Hague: Martinus Nijhoff, 1966], 277–296, quotation from 296). An audio file of the full speech is available at the website of

the Center for the Study of World Religions, http://www.hds.harvard
.edu/cswr/resources/lectures/radhakrishnan.html, accessed 23 October
2011. Quotations are drawn from the printed version. See also Steven
Wasserstrom, *Religion after Religion: Gershom Scholem, Mircea Eliade, and
Henry Corbin at Eranos* (Princeton, N.J.: Princeton University Press,
1999).

7. The Modern Origins of Ancient Religions

1. I have found few accounts of the development of "Greek religion" and
"Roman religion" as objects of study. On the Greek side, one can consult
Michel Despland, "Seven Decades of Writing on Greek Religion," *Religion* 4 (1974): 118–50. Despland commences with developments in the
late-nineteenth century and provides an overview of scholarship from
that point until the middle of the twentieth century. For Roman religion, see Guy G. Stroumsa, *A New Science: The Discovery of Religion in the
Age of Reason* (Cambridge, Mass.: Harvard University Press, 2010), 149–
57, and the literature cited there.

2. Augustine, *City of God*, 2.24–25. The notion probably goes back to the
apostle Paul (1 Cor. 10:20–22) and ultimately to the Septuagint's Greek
rendering of Ps. 95:5: "all the gods of the nations are demons" (*pantes hoi
theoi tōn ethnōn daimonia*).

3. For Lactantius, see Book 1 of *The Divine Institutes*, trans. Mary Francis
McDonald (Washington, D.C.: Catholic University of America Press,
1964). On Isidore, see the introduction, text, and commentary of Katherine Nell MacFarlane, "Isidore of Seville on the Pagan Gods (*Origines*
VIII.11)," *Transactions of the American Philosophical Society* 70:3 (1980):
1–40. Such a view can also be found in Augustine (*City of God*, 7.18).

4. See Luc Brisson, *How Philosophers Saved Myths: Allegorical Interpretation
and Classical Mythology*, trans. Catherine Tihanyi (Chicago: University
of Chicago Press, 2004 [French ed. 1996]), esp. 107–65.

5. See the images and analyses of Jean Seznec in *The Survival of the Pagan
Gods: The Mythological Tradition and Its Place in Renaissance Humanism and
Art*, trans. B. F. Sessions (New York: Pantheon, 1953). For a striking example of the pagan gods as church decor, see the fifteenth-century sculptures and bas reliefs of the church of San Francesco in Rimini (ibid.,
132–34).

6. Frank E. Manuel, *The Eighteenth Century Confronts the Gods* (Cambridge,
Mass.: Harvard University Press, 1959), 15–16.

7. José de Acosta, *The Naturall and Morall Historie of the East and West Indies, Intreating of the Remarkable Things of Heaven, of the Elements, Mettalls, Plants and Beasts which are Proper to that Country: Together with the Manners, Ceremonies, Lawes, Governments, and Warres of the Indians*, trans. (possibly) Edward Grimeston, 2nd ed. (London: V. Sims for Edward Blount and William Aspley, 1604), 337–38. The original Spanish edition appeared in 1590; there were also early translations of the work into Dutch, Latin, French, and Italian.

8. Although the *Apologética Historia* was not published until the nineteenth century, Las Casas's other works were published and well known, and manuscript copies of the *Apologética Historia* circulated already in the sixteenth century. See Henry Raup Wagner and Helen Rand Parish, *The Life and Writings of Bartolome de las Casas* (Albuquerque: University of New Mexico Press, 1967), 200–204 and 288–89.

9. See chapter 102 of the *Apologética Historia* in Bartolomé de Las Casas, *Obras Completas*, ed. Vidal Abril Castelló, 14 vols. (Madrid: Alianza, 1988–1994), 7.783–88. I owe the reference to Peter N. Miller, "Taking Paganism Seriously: Anthropology and Antiquarianism in Early Seventeenth-Century Histories of Religion," *Archiv für Religionsgeschichte* 3 (2001): 183–209, citation from 190.

10. Richard Blome, *The Present State of His Majesties Isles and Territories in America, viz. Jamaica, Barbadoes, S. Christophers, Mevis, Antego, S. Vincent, Dominica, New Jersey, Pensilvania, Monserat, Anguilla, Bermudas, Carolina, Virginia, New-England, Tobago, New Found-land, Mary-land, New-York. With new maps of every place. Together with astronomical tables, which will serve as a constant diary or calendar, for the use of the English inhabitants in those islands* (London: H. Clark for D. Newman, 1687), 199.

11. Ibid., 67–69.

12. I quote MacCormack's translation ("Gods, Demons, and Idols in the Andes," *Journal of the History of Ideas* 67 [2006]: 623–47, quotation from 626–27). The report is from Miguel Estete as recorded in the account of Francisco de Xeres.

13. Acosta, *The Naturall and Morall Historie*, 334–35.

14. Garcilaso de la Vega, *The Royal Commentaries of Peru, in Two Parts*, trans. Paul Rycaut (London: Miles Flesher for Jacob Tonson, 1688), 28–29. The original text, *Los Commentarios reales, que tratan del origen de los Yncas*, was published in two parts in 1609 and 1616 (the latter under the title of *Historia general del Peru*).

15. See Bernard Picart, *Ceremonies and Religious Customs . . .* , 7 vols. (London: William Jackson for Claude du Bosc, 1723–1739), 3.187–211, and Hurd, *A New Universal History of the Religious Rites . . .* (Blackburn: J. Hemmingway, 1799), 501–14.

16. Manuel, *The Eighteenth Century Confronts the Gods*, 18–19.

17. It is probably no accident that the word "polytheism," which had been rather rare in the European vernaculars, gained a newfound popularity in the late sixteenth and early seventeenth centuries (both Bodin and Purchas used it). See Francis Schmidt, "Polytheisms: Degeneration or Progress?," *History and Anthropology* 3 (1987): 9–60.

18. Alexander Ross, *Pansebeia: Or, A View of All Religions in the World . . .* (London: James Young and John Saywell, 1653), 95–107.

19. A related phenomenon is documented by John Scheid, "Polytheism Impossible; or, the Empty Gods: Reasons behind a Void in the History of Roman Religion," *History and Anthropology* 3 (1987): 303–25.

20. Basil Kennett, *Romae Antiquae Notitia: Or, The Antiquities of Rome. In Two Parts* (London: A. Swall and T. Child, 1696), 64. Later editions (a seventeenth edition was published in 1793) reworded the passage as follows: "a matter that is involved in so many endless Fictions, and yet has employed so many pens to explain it." The citation of Machiavelli is drawn from his discourses on Livy.

21. Ibid., 61.

22. I owe the phrase to Walter Burkert, *Greek Religion*, trans. John Raffan (Cambridge, Mass.: Harvard University Press, 1985 [German ed. 1977]), 1. Burkert refers only to the Greek material, but his statement holds for the treatment of Roman evidence as well.

23. Edward Gibbon, *The History of the Decline and Fall of the Roman Empire: Edited, with an Introduction and Appendices, by David Womersley*, 3 vols. (London: Allen Lane, Penguin, 1994), 1.57 and n. 3. The first volume of Gibbon's work was originally published in February 1776, the second and third in 1781, and the last three in 1788. The first volume quickly passed through two more editions (the second edition in June 1776 and the third in May 1777), both of which adjusted the discussion of "religion." See David Womersley, *Gibbon and the "Watchmen of the Holy City": The Historian and His Reputation, 1776–1815* (Oxford: Clarendon, 2002), particularly the first chapter, "Revision and Religion."

24. *The History of the Decline and Fall of the Roman Empire*, 1.58–59.

25. Ibid., 1.447.

26. Early responses to Gibbon demonstrate that his depiction of early Christianity was indeed understood as a critique of contemporary Christians and Christianity. See, for example, Richard Watson, *An Apology for Christianity: In a Series of Letters Addressed to Edward Gibbon, Esq., Author of the Decline and Fall of the Roman Empire* (Cambridge: F. Archdeacon for T. and J. Merrill et al., 1776); and James Chelsum, *Remarks on the Last Two Chapters of Mr. Gibbon's History, of the Decline and Fall of the Roman Empire, in a Letter to a Friend* (London: Printed for T. Payne and Son and J. Robson and Co., 1776). Both works went quickly through multiple printings. See also Shelby T. McCloy, *Gibbon's Antagonism to Christianity* (London: Williams and Norgate, 1933), and Womersley, *Gibbon and the "Watchmen of the Holy City."*

27. Gibbon, *The History of the Decline and Fall of the Roman Empire*, 1.61. And this revitalization of the Greek and Roman pantheons was not only a scholarly enterprise, as the work of the Romantic poets (most notably Friedrich Schiller in "Die Götter Griechenlandes") attests (see Schiller, "Die Götter Griechenlandes," *Der Teutsche Merkur* [March 1788]: 250–60). See also Richard Jenkyns, *The Victorians and Ancient Greece* (Oxford: Basil Blackwell, 1980), 174–91.

28. For a concise account of the resurgence of the notion of "myth" in the nineteenth century, see the third chapter ("The History of Myth from the Renaissance to the Second World War") of Bruce Lincoln, *Theorizing Myth: Narrative, Ideology, and Scholarship* (Chicago: University of Chicago Press, 1999).

29. The growth of philhellenism varied in Europe and the United States. For scholarship in Great Britain, see Frank M. Turner, "Why the Greeks and Not the Romans in Victorian Britain?," in *Rediscovering Hellenism: The Hellenic Inheritance and the English Imagination*, ed. G. W. Clarke (Cambridge: Cambridge University Press, 1989), 61–82. For the mood of Germany and the United States, see Thomas N. Habinek "Grecian Wonders and Roman Woe: The Romantic Rejection of Rome and Its Consequences for the Study of Latin Literature," in *The Interpretation of Roman Poetry: Empiricism or Hermeneutics?*, ed. Karl Galinsky (Frankfurt am Main: Peter Lang, 1992), 227–42. For an interesting example of the connections between what was happening in Great Britain and Germany with regard to the study of Greek antiquity, see the letters of Sir George Cornewall Lewis to Karl Otfried Müller, collected in *Teaching the English Wissenschaft*, ed. William M. Calder III et al. (Zürich: Georg Olms Verlag, 2002).

30. See Suzanne L. Marchand, *Down from Olympus: Archaeology and Philhellenism in Germany, 1750–1970* (Princeton, N.J.: Princeton University Press, 1996), 43–47 et passim.

31. On Müller's influence, see the essays collected in *Zwischen Rationalismus und Romantik: Karl Otfried Müller und die antike Kultur,* ed. William M. Calder III and Renate Schlesier (Hildesheim: Weidmann, 1998), particularly Robert Ackerman, "K. O. Müller in Britain," 1–17. On Wilamowitz, see the essays in *Wilamowitz und kein Ende: Wissenschaftsgeschichtliches Kolloquium Fondation Hardt, 9. bis 13. September 2002,* ed. Markus Mülke (Hildesheim: Georg Olms Verlag, 2003); and Friedrich Solmsen, "Wilamowitz in His Last Ten Years," *Greek, Roman, and Byzantine Studies* 20 (1979): 89–122. For a rather less celebratory evaluation of Wilamowitz's work on "religion," see Egon Flaig, "Towards 'Rassenhygiene': Wilamowitz and the German New Right," in *Out of Arcadia: Classics and Politics in Germany in the Age of Burckhardt, Nietzsche and Wilamowitz,* ed. Ingo Gildenhard and Martin Ruehl (London: Institute of Classical Studies, 2003), 105–27.

32. Both were translated into English by John Leitch, *Introduction to a Scientific System of Mythology* (London: Longman, Brown, Green, and Longmans, 1844); and *Ancient Art and Its Remains: Or A Manual of the Archaeology of Art,* 2nd ed. (London: A. Fullarton, 1850 [1847]). On the nexus of nationality, art, and religion, Müller writes: "The whole artistic activity, in so far as it depends on the spiritual life and habits of a single person, becomes *individual,* on those of an entire nation, *national . . .* The spiritual life which expresses itself in art is connected in the closest manner with the whole life of the spirit . . . However, art universally stands most especially in connexion with *religious life,* with the conceptions of deity, because religion opens up to man a spiritual world which does not appear externally in experience, and yet longs for an outward representation which it more or less finds in art according to the different tendency of nations" ("indem die Religion dem Menschen eine geistige Welt öffnet, welche in der Erfahrung nicht äußerlich erscheint, und doch eine außere Darstellung verlangt, die sie nach der verschiedenen Richtung der Völker mehr oder minder in der Kunst findet"). (English, *Ancient Art and Its Remains,* 11; German: *Handbuch der Archäologie der Kunst,* 2nd ed. [Breslau: Max und Romp, 1835 (1830)], 15–16).

33. Mommsen's work was first published as *Römische Geschichte,* 3 vols. (Berlin: Weidmannsche Buchhandlung, 1854–1856); the third edition,

which appeared in 1861, was first translated into English by W. P. Dickson as *The History of Rome*, 4 vols. (London: Richard Bentley, 1861–1866). I cite from this translation.

34. Mommsen, *The History of Rome*, 3.426.

35. The fullest statements of Fowler's outlook are his Gifford Lectures delivered in 1909–1910. My quotations are drawn from the published version: *The Religious Experience of the Roman People: From the Earliest Times to the Age of Augustus* (London: Macmillan, 1911), 92, 249, 3. Fowler quotes the comment about the Pharisees, with only some reservations, from M. Jean Réville by way of Franz Cumont.

36. Although it was not a study of the classical world, William Robertson Smith's *Lectures on the Religion of the Semites* (Edinburgh: A. and C. Black, 1889) also merits mention in this context because it appeared at exactly the same time and also evinces this turn toward an interest in ritual.

37. The intriguing story of the "on-and-off" influence of Harrison's work is available in Mary Beard, *The Invention of Jane Harrison* (Cambridge, Mass.: Harvard University Press, 2000). It should also be noted here that the works in English take a more comparative approach than those in German, which often keep strictly to the classical sources. The influence of the developing field of anthropology (à la E. B. Tylor and the so-called Cambridge ritualists) is certainly felt more among the English authors.

38. A focus on both ritual and origins is not surprising. Denis Feeney writes: "In many earlier studies, the focus on cult is perhaps rather grudging, as if the authors have regretfully come to the conclusion that they must concentrate on this, however repellent it may be, since there is after all nothing else which is native or authentic in Roman religious experience. An almost necessary corollary of such an approach to Roman ritual is an interest in origins at the expense of practice. The reality of ritual, according to this school, is to be found in its trace of an origin: meaningless and obsessive in its historical manifestation, at least Roman ritual holds up a promise of a recovery of a pristine, pure, and preferably rustic originary moment" (*Literature and Religion at Rome: Cultures, Contexts, and Beliefs* [New York: Cambridge University Press, 1998], 115). Wilamowitz's *Der Glaube der Hellenen*, 2 vols. (Berlin: Wiedmannsche Buchhandlung, 1931–1932), can be read as a reaction to this "anthropological" interest in ritual (and origins).

39. Mircea Eliade wrote the warm preface to the English translation published in 1970, *Archaic Roman Religion with an Appendix on the Religion of*

the Etruscans, 2 vols., trans. Philip Krapp (Chicago: University of Chicago Press, 1970).

40. Moses I. Finley, foreword to *Greek Religion and Society*, ed. P. E. Easterling and J. V. Muir (Cambridge: Cambridge University Press, 1985), xiv–xv.

41. Paul Cartledge, "Translator's Introduction" to Louise Bruit Zaidman and Pauline Schmitt Pantel, *Religion in the Ancient Greek City*, trans. Paul Cartledge (Cambridge: Cambridge University Press, 1992 [French ed. 1989]), xvii.

42. Ross, *Pansebeia*, 38–39.

43. Ibid., 39.

44. In what follows, I rely on the accounts of E. A. Wallis Budge, *The Rise & Progress of Assyriology* (London: Martin Hopkinson, 1925); C. Wade Meade, *Road to Babylon: Development of U.S. Assyriology* (Leiden: Brill, 1974); and Benjamin R. Foster, "The Beginnings of Assyriology in the United States," in *Orientalism, Assyriology and the Bible*, ed. Steven W. Holloway (Sheffield: Sheffield Phoenix Press, 2006), 44–73.

45. A number of other scholars had been at work on deciphering cuneiform scripts since the late eighteenth century, most importantly Georg Friedrich Grotefend and Christian Lassen. Budge's account tends to minimize their contributions, but this is not surprising given the nationalist thrust of his book: "The object of this book is to tell the general reader . . . how [the science of Assyriology] was established solely by the Trustees of the British Museum, and to show how the study of it passed from England into Germany and other European countries, and finally into America" (*The Rise & Progress of Assyriology*, xi).

46. Rawlinson's edition of the inscription was published as "The Persian Cuneiform Inscription at Behistun, Deciphered and Translated; with a Memoir," *Journal of the Royal Asiatic Society* 10–11 (1848–1849), though draft forms of his work had already been circulating in the scholarly community a decade before the publication.

47. Budge, *The Rise & Progress of Assyriology*, 155.

48. Morris Jastrow, *The Religion of Babylonia and Assyria* (Boston: Ginn and Company, 1898), ix, 690.

49. As far as I know, this ambitious project yielded only five books: Jastrow's own, Edward Washburn Hopkins's *Religions of India*, treatments of the religion of the Teutons and the religion of the Hebrews, and an introduction to the history of religions.

50. Niek Veldhuis, *Religion, Literature, and Scholarship: The Sumerian Composition Nanše and the Birds, with a catalogue of Sumerian bird names* (Leiden: Brill/Styx, 2004), 13–17.

51. Jacobsen's views find fullest expression in *The Treasures of Darkness: A History of Mesopotamian Religion* (New Haven, Conn.: Yale University Press, 1976), and the essays collected in *Toward the Image of Tammuz and Other Essays on Mesopotamian History and Culture*, ed. William L. Moran (Cambridge, Mass.: Harvard University Press, 1970). Oppenheim's classic statement is in his *Ancient Mesopotamia: Portrait of a Dead Civilization* (Chicago: University of Chicago, 1964). A lightly revised edition appeared in 1977 under the editorship of Erica Reiner; page citations here are from the later edition.

52. Excerpt from Erica Reiner, *An Adventure of Great Dimension: The Launching of the Chicago Assyrian Dictionary* (Philadelphia: American Philosophical Society, 2002), 109–14. I am indebted to Eckart Frahm for bringing this fascinating work to my attention.

53. Jacobsen, *The Treasures of Darkness*, 1–2.

54. See Jacobsen's essays "Ancient Mesopotamian Religion: The Central Concerns" and "Formative Tendencies in Sumerian Religion" in *Toward the Image of Tammuz*. The same unproblematized notion of religion (as any culture's reaction to "the supernatural, the sacred, the numinous," etc.) is found more recently in Jean Bottéro, *Mesopotamia: Writing, Reasoning, and the Gods*, trans. Zainab Bahrani and Marc Van De Mieroop (Chicago: University of Chicago Press, 1992 [French ed. 1987]), 203, and *Religion in Ancient Mesopotamia*, trans. Teresa Lavender Fagan (Chicago: University of Chicago Press, 2001 [French ed. 1998], a revision of his 1952 *La religion babylonienne*).

55. *The Treasures of Darkness*, 3.

56. Jacobsen summarizes as follows: "Applying this general chronological framework, we can distinguish three major aspects or phases of ancient Mesopotamian religion, each phase roughly corresponding to, and characterizing, a millennium; each reflecting the central hopes and fears of its times. In our presentation we shall consider therefore: 1. An early phase representative of the fourth millennium B.C. and centering on worship of powers in natural and other phenomena essential for economic survival. The dying god, power of fertility and plenty, is a typical figure. 2. A later phase, representative approximately of the third millennium which adds the concept of the ruler and the hope of security

against enemies. This phase has as typical figures the great ruler gods of the Nippur assembly. 3. Lastly, there is a phase representative of the second millennium B.C. in which the fortunes of the individual increase in importance until they rival those of communal economy and security. The typical figure is the personal god" (ibid., 21).

57. Ibid., 73.

58. Ibid., 79.

59. There is a tension in Jacobsen between his worry over importing modern categories (*Toward the Image of Tammuz*, 2) and his easy assumption that Mesopotamians, like all people, had a "religion" that focused on "salvation, which characterizes the human response to the numinous experience" (ibid., 10).

60. Oppenheim, *Ancient Mesopotamia*, 172.

61. Ibid., 175.

62. For Oppenheim's concern for the religious experience of "the common man," see, for example, ibid., 181.

63. Ibid., 177.

64. Ibid., 183.

65. It is not entirely clear how Oppenheim would have scholars proceed. In his epilogue to *Ancient Mesopotamia*, he writes, "My discussion of Mesopotamian religion represents a frankly polemic shift of interest from the tepid climate of sentimental and patronizing interest in which it is customarily treated. Purposely, the subject matter has not been set forth in what may be called its 'best light'—if light can indeed be called the frame of reference provided by our built-in Old and New Testament 'guidance system.' A de-westernization of the topic is aimed at, although I fully realize that the aim is utopian and that work in this direction will have to wait for a generation of Assyriologists free from emotional and institutionalized interests in the religions of the ancient near east. I shall offer the same excuse for not making full use of the textual evidence to present the several Mesopotamian concepts of the divine, ranging from the great celestial figures to the fallen gods, demons, and evil spirits" (333).

66. See *Forgotten Religions (Including Some Living Primitive Religions*, ed. Virgilius Ferm (New York: Philosophical Library, 1950), 63–79, republished as *Ancient Religions* (New York: Citadel, 1965). He covers much of the same ground as in *Ancient Mesopotamia*, but the presentation is more schematic, with subheadings for "Assyria and Babylonia," "The Pantheon," "The Divine," "The Temple," and "The Common Man."

67. Oppenheim, *Ancient Mesopotamia*, 176–82.

68. Jacobsen, *Toward the Image of Tammuz*, 38.

69. Again, the problem is not that their picture is modern (all products of our scholarly work always will be); it is that they are unaware of that fact. The phenomenon of the so-called personal gods as evidence of a developed "personal religion" is overplayed by Jacobsen (*The Treasures of Darkness*, 152–64). Oppenheim's treatment of this phenomenon under the rubric "Psychology" (by which he seems to mean "physiology and anatomy") seems more appropriate and illuminating (*Ancient Mesopotamia*, 198–206).

70. Simon Price, *Religions of the Ancient Greeks* (Cambridge: Cambridge University Press, 1999), 89. For an extensive collection of examples of this phenomenon and a more in-depth assessment, see Brent Nongbri, "Dislodging 'Embedded' Religion: A Brief Note on a Scholarly Trope," *Numen* 55 (2008): 440–60.

71. In the study of Asian "religions," another rhetorical move accomplishes a similar feat, the trope of "diffused religion." This particular phrase is especially associated with the work of C. K. Yang (*Religion in Chinese Society: A Study of Contemporary Social Functions of Religion and Some of Their Historical Factors*, repr. ed. [Berkeley: University of California Press, 1967 (1961)]). In the middle of the twentieth century, Yang wrote to correct what he regarded as the erroneous views of earlier scholars that the historical record of China indicated that Chinese culture lacked a notion of religion. He cites several such claims: "Whether China has a religion or not is a question that merits serious study," "the educated people of China are indifferent to religion," "China is a country without religion" (*Religion in Chinese Society*, 5–6). Yang attempted to argue that religion was extremely important in China by highlighting the presence and importance in Chinese society of things that were, to him, self-evidently religious (the numerous temples and household shrines, the "institutional religions" of Buddhism and Taoism). He argued that previous students of Chinese religion had underestimated the importance of "religion" because they did not take account of "diffused religion," which was "intimately merged with the concepts and structure of secular institutions and other aspects of the social order" and "was a pervasive factor in all major aspects of social life" (ibid., 20 and 295–96). Here again, a rhetorical trope promotes confusion between descriptive and redescriptive usages of "religion." The claim that religion was "intimately merged" with "secular institutions" and "pervaded" all

aspects of social life suggests that, at a descriptive level, religion was not something that was independently recognized in Chinese society.

72. Russell T. McCutcheon, *The Discipline of Religion: Structure, Meaning, Rhetoric* (London: Routledge, 2003), 255.

Conclusion

1. On this phenomenon, see Jonathan Z. Smith, "Tillich['s] Remains," *Journal of the American Academy of Religion* 78 (2010): 1139–70.

2. Benson Saler, *Conceptualizing Religion: Immanent Anthropologists, Transcendent Natives, and Unbounded Categories* (Leiden: Brill, 1993), 157.

3. Jonathan Z. Smith, "God Save This Honourable Court: Religion and Civic Discourse," in *Relating Religion: Essays in the Study of Religion* (Chicago: University of Chicago Press, 2004), 375–90.

4. I take this to be one of the basic suggestions of Russell T. McCutcheon in *The Discipline of Religion: Structure, Meaning, Rhetoric* (London: Routledge, 2003), and *Religion and the Domestication of Dissent: Or, How to Live in a Less Than Perfect Nation* (London: Equinox, 2005).

5. For eye-opening examples of this sort of scholarship, see David Chidester, *Authentic Fakes: Religion and American Popular Culture* (Berkeley: University of California Press, 2005), and Kathryn Lofton, *Oprah: The Gospel of an Icon* (Berkeley: University of California Press, 2011).

6. I am thus not persuaded by those who discourage any use of the concept of religion in the study of the modern world. When Wilfred Cantwell Smith advocated abandoning the term "religion" in the 1960s, he did so because he claimed that it compromised the sacred integrity of an inner disposition he called "faith" and that it failed to accurately describe people who have "been religious" throughout history and in the modern world. I have argued that what was involved in the formation of religion was the very possibility of conceiving of the idea of "being religious." So I cannot agree with Smith's reasoning for ceasing to speak of religion. More recently, there has been a renewed call for abandoning the term, but for reasons beyond those that Smith offered. The most vocal advocate for discarding the concept of religion has been Timothy Fitzgerald, who has argued his point in two books, *The Ideology of Religious Studies* (New York: Oxford University Press, 2000), and *Discourse of Civility and Barbarity: A Critical History of Religion and Related Categories* (New York: Oxford University Press, 2007). His case deserves more detailed interaction that I can provide here, and I am

sympathetic to much of Fitzgerald's argument, but as the brief examples I have provided here suggest, I have not been persuaded by his call to renounce the study of religion in the modern world.

7. Judge is one among a small group of historians who has seriously considered these problems. For his more recent thoughts on the topic, see Edwin Judge, "The Absence of Religion, Even in Ammianus?," in *Jerusalem and Athens: Cultural Transformation in Late Antiquity*, ed. Alanna Nobbs (Tübingen: Mohr Siebeck, 2010), 264–75, and "Was Christianity a Religion?," in *The First Christians in the Roman World: Augustan and New Testament Essays*, ed. James R. Harrison (Tübingen: Mohr Siebeck, 2008), 404–9.

8. The bibliographies on these troublesome terms are large. The following are good introductions to the problems. On culture, see the discussion in Kathryn Tanner, *Theories of Culture: A New Agenda for Theology* (Minneapolis: Fortress, 1997), 3–58. On society, see John Bossy, "Some Elementary Forms of Durkheim," *Past and Present* 95 (1982): 3–18. On ethnicity, see John Hutchinson and Anthony D. Smith (eds.), *Ethnicity* (New York: Oxford University Press, 1996).

9. Jonathan Z. Smith, "Bible and Religion," *Bulletin of the Council of Societies for the Study of Religion* 29 (2000): 87–93, reprinted in Smith, *Relating Religion*, 197–214; the quotation is from the latter at 208.

10. See Stanley Stowers, "The Ontology of Religion," in *Introducing Religion: Essays in Honor of Jonathan Z. Smith*, ed. Willi Braun and Russell T. McCutcheon (London: Equinox, 2008), 434–49. For an example of Stowers's theory put into practice, see Stowers, "Theorizing the Religion of Ancient Households and Families," in *Household and Family Religion in Antiquity*, ed. John Bodel and Saul M. Olyan (Oxford: Blackwell, 2008), 5–19.

11. Stowers, "The Ontology of Religion," 443.

12. The best example known to me of the creative use of anachronism for the study of ancient texts is Stephen Moore, *God's Gym: Divine Male Bodies of the Bible* (New York: Routledge, 1996).

13. Despite its title, Niek Veldhuis's *Religion, Literature, and Scholarship: The Sumerian Composition* Nanše and the Birds (Leiden: Brill/Styx, 2004) provides a good model of what I mean by disaggregation of the concept of religion. I see a similar shift in Andrew Wallace-Hadrill's recent book *Rome's Cultural Revolution* (Cambridge: Cambridge University Press, 2008), which does not contain a great deal of detailed reflection

on the concept of religion but instead focuses on Romans' concern for and use of the idea of ancestors. The essays of Clifford Ando collected in *The Matter of the Gods: Religion and the Roman Empire* (Berkeley: University of California Press, 2008) also move (again, despite the volume's title) in a helpful direction by scrutinizing the ways in which Romans established knowledge about divine beings in a variety of contexts (legal, philosophical, and military, to name three). The way ahead lies in studies like these.

BIBLIOGRAPHY

Edited collections or translations containing ancient texts by multiple authors are listed under the name of the modern editor, as are collections of ancient inscriptions. For biblical texts, I have relied on the editions of the Deutsche Bibelgesellschaft.

Ackerman, Robert. "K. O. Müller in Britain." Pages 1–17 in *Zwischen Rationalismus und Romantik: Karl Otfried Müller und die antike Kultur.* Edited by William M. Calder III and Renate Schlesier. Hildesheim: Weidmann, 1998.

Acosta, José de. *The Naturall and Morall Historie of the East and West Indies.* Translated by (possibly) Edward Grimeston. 2nd ed. London: V. Sims for Edward Blount and William Aspley, 1604 [Spanish ed. 1590].

Adler, Joseph A. (revising and expanding Daniel L. Overmyer). "Chinese Religion: An Overview." Pages 1580–1613 in *Encyclopedia of Religion*, Vol. 3. Edited by Lindsay Jones. 2nd ed. Detroit: Macmillan, 2005.

Al-Biruni. *Chronologie orientalischer Völker von Alberuni.* Edited by C. Eduard Sachau. Leipzig: F. A. Brockhaus, 1878.

———. *The Chronology of Ancient Nations: An English version of the Arabic Text of the Athar-ul-bakiya of Albiruni.* Translated by C. Eduard Sachau. London: William H. Allen, 1879.

Albright, William F. "The Goddess of Life and Wisdom." *American Journal of Semitic Languages and Literatures* 36 (1920): 258–94.

Alexander of Lycopolis. *An Alexandrian Platonist against Dualism: Alexander of Lycopolis' Treatise 'Critique of the Doctrines of Manichaeus.'* Edited and Translated by Pieter Willem van der Horst and Jaap Mansfeld. Leiden: Brill, 1974.

Ali, Abdullah Yusuf. *The Holy Qur-an: Text, Translation, and Commentary.* Reprint ed. 3 vols. Lahore: Ashraf, 1969.

Allan, David. "'An Ancient Sage Philosopher': Alexander Ross and the Defence of Philosophy." *Seventeenth Century* 16 (2001): 68–94.

Allen, Michael J. B. "Marsilio Ficino, Hermes Trismegistus and the *Corpus Hermeticum.*" Pages 38–47 in *New Perspectives on Renaissance Thought. Essays in the History of Science, Education and Philosophy: In Memory of Charles*

B. Schmitt. Edited by John Henry and Sarah Hutton. London: Duckworth, 1990. Reprinted with added notes in Michael J. B. Allen, *Plato's Third Eye: Studies in Marsilio Ficino's Metaphysics and Its Sources.* Aldershot: Variorum, 1995.

Almond, Philip C. *The British Discovery of Buddhism.* Cambridge: Cambridge University Press, 1988.

———. "The Buddha in the West, 1800–1860." Pages 381–92 in *Perspectives on Language and Text: Essays and Poems in Honor of Francis I. Andersen's Sixtieth Birthday.* Edited by Edgar W. Conrad and Edward G. Newing. Winona Lake, Ind.: Eisenbrauns, 1987.

———. "The Buddha of Christendom: A Review of the Legend of Barlaam and Josaphat." *Religious Studies* 23 (1987): 391–406.

Ando, Clifford. "Introduction: Religion, Law and Knowledge in Classical Rome." Pages 1–15 in *Roman Religion.* Edited by Clifford Ando. Edinburgh: Edinburgh University Press, 2003.

———. *The Matter of the Gods: Religion and the Roman Empire.* Berkeley: University of California Press, 2008.

Andreas, F. C., and Walter Henning. *Mitteliranische Manichaica aus Chinesisch-Turkestan II.* Berlin: Verlag der Akademie der Wissenschaften, 1933.

[Anonymous]. *A Booke of Christian Questions and Answeres. Wherein are set foorthe the chiefe pointes of Christian Religion. A woorke right necessarie and profitable, for all such as shall have to deale with the captious quarellinges of the wrangling adversaries of Gods truth.* London: John Harrison, 1578.

[Anonymous]. "First Report from the Select Committee on Indian Territories; Together with the Minutes of Evidence." In *Reports from Committees.* London: House of Commons, 1853.

Aquilecchia, Giovanni. "Giordano Bruno as Philosopher of the Renaissance." Pages 3–14 in *Giordano Bruno: Philosopher of the Renaissance.* Edited by Hillary Gatti. Aldershot: Ashgate, 2002.

Arberry, Arthur J. *The Koran Interpreted.* Reprint ed. London: Oxford University Press, 1964 [1955].

Armstrong, Karen. *Islam: A Short History.* London: Phoenix, 2001.

Arnobius of Sicca. *Arnobii Adversus Nationes Libri VII.* Edited by Concetto Marchesi. 2nd ed. Turin: Società per Azione G. B. Paravia, 1953 [1934].

———. *Arnobius of Sicca: The Case against the Pagans.* Translated by George E. McCracken. 2 vols. Westminster, Md.: Newman, 1949.

Asad, Talal. *Genealogies of Religion: Disciplines and Reasons of Power in Christianity and Islam.* Baltimore, Md.: Johns Hopkins University Press, 1993.

———. "Reading a Modern Classic: W. C. Smith's *The Meaning and End of Religion.*" *History of Religions* 40 (2001): 205–22.

Aśvaghoṣa. *Aśvaghoṣa's Buddhacarita or Acts of the Buddha.* Edited and translated by E. H. Johnston. Reprint ed. Delhi: Motilal Banarsidass, 1992.

Auffarth, Christoph. "'Weltreligion' als ein Leitbegriff der Religionswissenschaft im Imperialismus." Pages 17–36 in *Mission und Macht im Wandel politischer Orientierungen: Europäische Missionsgesellschaften in politischen Spannungsfeldern in Afrika und Asien zwischen 1800 und 1945.* Edited by Ulrich van der Heyden and Holger Stoecker. Stuttgart: Franz Steiner, 2005.

Augustine of Hippo. *Augustine: City of God.* Edited and translated by George E. McCracken, William M. Green, Eva Matthews Sanford, David S. Wiesen, Philip Levine, and William Chase Greene. 7 vols. Cambridge, Mass.: Harvard University Press, 1957–1972.

———. *Augustine: Earlier Writings.* Translated by John H. S. Burleigh. Philadelphia: Westminster, 1953.

———. *Sancti Aurelii Augustini: De doctrina christiana, De vera religione.* Edited by K.-D. Daur. Turnhout: Brepols, 1962.

———. *Sancti Aureli Augustini: De utilitate credendi, De duabus animabus, Contra Fortunatum, Contra Adimantum, Contra epistulam fundamenti, Contra Faustum.* Edited by Joseph Zycha. Vienna: F. Tempsky, 1891.

———. *Sancti Aurelii Augustini: Retractationum libri II.* Edited by Almut Mutzenbecher. Turnhout: Brepols, 1984.

Balagangadhara, S. N. *"The heathen in his blindness": Asia, the West, and the Dynamic of Religion.* Leiden: Brill, 1994.

Barnes, Timothy David. *Tertullian: A Historical and Literary Study.* Corrected ed. Oxford: Clarendon, 1985.

Baronius, Caesar. *Martyrologium Romanum. Ad novam Kalendarii rationem, & Ecclesiasticae historiae vertitatem restitutum. Gregorii XIII. Pont. Max. iussu editum.* Salamanca: Apud Lucam Iuntam, 1584; Venice: Apud Marcum Antonium Zalterium, 1597.

Baynes, Norman H. *Constantine the Great and the Christian Church.* 2nd ed. Oxford: Oxford University Press, 1977.

Beard, Mary. "Cicero and Divination: The Formation of a Latin Discourse." *Journal of Roman Studies* 76 (1986): 33–46.

———. *The Invention of Jane Harrison.* Cambridge, Mass.: Harvard University Press, 2000.

Beard, Mary, John North, and Simon Price. *Religions of Rome*. 2 vols. Cambridge: Cambridge University Press, 1998.

BeDuhn, Jason David. *Augustine's Manichaean Dilemma, I: Conversion and Apostasy, 373–388 C.E.* Philadelphia: University of Pennsylvania Press, 2010.

Bell, Catherine. "Paradigms behind (and before) the Modern Concept of Religion." *History and Theory* 45 (2006): 27–46.

Benveniste, Émile. *Indo-European Language and Society*. Translated by Elizabeth Palmer. London: Farber and Farber, 1973 [French ed. 1969].

Bickerman, Elias. *The God of the Maccabees: Studies on the Meaning and Origin of the Maccabean Revolt*. Translated by H. R. Moehring. Leiden: Brill, 1979 [German ed. 1937].

Biddle, John C. "Locke's Critique of Innate Principles and Toland's Deism." *Journal of the History of Ideas* 37 (1976): 411–22.

Biechler, James E. "Interreligious Dialogue." Pages 270–96 in *Introducing Nicholas of Cusa: A Guide to a Renaissance Man*. Edited by Christopher M. Bellitto, Thomas M. Izbicki, and Gerald Christianson. New York: Paulist Press, 2004.

Biller, Peter. "Words and the Medieval Notion of Religion." *Journal of Ecclesiastical History* 36 (1985): 351–69.

Blaise, Albert, ed. *Dictionnaire Latin-Français des auteurs du Moyen-Age*. Turnhout: Brepols, 1975.

Bloch, Maurice. "Why Religion Is Nothing Special But Is Central." *Philosophical Transactions of the Royal Society B* 363 (2008): 2055–61.

Blois, François de. "On the Sources of the Barlaam Romance, or: How the Buddha Became a Christian Saint." Pages 7–26 in *Literarische Stoffe und ihre Gestaltung in mitteliranischer Zeit: Kolloquium anlässlich des 70. Geburtstages von Werner Sundermann*. Edited by Desmond Durkin-Meistererernst, Christiane Reck, and Dieter Weber. Wiesbaden: Dr. Ludwig Reichert, 2009.

Blome, Richard. *The Present State of His Majesties Isles and Territories in America*. London: H. Clark for D. Newman, 1687.

Bobzin, Hartmut. "Translations of the Qur'ān." Pages 340–58 in *Encyclopaedia of the Qur'ān*, Vol. 5. Edited by Jane Dammen McAuliffe. Leiden: Brill, 2006.

Bodin, Jean. *Colloquium of the Seven about Secrets of the Sublime*. Translated by Marion L. Kuntz. Princeton, N.J.: Princeton University Press, 1975. Originally published as *Colloquium heptaplomeres de rerum sublimium arcanis abditis*. Edited by Ludovicus Noack (Schwerin: F. G. Baerensprung, 1857).

———. *Six Bookes of a Commonweale: A Facsimile Reprint of the English Translation of 1606*. Translated by Richard Knolles and edited by Kenneth Douglas McRae. Cambridge, Mass.: Harvard University Press, 1962. Originally published as *Les six livres de la republique* (Paris: Chez Jacques du Puys, 1576), and in Latin as *De Republica libri sex* (Paris: Jacobum Du-puys, 1586).

Bossy, John. "Some Elementary Forms of Durkheim." *Past and Present* 95 (1982): 3–18.

Bottéro, Jean. *Mesopotamia: Writing, Reasoning, and the Gods*. Translated by Zainab Bahrani and Marc Van De Mieroop. Chicago: University of Chicago Press, 1992 [French ed. 1987].

———. *Religion in Ancient Mesopotamia*. Translated by Teresa Lavender Fagan. Chicago: University of Chicago Press, 2001 [French ed. 1998].

Boyarin, Daniel. *Border Lines: The Partition of Judaeo-Christianity*. Philadelphia: University of Pennsylvania Press, 2004.

———. "Rethinking Jewish Christianity: An Argument for Dismantling a Dubious Category (to which is appended a correction of my *Border Lines*)." *Jewish Quarterly Review* 99 (2009): 7–36.

———. "Semantic Differences; or, 'Judaism'/'Christianity.'" Pages 65–85 in *The Ways That Never Parted: Jews and Christians in Late Antiquity and the Early Middle Ages*. Edited by Adam H. Becker and Annette Yoshiko Reed. Tübingen: Mohr Siebeck, 2003.

Boyce, Mary. *A Word-List of Manichaean Middle Persian and Parthian*. Leiden: Brill, 1977.

Bremmer, Jan N. "Methodologische en terminologische notities bij de opkomst van de godsdienstgeschiedenis in de achttiende en negentiende eeuw." *Nederlands Theologisch Tijdschrift* 57 (2003): 308–20.

———. "Secularization: Notes toward a Genealogy." Pages 432–37 in *Religion: Beyond a Concept*. Edited by Hent de Vries. New York: Fordham University Press, 2008.

Brisson, Luc. *How Philosophers Saved Myths: Allegorical Interpretation and Classical Mythology*. Translated by Catherine Tihanyi. Chicago: University of Chicago Press, 2004 [French ed. 1996].

Brodeur, Patrice C. "Religion." Pages 395–98 in *Encyclopaedia of the Qur'ān*, Vol. 4. Edited Jane Dammen McAuliffe. Leiden: Brill, 2004.

Broughton, Thomas. *An Historical Dictionary of All Religions from the Creation of the World to this Present Time*. 2 vols. London: C. Davis and T. Harris, on London-Bridge, 1742.

Brown, Peter. *Augustine of Hippo: A Biography*. Revised ed. Berkeley: University of California Press, 2000 [1967].

————. *The Body and Society: Men, Women, and Sexual Renunciation in Early Christianity.* New York: Columbia University Press, 1988.

Bruno, Giordano. *The Ash Wednesday Supper: La cena de le ceneri.* Translated by Edward A. Gosselin and Lawrence S. Lerne. Reprint ed. Toronto: University of Toronto Press, 1995. Originally published as *La Cena de le Ceneri Descritta in cinque dialogi.* ([London: John Charlewood], 1584).

————. *The Expulsion of the Triumphant Beast.* Translated by Arthur D. Imerti. New Brunswick, N.J.: Rutgers University Press, 1964. Originally published as *Spaccio de la bestia trionfante, proposto da Giove, effettuato dal conseglo, Revelato da Mercurio, Recitato da Sophia, Udito da Saulino, Registrato dal Nolano.* ([London: John Charlewood], 1584), and in English as *Spaccio della bestia trionfante, Or the Expulsion of the Triumphant Beast* (translator unknown) (London: n.p., 1713).

Budge, E. A. Wallis. *The Rise & Progress of Assyriology.* London: Martin Hopkinson, 1925.

Buell, Denise Kimber. *Why This New Race: Ethnic Reasoning in Early Christianity.* New York: Columbia University Press, 2005.

Burkert, Walter. *Greek Religion: Archaic and Classical.* Translated by John Raffan. Oxford: Blackwell, 1985. Originally published as *Griechische Religion der archaischen und klassischen Epoche* (Stuttgart: Verlag W. Kohlhammer, 1977).

Burman, Thomas E. *Reading the Qur'ān in Latin Christendom, 1140–1560.* Philadelphia: University of Pennsylvania Press, 2007.

Byrne, Peter. *Natural Religion and the Nature of Religion: The Legacy of Deism.* London: Routledge, 1989.

Calder, William M., III, and Renate Schlesier, eds. *Zwischen Rationalismus und Romantik: Karl Otfried Müller und die antike Kultur.* Hildesheim: Weidmann, 1998.

Calder, William M., III, R. Scott Smith, John Vaio, eds. *Teaching the English Wissenschaft: The Letters of Sir George Cornewall Lewis to Karl Otfried Müller (1828–1839).* Zürich: Georg Olms Verlag, 2002.

Carratelli, G. Pugliese, and G. Garbini, eds. *A Bilingual Graeco-Aramaic Edict by Aśoka: The First Greek Inscription Discovered in Afghanistan.* Rome: Istituto Italiano per il Medio ed Estremo Oriente, 1964.

Cartledge, Paul. "Translator's Introduction" to *Religion in the Ancient Greek City,* by Louise Bruit Zaidman and Pauline Schmitt Pantel. Translated by Paul Cartledge. Cambridge: Cambridge University Press, 1992 [French ed. 1989].

Casadio, Giovanni. "*Religio* versus Religion." Pages 301–26 in *Myths, Martyrs, and Modernity: Studies in the History of Religions in Honour of Jan N. Bremmer.* Edited by Jitse Dijkstra, Justin Kroesen, and Yme Kuiper. Leiden: Brill, 2010.

Casas, Bartolomé de Las. *Obras Completas.* Edited by Paulino Castañeda Delgado. 14 vols. Madrid: Alianza, 1988–1994.

Casaubon, Isaac. *De rebus sacris et ecclesiasticis exercitationes XVI.* London: Nortoniana apud Jo. Billium, 1614.

Cassirer, Ernst. *The Platonic Renaissance in England.* Translated by James P. Pettegrove. Austin: University of Texas Press, 1953 [German ed. 1932].

Cavanaugh, William T. "'A Fire Strong Enough to Consume the House': The Wars of Religion and the Rise of the State." *Modern Theology* 11 (1995): 397–420.

———. *The Myth of Religious Violence.* New York: Oxford University Press, 2009.

Champion, Justin. *Republican Learning: John Toland and the Crisis of Christian Culture, 1696–1722.* New York: Palgrave, 2003.

———. "Toleration and Citizenship in Enlightenment England: John Toland and the Naturalization of the Jews, 1714–1753." Pages 133–56 in *Toleration in Enlightenment Europe.* Edited by Ole Peter Grell and Roy Porter. Cambridge: Cambridge University Press, 2000.

Chaucer, Geoffrey. *The Works of our Ancient, Learned, & Excellent English Poet, Jeffrey Chaucer, As they have lately been Compar'd with the best Manuscripts.* Edited by Thomas Speght. London: n.p., 1687.

Chelsum, James. *Remarks on the Last Two Chapters of Mr. Gibbon's History, of the Decline and Fall of the Roman Empire, in a Letter to a Friend.* London: Printed for T. Payne and Son and J. Robson and Co., 1776.

Chi, Tsui. "Mo Ni Chiao Hsia Pu Tsan 'The Lower (Second?) Section of the Manichaean Hymns.'" *Bulletin of the School of Oriental and African Studies* 11 (1943): 174–219.

Chidester, David. *Authentic Fakes: Religion and American Popular Culture.* Berkeley: University of California Press, 2005.

———. *Savage Systems: Colonialism and Comparative Religion in Southern Africa.* Charlottesville: University Press of Virginia, 1996.

Cicero. *Cicero: On Fate & Boethius: The Consolation of Philosophy IV.5–7, V.* Edited by R. W. Sharples. Warminster: Aris and Phillips, 1991.

———. *Cicero: On the Nature of the Gods.* Translated by Patrick Gerard Walsh. Oxford: Oxford University Press, 1998.

———. *On Divination.* Edited and translated by William Armistead Falconer. Reprint ed. Cambridge, Mass.: Harvard University Press, 1971 [1923].

———. *On the Nature of the Gods.* Edited and translated by H. Rackham. Reprint ed. London: William Heinemann, 1972 [1933].

———. *Cicero: The Verrine Orations.* 2 vols. Edited and translated by L. H. G. Greenwood. London: William Heinemann, 1935.

Clement of Alexandria. *Clément d'Alexandrie: Les Stromates.* 7 vols. Edited by Claude Mondésert, Marcel Caster, P. Th. Camelot, Anneweis van den Hoek, Alain Le Boulluec, Pierre Voulet, and Patrick Descourtieux. Paris: Editions du Cerf, 1951–2009.

Cohen, Shaye J. D. *The Beginnings of Jewishness: Boundaries, Varieties, Uncertainties.* Berkeley: University of California Press, 1999.

Cook, Michael. *Muhammad.* Oxford: Oxford University Press, 1996.

Copenhaver, Brian P. *Hermetica: The Greek Corpus Hermeticum and the Latin Asclepius in a New English Translation.* Cambridge: Cambridge University Press, 1992.

Coyle, J. Kevin. "Foreign and Insane: Labelling Manichaeism in the Roman Empire." *Studies in Religion/Sciences Religieuses* 33 (2004): 217–34. Reprinted in J. Kevin Coyle, *Manichaeism and Its Legacy.* Leiden: Brill, 2009, 3–23.

Cranston, Maurice. *John Locke: A Biography.* Reprint ed. London: Longmans, 1966 [1957].

Creppell, Ingrid. *Toleration and Identity: Foundations in Early Modern Thought.* London: Routledge, 2003.

Creveld, Martin van. *The Rise and Decline of the State.* Cambridge: Cambridge University Press, 1999.

Crone, Patricia, and Michael Cook. *Hagarism: The Making of the Islamic World.* Cambridge: Cambridge University Press, 1977.

Cyprian. *The Letters of St. Cyprian of Carthage.* Translated by G. W. Clarke. 4 vols. New York: Newman, 1984–1989.

———. *Sancti Cypriani Episcopi Epistularium.* Edited by G. F. Diercks. Turnhout: Brepols, 1994–1999.

Daniel, Norman. *Islam and the West: The Making of an Image.* Revised ed. Oxford: Oneworld, 2009 [1960].

Dati, Giuliano. *Lettera delle isole che ha trovato il re di Spagna.* Florence: Lorenzo Morgiani and Johannes Petri, 1493.

Davids, Thomas William Rhys, trans. *Buddhist Birth Stories; or, Jātaka Tales.* Edited by V. Fausböll. London: Trübner, 1880.

Davies, Martin. *Columbus in Italy: An Italian Versification of the Letter on the Discovery of the New World*. London: British Library, 1991.

Davis, Stephen J., Samuel Noble, and Bilal Orfali. *A Disputation over a Fragment of the Cross: A Medieval Arabic Text from the History of Christian-Jewish-Muslim Relations in Egypt*. Beiruter Texte und Studien. Forthcoming.

Dawood, N. J. *The Koran Translated*. Revised ed. London: Penguin, 2003 [1956].

de León-Jones, Karen Silvia. *Giordano Bruno and the Kabbalah: Prophets, Magicians, and Rabbis*. New Haven, Conn.: Yale University Press, 1997.

den Boer, Pim. "Europe to 1914: The Making of an Idea." Pages 13–82 in *The History of the Idea of Europe*. Edited by Kevin Wilson and Jan van der Dussen. London: Routledge, 1995.

Denny, Frederick Mathewson. "The Meaning of 'Ummah' in the Qur'ān." *History of Religions* 15 (1975): 34–70.

Despland, Michel. *La religion en occident: Évolution des idées et du vécu*. Reprint ed. Montreal: Fides, 1988 [1979].

———. "Seven Decades of Writing on Greek Religion." *Religion* 4 (1974): 118–50.

Dickens, A. G. *Reformation and Society in Sixteenth-Century Europe*. London: Thames and Hudson, 1966.

Diehl, Peter, and Scott L. Waugh, eds. *Christendom and Its Discontents: Exclusion, Persecution, and Rebellion, 1000–1500*. Cambridge: Cambridge University Press, 1996.

Dionysius of Halicarnassus. *The Roman Antiquities of Dionysius of Halicarnassus*. Edited and translated by Earnest Cary. 7 vols. London: William Heinemann, 1937–1950.

Donner, Fred M. "From Believers to Muslims: Confessional Self-Identity in the Early Islamic Community." *Al-Abhath* 50–51 (2002–2003): 9–53.

———. *Muhammad and the Believers: At the Origins of Islam*. Cambridge, Mass.: Belknap, 2010.

Dubuisson, Daniel. *The Western Construction of Religion: Myths, Knowledge, and Ideology*. Translated by William Sayers. Baltimore: Johns Hopkins University Press, 2003 [French ed. 1998].

Du Cange, Charles Du Fresne. *Glossarium Mediae et infimae latinitatis*. Reprint ed. Paris: Librairie des sciences et des arts, 1938.

Dumézil, Georges. *Archaic Roman Religion with an Appendix on the Religion of the Etruscans.* Translated by Philip Krapp. 2 vols. Chicago: University of Chicago Press, 1970 [French ed. 1966].

Dunn, Richard S. *The Age of Religious Wars: 1559–1715.* 2nd ed. New York: Norton, 1979 [1970].

du Ryer, André. *L'Alcoran de Mahomet: Translaté d'Arabé en François.* Paris: Antoine de Sommaville, 1672.

Edgerton, Franklin. "Edward Washburn Hopkins, 1857–1932." *Journal of the American Oriental Society* 52 (1932): 311–15.

Edwards, John. *The Doctrines Controverted Between Papists and Protestants Particularly and Distinctly Consider'd: And Those which are held by the Former Confuted.* London: Printed for James Roberts, 1724.

———. *The Socinian Creed: Or, A Brief Account of the Professed Tenets and Doctrines of the Foreign and English Socinians.* London: Printed for J. Robinson and J. Wyat, 1697.

———. *POLUPOIKILOS SOPHIA: A Compleat History or Survey of all the Dispensations and Methods of Religion.* London: Printed for Daniel Brown . . . and E. Harris, 1699.

Elliott, J. H. *The Old World and the New: 1492–1650.* Cambridge: Cambridge University Press, 1970.

Elverskog, Johan. *Buddhism and Islam on the Silk Road.* Philadelphia: University of Pennsylvania Press, 2010.

Esposito, John L., Darrell J. Fasching, and Todd Lewis. *World Religions Today.* 3rd ed. New York: Oxford University Press, 2009.

Eusebius of Caesarea. *Die Demonstratio Evangelica.* Edited by Ivar A. Heikel. Leipzig: J. C. Hinrichs'sche Buchhandlung, 1913.

———. *Die Praeparatio Evangelica.* Edited by Karl Mras and Édouard Des Places. 2 vols. 2nd ed. Berlin: Akademie-Verlag, 1982–1983 [1954–1956].

———. *Eusebius: The Ecclesiastical History.* Edited and translated by Kirsopp Lake, J. E. L. Oulton, and H. J. Lawlor. 2 vols. London: William Heinemann, 1926–1932.

———. *Über das Leben Constantins.* Edited by Ivar A. Heikel. Leipzig: J. C. Hinrichs'sche, 1902.

———. *Die Kirchengeschichte.* Edited by Eduard Schwartz. 3 vols. Leipzig: J. C. Hinrichs'sche, 1903–1909.

Evodius. *Sancti Aureli Augustini: Contra Felicem de natura boni, Epistula secundini contra Secundinum, accedunt Euodii De Fide Contra Manichaeos.* Edited by Joseph Zycha. Vienna: F. Tempsky, 1892.

Feeney, Denis. *Literature and Religion at Rome: Cultures, Contexts, and Beliefs.* New York: Cambridge University Press, 1998.

Feil, Ernst. *Religio: Die Geschichte eines neuzeitlichen Grundbegriffs.* 4 vols. Göttingen: Vandenhoeck and Ruprecht, 1986–2007.

Ficino, Marsilio. *La religione Cristiana.* Translated by Roberto Zanzarri. Rome: Città Nuova, 2005.

———. *Marsilio Ficino: Opera Omnia.* Reprint ed. Turrin: Bottega d'Erasmo, 1959.

———. *Mercurii Trismegisti, Liber de potestate et sapientia Dei: Pimander.* Reprint ed. Firenze: S.P.E.S., 1989; 1st ed., Treviso: Gerardus de Lisa, 1471.

———. *Platonic Theology.* Edited and translated by Michael J. B. Allen, James Hankins, William Bowen, and John Warden. 6 vols. Cambridge, Mass.: Harvard University Press, 2001–2006.

Finley, Moses I. Foreword to *Greek Religion and Society.* Edited by P. E. Easterling and J. V. Muir. Cambridge: Cambridge University Press, 1985.

Firmicus Maternus. *Firmicus Maternus: L'erreur des religions paiennes.* Edited by Robert Turcan. Paris: Les belles lettres, 1982.

Fitzgerald, Timothy. *Discourse on Civility and Barbarity: A Critical History of Religion and Related Categories.* New York: Oxford University Press, 2007.

———. *The Ideology of Religious Studies.* New York: Oxford University Press, 2000.

Flaig, Egon. "Towards 'Rassenhygiene': Wilamowitz and the German New Right." Pages 105–27 in *Out of Arcadia: Classics and Politics in Germany in the Age of Burckhardt, Nietzsche and Wilamowitz.* Edited by Ingo Gildenhard and Martin Ruehl. London: Institute of Classical Studies, 2003.

Foschia, Laurence. "Le nom du culte, *thrēskeia,* et ses dérivés à l'époque impériale." Pages 15–35 in *L'hellénisme d'époque romaine: Nouveaux documents, nouvelles approches (Ier s.a.C.—IIIe s.p.C.).* Edited by Simon Follet. Paris: de Boccard, 2004.

Foster, Benjamin R. "The Beginnings of Assyriology in the United States." Pages 44–73 in *Orientalism, Assyriology and the Bible.* Edited by Steven W. Holloway. Sheffield: Sheffield Phoenix Press, 2006.

Fowler, W. Warde. *The Religious Experience of the Roman People: From the Earliest Times to the Age of Augustus.* London: Macmillan, 1911.

Frazer, James George. *The Golden Bough: A Study in Comparative Religion.* 2 vols. London: Macmillan, 1890.

Frykenberg, Robert Eric. "The Emergence of Modern 'Hinduism' as a Concept and as an Institution: A Reappraisal with Special Reference to

South India." Pages 82–107 in *Hinduism Reconsidered*. Edited by Günther-Dietz Sontheimer and Hermann Kulke. Revised ed. New Delhi: Manohar, 2005 [1989].

Funk, Wolf-Peter. *Kephalaia I, Zweite Hälfte*. Stuttgart: Kohlhammer, 1999–2000.

———. "Mani's Account of Other Religions According to the Coptic *Synaxeis* Codex." Pages 115–27 in *New Light on Manichaeism: Papers from the Sixth International Congress on Manichaeism*. Edited by Jason David BeDuhn. Leiden: Brill, 2009.

Gandhi, Mahatma. *An Autobiography or The Story of My Experiments with Truth*. Reprint ed. Ahmedabad: Navajivan, 1996 [1927].

Gardet, Louis. "dīn." Pages 293–96 in *Encyclopaedia of Islam*, Vol. 2. Edited by Bernard Lewis, Charles Pellat, and Joseph Schacht. Leiden: Brill, 1965.

Gardner, Iain. *Kellis Literary Texts*. 2 vols. Oxford: Oxbow, 1996 and 2007.

Gardner, Iain, Anthony Alcock, and Wolf-Peter Funk. *Coptic Documentary Texts from Kellis*, Vol. 1. Oxford: Oxbow, 1999.

Gardner, Iain, and Samuel N. C. Lieu, eds. *Manichaean Texts from the Roman Empire*. Cambridge: Cambridge University Press, 2004.

Gatti, Hilary. *Giordano Bruno and Renaissance Science*. Ithaca, N.Y.: Cornell University Press, 1999.

Geertz, Clifford. "Religion as a Cultural System." Pages 1–46 in *Anthropological Approaches to the Study of Religion*. Edited by Michael Banton. New York: Frederick A. Praeger, 1966. Reprinted in *The Interpretation of Cultures*. New York: Basic Books, 1973.

Gibbon, Edward. *The History of the Decline and Fall of the Roman Empire: Edited, with an Introduction and Appendices, by David Womersley*. 3 vols. London: Allen Lane, Penguin, 1994.

Gignoux, Philippe. "*Dēnkard*." Pages 284–89 in *Encyclopaedia Iranica*, Vol. 7. Edited by Ehsan Yarshater. Costa Mesa, Calif.: Mazda, 1996.

Glausser, Wayne. "Three Approaches to Locke and the Slave Trade." *Journal of the History of Ideas* 51 (1990): 199–216.

Good, Anne. "The Construction of an Authoritative Text: Peter Kolb's Description of the Khoikhoi at the Cape of Good Hope in the Eighteenth Century." *Journal of Early Modern History* 10 (2006): 61–94.

Gouge, Thomas. *The Principles of Christian Religion, Explained to the Capacity of the Meanest*. London: John Wright, 1668.

Gradel, Ittai. *Emperor Worship and Roman Religion*. Oxford: Clarendon, 2002.

Graf, Fritz. *Magic in the Ancient World*. Translated by Franklin Philip. Cambridge, Mass.: Harvard University Press, 1997 [French ed. 1994].

Grapard, Allan G. "Japan's Ignored Cultural Revolution: The Separation of Shinto and Buddhist Divinities in Meiji (*shimbutsu bunri*) and a Case Study: Tōnomine." *History of Religions* 23 (1984): 240–65.

Gregory of Nyssa. *Contra Eunomium libri*. Edited by Werner Jaeger. 2 vols. Leiden: Brill, 1960.

Grotius, Hugo. *De Veritate Religionis Christianae*. 2nd ed. Leiden: Ioannis Maire, 1629 [1627].

———. *Hugo Grotius: On the Truth of Christianity*. Translated by Spencer Madan. London: J. Dodsley, 1782.

———. *The Truth of Christian Religion in Six Books*. Translated by Symon Patrick. London: Rich, Royston, 1683.

Habinek, Thomas N. "Grecian Wonders and Roman Woe: The Romantic Rejection of Rome and Its Consequences for the Study of Latin Literature." Pages 227–42 in *The Interpretation of Roman Poetry: Empiricism or Hermeneutics?* Edited by Karl Galinsky. Frankfurt am Main: Peter Lang, 1992.

Haddad, Yvonne Yazbeck. "The Conception of the Term *dīn* in the Qur'ān." *Muslim World* 64 (1974): 114–23.

Haloun, G., and W. B. Henning. "The Compendium of the Doctrines and Styles of the Teaching of Mani, the Buddha of Light." *Asia Minor, N.S.* 3 (1952): 184–212.

Hankins, James. *Plato in the Italian Renaissance*. 2 vols. Leiden: Brill, 1990.

Hardacre, Helen. *Shintō and the State, 1868–1988*. Princeton, N.J.: Princeton University Press, 1989.

Harris, J. Rendel. Review of several books on the Didache. *American Journal of Philology* 6 (1885): 102–5.

Harrison, Jane. *Prolegomena to the Study of Greek Religion*. Cambridge: The University Press, 1903.

Harrison, Peter. *"Religion" and the Religions in the English Enlightenment*. Cambridge: Cambridge University Press, 1990.

Heering, Jan-Paul. "Hugo Grotius' De Veritate Religionis Christianae." Pages 41–52 in *Hugo Grotius: Theologian: Essays in Honour of G. H. M. Posthumus Meyjes*. Edited by Henk J. M. Nellen and Edwin Rabbie. Leiden: Brill, 1994.

———. *Hugo Grotius as Apologist for the Christian Religion: A Study of His Work De Veritate Religionis Christianae*. Translated by J. C. Grayson. Leiden: Brill, 2004 [Dutch ed. 1992].

Hegemonius. *Hegemonius: Acta Archelai*. Edited by Charles Henry Beeson. Leipzig: J. C. Hinrichs'sche, 1906.

Henning, W. B. "Persian Poetical Manuscripts from the Time of Rūdakī." Pages 89–104 in *A Locust's Leg: Studies in Honor of S. H. Taqizadeh*. London: Percy Lund, Humphries, 1962. Reprinted in W. B. Henning, *Selected Papers*. 2 vols. Leiden: Brill, 1977, 2.559–74.

Henrichs, Albert, and Ludwig Koenen. "Ein griechischer Mani-Codex (P. Colon. Inv. nr. 4780)." *Zeitschrift für Papyrologie und Epigraphik* 5 (1970): 97–216.

Herbert of Cherbury, Edward, 1st Lord. *The Antient Religion of the Gentiles, and Causes of their Errors Consider'd*. Translated by William Lewis. London: William Taylor, 1711 [1705]. Originally published as *De religione gentilium, errorumque apud eos causis*. Amsterdam: Typis Blaeviorum, 1663.

―――. *The Autobiography of Edward, Lord Herbert of Cherbury*. Edited by Sidney Lee. Reprint ed. Westport, Conn.: Greenwood, 1970.

―――. *De Veritate by Edward, Lord Herbert of Cherbury*. Translated by Meyrick H. Carré. Bristol: J. W. Arrowsmith, 1937. Originally published as *De Veritate, prout distinguitur a Revelatione, a Verisimili, a Possibili, et a Falso*. Paris: n.p., 1624.

―――. *Pagan Religion: A Translation of De religione gentilium*. Translated by John Anthony Butler. Ottawa: Dovehouse, 1996.

Herodotus. *Herodotus*. Edited and translated by A. D. Godley. Reprint revised ed. 4 vols. Cambridge, Mass.: Harvard University Press, 1981 [1921–1924].

Hesychius. *Hesychii Alexandrini lexicon*. Edited by Kurt Latte. 4 vols. Copenhagen and Berlin: Munksgaard and de Gruyter, 1953–2009.

Hick, John. *An Interpretation of Religion: Human Responses to the Transcendent*. 2nd ed. New Haven, Conn.: Yale University Press, 2004 [1989].

Hirai Naofusa. "Shinto." Translated by Helen Hardacre. Pages 13.280–94 in *Encyclopedia of Religion*. Edited by Mircea Eliade. 16 vols. New York: Macmillan, 1987.

Hirsh, John C. *Barlam and Iosaphat: A Middle English Life of Buddha*. London: Oxford University Press, 1986.

Historia Compostellana. Edited by Emma Falque Rey. Turnhout: Brepols, 1988.

Hopkins, Edward Washburn. *The Religions of India*. Boston: Ginn and Company, 1895.

Hoyland, Robert G. *Seeing Islam as Others Saw It: A Survey and Evaluation of Christian, Jewish, and Zoroastrian Writings on Early Islam*. Princeton, N.J.: Darwin Press, 1997.

Hume, David. *Four Dissertations.* London: Printed for A. Millar, 1757.

Hunt, Lynn, Margaret C. Jacob, and Wijnand Mijnhardt. *The Book That Changed Europe: Picart and Bernard's Religious Ceremonies of the World.* Cambridge, Mass.: Belknap, 2010.

Hurd, William. *A New Universal History of the Religious Rites, Ceremonies and Customs of the Whole World; Or, A Complete and Impartial View of All the Religions in the Various Nations of the Universe; Both Ancient and Modern, From the Creation Down to the Present Time.* Blackburn: J. Hemmingway, 1799.

Hutchinson, John, and Anthony D. Smith, eds. *Ethnicity.* New York: Oxford University Press, 1996.

Hyamson, M., ed. *Mosaicarum et Romanarum Legum Collatio.* London: Oxford University Press, 1913.

Idel, Moshe. "Kabbalah, Platonism, and Prisca Theologia: The Case of R. Menasseh ben Israel." Pages 207–19 in *Menasseh ben Israel and His World.* Edited by Yosef Kaplan, Henry Méchoulan, and Richard H. Popkin. Leiden: Brill, 1989.

Ingegno, Alfonso. *La Sommersa nave della religione: Studio sulla polemica anticristiana del Bruno.* Naples: Bibliopolis, 1985.

Isidore of Seville. "Isidore of Seville on the Pagan Gods (*Origines* VIII.11)." Edited by Katherine Nell MacFarlane. *Transactions of the American Philosophical Society* 70:3 (1980): 1–40.

Isocrates. *Isocrates.* Edited and translated by George Norlin. 3 vols. London: W. Heinemann, 1928–1945.

Jackson, Peter. *The Mongols and the West, 1221–1410.* New York: Pearson Longman, 2005.

Jacobsen, Knut A. "Introduction." Pages xxxiii–xliii in *Brill's Encyclopedia of Hinduism.* Leiden: Brill, 2009.

Jacobsen, Thorkild. *The Treasures of Darkness: A History of Mesopotamian Religion.* New Haven, Conn.: Yale University Press, 1976.

———. *Toward the Image of Tammuz and Other Essays on Mesopotamian History and Culture.* Edited by William L. Moran. Cambridge, Mass.: Harvard University Press, 1970.

James, William. *The Varieties of Religious Experience: A Study in Human Nature.* London: Longmans, Green, 1902.

Jastrow, Morris. *The Religion of Babylonia and Assyria.* Boston: Ginn and Company, 1898.

Jeffery, Arthur. *The Foreign Vocabulary of the Qur'ān.* Reprint ed. Leiden: Brill, 2007 [1938].

Jenkyns, Richard. *The Victorians and Ancient Greece.* Oxford: Basil Blackwell, 1980.

John of Damascus. *Jean Damascène: Écrits sur l'Islam.* Edited by Raymond Le Coz. Paris: Éditions du Cerf, 1992.

———. *Die Schriften des Johannes von Damaskos.* Edited by P. Bonifatius Kotter and Robert Volk. 7 vols. Berlin: de Gruyter, 1969–2009.

[———]. *The Balavariani (Barlaam and Josaphat): A Tale from the Christian East Translated from the Old Georgian.* Translated by David M. Lang. London: George Allen and Unwin, 1966.

[———]. *St. John Damascene: Barlaam and Ioasaph.* Edited and translated by G. R. Woodward and H. Mattingly. Revised ed. London: William Heinemann, 1967 [1914].

[———]. *The Wisdom of Balahvar: A Christian Legend of the Buddha.* Translated by David M. Lang. London: George Allen and Unwin, 1957.

Johnson, Aaron P. *Ethnicity and Argument in Eusebius' Praeparatio Evangelica.* Oxford: Oxford University Press, 2006.

Joosten, Jan. "The *Gospel of Barnabas* and the Diatessaron." *Harvard Theological Review* 95 (2002): 73–96.

Josephus. *Flavii Iosephi Opera.* Edited by Benedictus Niese. 7 vols. Reprint ed. Berlin: Weidmannos, 1955 [1885–1895].

Judge, Edwin. "The Absence of Religion, Even in Ammianus?" Pages 264–75 in *Jerusalem and Athens: Cultural Transformation in Late Antiquity.* Edited by Alanna Nobbs. Tübingen: Mohr Siebeck, 2010.

———. "Was Christianity a Religion?" Pages 404–9 in *The First Christians in the Roman World: Augustan and New Testament Essays.* Edited by James R. Harrison. Tübingen: Mohr Siebeck, 2008.

Just, Arthur, Jr., ed. *Ancient Christian Commentary on Scripture: Luke.* Downers Grove, Ill.: InterVarsity, 2003.

Kennett, Basil. *Romae Antiquae Notitia: Or, The Antiquities of Rome. In Two Parts.* London: A. Swall and T. Child, 1696.

King, Richard. *Orientalism and Religion: Post-Colonial Theory, India and 'the Mystic East.'* New York: Routledge, 1999.

Kippenberg, Hans G. *Discovering Religious History in the Modern Age.* Translated by Barbara Harshav. Princeton: Princeton University Press, 2002 [German ed. 1997].

Knight, W. S. M. *The Life and Works of Hugo Grotius.* London: Sweet and Maxwell, 1925.

Koenen, Ludwig, and Cornelia Römer. *Der Kölner Mani-Kodex: Abbildungen und diplomatischer Text.* Bonn: Habelt, 1985.

Kolb, Peter. *The Present State of the Cape of Good-Hope: Or, A Particular Account of the Several Nations of the Hottentots: Their Religion, Government, Laws, Customs, Ceremonies, and Opinions: Their Art of War, Professions, Language, Genesis, &c.* Translated by Mr. Medley. 2nd ed. London: W. Innys, 1738 [1731]. Originally published as *Caput Bonae Spei hodiernum. Das ist, völlstandige Beschreibung des afrikanischen Vorgebürges der Guten Hofnung.* Nürnberg: Peter Conrad Monath, 1719.

Konstan, David. "Defining Ancient Greek Ethnicity." *Diaspora* 6 (1997): 97–110.

Kristeller, Paul Oskar. *The Philosophy of Marsilio Ficino.* Translated by Virginia Conant. New York: Columbia University Press, 1943.

———. *Supplementum Ficinianum.* 2 vols. Florence: Leonis S. Olschki, 1937.

Kuenen, Abraham. *National Religions and Universal Religions.* New York: C. Scribner's Sons, 1882.

———. *Volksreligion und Weltreligion: Fünf Hibbert-Vorlesungen.* Berlin: G. Reimer, 1883.

Kuntz, Marion L. "Bodin's Demons." *New York Review of Books* (24) 1977. http://www.nybooks.com/articles/8723 (accessed 23 October 2011).

Kuroda Toshio. "Shinto in the History of Japanese Religion." Translated by James C. Dobbins and Suzanne Gay. *Journal of Japanese Studies* 7 (1981): 1–21.

Laboulaye, Édouard. Review of Stanislaus Julien, *Les Avadānas* in *Journal des Débats* (26 July 1859): 2–3.

Lactantius. *L. Caeli Firmiani Lactanti: Opera Omnia.* Edited by Samuel Brandt and Georgius Laubmann. Vienna/Leipzig: F. Tempsky/G. Freytag, 1890–1897.

———. *Lactantius: The Divine Institutes Books I–VII.* Translated by Mary Francis McDonald. Washington, D.C.: Catholic University of America Press, 1964.

———. *Lactantius: Divine Institutes.* Translated by Anthony Bowen and Peter Garnsey. Liverpool: Liverpool University Press, 2003.

———. *Lactantius: The Minor Works.* Translated by Mary Francis McDonald. Washington, D.C.: Catholic University of America Press, 1965.

Lalande, André. "Philosophy in France, 1934–1935." *Philosophical Review* 45 (1936): 1–25.

Lang, David M. "Bilawhar wa-Yūdāsaf." Pages 1215–17 in *Encyclopaedia of Islam,* Vol. 1. Edited by Bernard Lewis, Charles Pellat, and Joseph Schacht. Leiden: Brill, 1960.

Lecker, Michael. *The "Constitution of Medina": Muḥammad's First Legal Document.* Princeton, N.J.: Darwin Press, 2004.

Leuba, James H. *A Psychological Study of Religion: Its Origin, Function, and Future.* New York: Macmillan, 1912.

Lewis, Bernard. *The Jews of Islam.* Princeton, N.J.: Princeton University Press, 1984.

Lewis, Robert E., ed. *Middle English Dictionary.* Ann Arbor: University of Michigan Press, 1985.

Lieu, Samuel N. C. "Manichaean Art and Texts from the Silk Road." Pages 261–312 in *Studies in Silk Road Coins and Culture, Papers in Honour of Professor Ikuo Hirayama on his 65th Birthday.* Edited by Katsumi Tanabe, Joe Cribb, and Helen Wang. Kamakura: Institute of Silk Road Studies, 1997.

———. *Manichaeism in Central Asia and China.* Leiden: Brill, 1998.

———. *Manichaeism in the Later Roman Empire and Medieval China.* 2nd revised ed. Tübingen: Mohr Siebeck, 1992 [1985].

———. "'My Church Is Superior . . .': Mani's Missionary Statement in Coptic and Middle Persian." Pages 519–27 in *Coptica Gnostica Manichaica: Mélanges offerts à Wolf-Peter Funk.* Edited by Louis Painchaud and Paul-Hubert Poirier. Louvain: Peeters, 2006.

———. "The Self-Identity of the Manichaeans in the Roman East." *Mediterranean Archaeology* 11 (1998): 205–27.

Lilla, Mark. *The Stillborn God: Religion, Politics, and the Modern West.* New York: Alfred A. Knopf, 2007.

Lincoln, Bruce. *Holy Terrors: Thinking about Religion after September 11.* 2nd ed. Chicago: University of Chicago Press, 2006.

———. *Theorizing Myth: Narrative, Ideology, and Scholarship.* Chicago: University of Chicago Press, 1999.

Livy. *Livy.* Edited and translated by B. O. Foster, Frank Gardner Moore, Evan T. Sage, and Alfred C. Schlesinger. 14 vols. Cambridge, Mass.: Harvard University Press, 1919–1959.

Llewellyn, J. E. *Defining Hinduism: A Reader.* New York: Routledge, 2005.

Locke, John. *Epistola de tolerantia ad clarissimum Virum.* Gouda: Justus van der Hoeve, 1689.

———. *Epistola de Tolerantia: A Letter on Toleration.* Edited and translated by Raymond Klibansky and J. W. Gough. Oxford: Clarendon, 1968.

———. *A Letter Concerning Toleration: Humbly Submitted &c.* Translated by William Popple. London: Printed for Awnsham Churchill, 1689.

Lofton, Kathryn. *Oprah: The Gospel of an Icon.* Berkeley: University of California Press, 2011.

Lopez, Donald S. *Curators of the Buddha: The Study of Buddhism under Colonialism*. Chicago: University of Chicago Press, 1995.

Lord, Henry. *A Display of Two Forraigne Sects in the East Indes*. London: T. and R. Cotes for Francis Constable, 1630.

Louth, Andrew. *St. John Damascene: Tradition and Originality in Byzantine Theology*. Oxford: Oxford University Press, 2002.

Lucretius. *Lucretius: De rerum natura*. Edited and translated by W. H. D. Rouse and Martin Ferguson Smith. Revised ed. Cambridge, Mass.: Harvard University Press, 1975 [1924].

MacCormack, Sabine. "Gods, Demons, and Idols in the Andes." *Journal of the History of Ideas* 67 (2006): 623–47.

MacMullen, Ramsay. *Constantine*. London: Weidenfeld and Nicolson, 1970.

Majamdar, R. C. *The Classical Accounts of India*. Calcutta: Mukhopadhyay, 1960.

Mandair, Arvind-pal S. *Religion and the Specter of the West: Sikhism, India, Postcoloniality, and the Politics of Translation*. New York: Columbia University Press, 2009.

Manuel, Frank E. *The Eighteenth Century Confronts the Gods*. Cambridge, Mass.: Harvard University Press, 1959.

Marchand, Suzanne L. *Down from Olympus: Archaeology and Philhellenism in Germany, 1750–1970*. Princeton, N.J.: Princeton University Press, 1996.

Marshall, John. *John Locke: Resistance, Religion and Responsibility*. Cambridge: Cambridge University Press, 1994.

———. *John Locke, Toleration and Early Enlightenment Culture: Religious Intolerance and Arguments for Religious Toleration in Early Modern and 'Early Enlightenment' Europe*. Cambridge: Cambridge University Press, 2006.

Martin, Craig. *Masking Hegemony: A Genealogy of Liberalism, Religion, and the Private Sphere*. London: Equinox, 2010.

Martin, Dale B. *Inventing Superstition: From the Hippocratics to the Christians*. Cambridge, Mass.: Harvard University Press, 2004.

Mason, Steve. "Jews, Judaeans, Judaizing, Judaism: Problems of Categorization in Ancient History." *Journal for the Study of Judaism* 38 (2007): 457–512.

Masuzawa, Tomoko. *The Invention of World Religions: Or, How European Universalism Was Preserved in the Language of Pluralism*. Chicago: University of Chicago Press, 2005.

———. "Rejoinder." *Bulletin of the Council of Societies for the Study of Religion* 35 (2006): 14–16.

———. "What Do the Critics Want?—A Brief Reflection on the Difference between a Disciplinary History and a Discourse Analysis." *Method and Theory in the Study of Religion* 20 (2008): 139–49.

Matar, Nabil. "Alexander Ross and the First English Translation of the Qur'ān." *Muslim World* 88 (1998): 81–92.

McCloy, Shelby T. *Gibbon's Antagonism to Christianity.* London: Williams and Norgate, 1933.

McCutcheon, Russell T. *The Discipline of Religion: Structure, Meaning, Rhetoric.* London: Routledge, 2003.

———. *Manufacturing Religion: The Discourse on Sui Generis Religion and the Politics of Nostalgia.* New York: Oxford University Press, 1997.

———. "The Perils of Having One's Cake and Eating It Too: Some Thoughts in Response." *Religious Studies Review* 31 (2005): 32–36.

———. *Religion and the Domestication of Dissent: Or, How to Live in a Less Than Perfect Nation.* London: Equinox, 2005.

———. "Religion before 'Religion'?" Pages 285–301 in *Chasing Down Religion: In the Sights of History and the Cognitive Sciences. Essays in Honor of Luther H. Martin.* Edited by Panayotis Pachis and Donald Wiebe. Thessaloníki: Barbounakis, 2010.

———. "Religion, Ire, and Dangerous Things." *Journal of the American Academy of Religion* 72 (2004): 173–93.

———. *Studying Religion: An Introduction.* London: Equinox, 2007.

———, ed. *The Insider/Outsider Problem in the Study of Religion: A Reader.* London: Cassell, 1998.

Meade, C. Wade. *Road to Babylon: Development of U.S. Assyriology.* Leiden: Brill, 1974.

Merrill, John E. "Of the Tractate of John of Damascus on Islam." *Moslem World* 41 (1951): 88–97.

Mikkelsen, Gunner B. *Dictionary of Manichaean Texts. Vol. 3: Texts from Central Asia and China, Part 4: Dictionary of Manichaean Texts in Chinese.* Turnhout: Brepols, 2006.

Miller, Peter N. "Taking Paganism Seriously: Anthropology and Antiquarianism in Early Seventeenth-Century Histories of Religion." *Archiv für Religionsgeschichte* 3 (2001): 183–209.

Minucius Felix. *M. Minuci Felicis Octavius.* Edited by Bernhard Kytzler. Leipzig: Teubner, 1982.

———. *Tertullian: Apologetical Works and Minucius Felix: Octavius.* Translated by Rudolph Arbesmann, Emily Joseph Daly, and Edwin A. Quain. New York: Fathers of the Church, 1950.

Momigliano, Arnaldo. "The Theological Efforts of the Roman Upper Classes in the First Century B.C." *Classical Philology* 79 (1984): 199–211.

Mommsen, Theodor. *The History of Rome*. Translated by W. P. Dickson. 4 vols. London: Richard Bentley, 1861–1866 [3rd German ed. 1861].

———. *Römische Geschichte*. 3 vols. Berlin: Weidmannsche Buchhandlung, 1854–1856.

Mommsen, Theodor, Paul Krueger, Wilhelm Kroll, and Rudolf Schöll, eds. *Corpus iuris civilis*. 3 vols. Berlin: Weidmann's, 1928–1929.

Moore, Stephen D. *God's Gym: Divine Male Bodies of the Bible*. New York: Routledge, 1996.

Mori Arinori. *Religious Freedom in Japan: A Memorial and Draft of Charter*. Washington, D.C.: privately published, 1872. Reprinted in John E. Van Sant, *Mori Arinori's Life and Resources in America*. Lanham, Md.: Lexington Books, 2004, 143–49.

Mülke, Markus, ed. *Wilamowitz und kein Ende: Wissenschaftsgeschichtliches Kolloquium Fondation Hardt, 9. bis 13. September 2002*. Hildesheim: Georg Olms Verlag, 2003.

Müller, F. Max. *Chips from a German Workshop*. 4 vols. London: Longmans, Green, 1867–1875.

———. *Introduction to the Science of Religion: Four Lectures Delivered at the Royal Institution with Two Essays on False Analogies, and the Philosophy of Mythology*. London: Longmans and Green, 1873.

———. *Natural Religion: The Gifford Lectures delivered before the University of Glasgow in 1888*. London: Longmans, Green, 1889.

Müller, Karl Otfried. *Introduction to a Scientific System of Mythology*. Translated by John Leitch. London: Longman, Brown, Green, and Longmans, 1844 [German ed. 1825].

———. *Ancient Art and Its Remains: Or A Manual of the Archaeology of Art*. Translated by John Leitch. 2nd ed. London: A. Fullarton, 1850 [1847; German ed. 1830].

Myres, John L. "*Mēdizein: mēdismos*." Pages 97–105 in *Greek Poetry and Life: Essays Presented to Gilbert Murray on His Seventieth Birthday*. Edited by Cyril Bailey, E. A. Barber, C. M. Bowra, J. D. Denniston, and D. L. Page. Oxford: Clarendon, 1936.

Nicetas of Byzantium. *Niketas von Byzanz, Schriften zum Islam*. Edited by Karl Förstel. Würzburg: Echter Verlag, 2000.

Nicholas of Cusa. *Nicholas of Cusa on Interreligious Harmony: Text, Concordance and Translation of De Pace Fidei*. Edited and translated by

James E. Biechler and H. Lawrence Bond. Lewiston, N.Y.: Edwin Mellen, 1990.

Nongbri, Brent. "Dislodging 'Embedded' Religion: A Brief Note on a Scholarly Trope." *Numen* 55 (2008): 440–60.

———. "The Motivations of the Maccabees and Judean Rhetoric of Ancestral Tradition." Pages 85–111 in *Ancient Judaism in Its Hellenistic Context*. Edited by Carol Bakhos. Leiden: Brill, 2005.

———. "Paul without Religion: The Creation of a Category and the Search for an Apostle Beyond the New Perspective." Ph.D. dissertation, Yale University, 2008.

Oddie, Geoffrey A. *Imagined Hinduism: British Protestant Missionary Constructions of Hinduism, 1793–1900*. New Delhi: Sage, 2006.

Olschki, Leonardo. "Manichaeism, Buddhism, and Christianity in Marco Polo's China." *Asiatische Studien* 5 (1951): 1–21.

Omerod, Oliver. *The Picture of a Papist: Or, A relation of the damnable heresies, detestable qualities, and diabolicall practises of sundry hereticks in former ages, and of the papists in this age*. London: Printed for Nathaniel Fosbrooke, 1606.

Oppenheim, A. Leo. "Assyro-Babylonian Religion." Pages 63–79 in *Forgotten Religions (including Some Living Primitive Religions)*. Edited by Virgilius Ferm. New York: Philosophical Library, 1950. Reprinted as *Ancient Religions*. Edited by Virgilius Ferm. New York: Citadel, 1965.

———. *Ancient Mesopotamia: Portrait of a Dead Civilization*. Edited by Erica Reiner. Chicago: University of Chicago Press, 1977 [1964].

Origen. *Die Schrift vom Martyrium Buch I–IV gegen Celsus*. Edited by Paul Koetschau. Leipzig: J. C. Hinrichs'sche, 1899.

Otto, Rudolf. *The Idea of the Holy: An Inquiry into the Non-rational Factor in the Idea of the Divine and Its Relation to the Rational*. Translated by John W. Harvey. 2nd ed. New York: Oxford University Press, 1958 [German ed. 1917].

Oxtoby, Willard G., and Alan F. Segal, eds. *A Concise Introduction to World Religions*. Oxford: Oxford University Press, 2007.

Pagitt, Ephraim. *Christianographie, Or The Description of the multitude and sundry sorts of Christians in the World not subiect to the Pope*. London: Matthew Costerden, 1635.

Pailin, David A. *Attitudes to Other Religions: Comparative Religion in Seventeenth- and Eighteenth-Century Britain*. Manchester: Manchester University Press, 1984.

———. "The Confused and Confusing Story of Natural Religion." *Religion* 24 (1994): 199–212.

Pecock, Reginald. *The Repressor of Over Much Blaming of the Clergy.* 2 vols. Edited by Churchill Babington. London: Longman, Green, Longman, and Roberts, 1860.

Penn, Nigel. "The Voyage Out: Peter Kolb and the VOC Voyages to the Cape." Pages 72–91 in *Many Middle Passages: Forced Migration and the Making of the Modern World.* Edited by Emma Christopher, Cassandra Pybus, and Marcus Rediker. Berkeley: University of California Press, 2007.

Pennington, L. E. *The Purchas Handbook: Studies in the Life, Times and Writings of Samuel Purchas 1577–1626.* 2 vols. London: Hakluyt Society, 1997.

Peter the Venerable. *Against the Sect or Heresy of the Saracens.* Edited by J. P. Migne in *Patrologia Latina,* Vol. 189, cols. 669–70.

Pharo, Lars Kirkhusmo. "The Concept of 'Religion' in Mesoamerican Languages." *Numen* 54 (2007): 28–70.

Philo of Alexandria. *Philo: The Embassy to Gaius.* Edited and translated by F. H. Colson. Reprint ed. London: Harvard University Press, 1991 [1962].

Photius. *Photius: Bibliothèque.* Edited by René Henry. 9 vols. Paris: Les belles lettres, 1959–1991.

Picard, Bernard. *Cérémonies et coutumes religieuses de tous les peuples du monde representées par des figures dessinées de la main de Bernard Picard: avec une explication historique & quelques dissertations curieuses.* 9 vols. Amsterdam: J.-F. Bernard, 1723–1737.

Picart, Bernard. *The Ceremonies and Religious Customs of the Various Nations of the Known World Together with Historical Annotations and several Curious Discourses Equally Informative and Entertaining.* 7 vols. London: William Jackson for Claude du Bosc, 1733–1739.

Plato. *Platonis Rempublicam.* Edited by S. R. Slings. New York: Oxford University Press, 2003.

Plautus. *Plautus with an English Translation.* Edited and translated by Paul Nixon. 5 vols. London: William Heinemann, 1916–1938.

Preus, J. Samuel. *Explaining Religion: Criticism and Theory from Bodin to Freud.* New Haven, Conn.: Yale University Press, 1987.

Price, Simon. "Latin Christian Apologetics: Minucius Felix, Tertullian, and Cyprian." Pages 105–29 in *Apologetics in the Roman Empire: Pagans, Jews, and Christians.* Edited by Mark Edwards, Martin Goodman, Simon Price, and Christopher Rowland. Oxford: Oxford University Press, 1999.

———. *Religions of the Ancient Greeks.* Cambridge: Cambridge University Press, 1999.

Pullapilly, Cyriac K. *Caesar Baronius: Counter-Reformation Historian.* Notre Dame, Ind.: University of Notre Dame Press, 1975.

Purchas, Samuel. *Purchas his Pilgrimage: Or Relations of the World and the Religions Observed in all Ages and Places discovered, from Creation unto this Present: In Foure Partes.* London: William Stansby for Henrie Fetherstone, 1613.

Radhakrishnan, Sarvepalli. "Fellowship of the Spirit." Pages 277–96 in *Philosophy, Religion, and the Coming World Civilization: Essays in Honor of William Ernest Hocking.* Edited by Leroy S. Rouner. The Hague: Martinus Nijhoff, 1966.

Ragg, Lonsdale, and Laura Ragg, eds. and trans. *The Gospel of Barnabas: Edited and Translated from the Italian Ms. in the Imperial Library at Vienna.* Oxford: Clarendon, 1907.

Rawlinson, Henry Creswicke. "The Persian Cuneiform Inscription at Behistun, Deciphered and Translated; with a Memoir." *Journal of the Royal Asiatic Society* 10–11 (1848–1849).

Rawson, Elizabeth. *Intellectual Life in the Late Roman Republic.* London: Duckworth, 1985.

Reiner, Erica. *An Adventure of Great Dimension: The Launching of the Chicago Assyrian Dictionary.* Philadelphia: American Philosophical Society, 2002.

Robert of Ketton. *Machumetis Saracenorum principis eiusque successorum vitae, doctrina, ac ipse Alcoran.* Edited by Theodore Bibliander. Zurich[?], 1550 [1543].

Robinson, James M. "The Fate of the Manichaean Codices of Medinet Madi 1929–1989." Pages 19–62 in *Studia Manichaica: II. Internationaler Kongreß zum Manichäismus.* Edited by Gernot Wießner and Hans-Joachim Klimkeit. Wiesbaden: Otto Harrassowitz, 1992.

Roggema, Barbara. "The Legend of Sergius-Baḥīrā: Some Remarks on Its Origin in the East and Its Traces in the West." Pages 107–23 in *East and West in the Crusader States: Contexts, Contacts, Confrontations III: Acta of the Congress Held at Hernen Castle in September 2000.* Edited by Krijnie Ciggaar and Herman Teule. Leuven: Peeters, 2003.

Rorty, Richard. *Philosophy as Cultural Politics: Philosophical Papers, Vol. 4.* Cambridge: Cambridge University Press, 2007.

Rose, Paul Lawrence. "The *Politique* and the Prophet: Bodin and the Catholic League, 1589–1594." *Historical Journal* 21 (1978): 783–808.

Ross, Alexander. *The Alcoran of Mahomet, translated out of Arabique into French; by the sieur Du Ryer, Lord of Malezair, and resident for the King of France, at Alexandria. And newly Englished, for the satisfaction of all that desire to look into the Turkish vanities.* London: n.p., 1649.

———. *The Alcoran of Mahomet, translated out of Arabick . . . To which is prefixed, the life of Mahomet, the prophet of the Turks, and author of the Alcoran.*

With A needful caveat, or admonition, for them who desire to know what use may be made of, or if there be danger in reading the Alcoran. London: Randal Taylor, 1688.

———. *Pansebeia: Or, A View of All Religions in the World, with the Several Church-Governments, from the Creation, to These Times. Together with a Discovery of All Known Heresies, in All Ages and Places, Throughout Asia, Africa, America, and Europe.* London: James Young and John Saywell, 1653.

Rossi, Mario M. *La vita, le opere, i tempi di Edoardo Herbert di Chirbury.* 3 vols. Florence: G. C. Sansoni, 1947.

Sabbatucci, Dario. *La prospettiva storico-religiosa: Fede, religione e cultura.* Milan: Saggiatore, 1990.

Sahas, Daniel J. *John of Damascus on Islam: The "Heresy of the Ishmaelites."* Leiden: Brill, 1972.

———. "The Notion of 'Religion' with Reference to Islam in the Byzantine Anti-Islamic Literature." Pages 523–30 in *The Notion of "Religion" in Comparative Research: Selected Proceedings of the XVIth Congress of the International Association for the History of Religions.* Edited by Ugo Bianchi. Rome: "L'Erma" di Bretscneider, 1994.

Saler, Benson. *Conceptualizing Religion: Immanent Anthropologists, Transcendent Natives, and Unbounded Categories.* Leiden: Brill, 1993.

Salvianus of Marseilles. *Salvien de Marseille: Oeuvres.* Edited by Georges Lagarrigue. 2 vols. Paris: Éditions du Cerf, 1971–1975.

Scheid, John. "Polytheism Impossible; or, the Empty Gods: Reasons behind a Void in the History of Roman Religion." *History and Anthropology* 3 (1987): 303–25.

Schiller, Johann Christoph Friedrich von. "Die Götter Griechenlandes." *Der Teutsche Merkur* (March 1788): 250–60.

Schmidt, Francis. "Polytheisms: Degeneration or Progress?" *History and Anthropology* 3 (1987): 9–60.

Schmidt, Karl Ludwig. "*thrēskeia, thrēskos, ethelothrēskeia.*" Pages 155–59 in *Theological Dictionary of the New Testament.* Edited and translated by Geoffrey W. Bromiley. Vol. 3. Grand Rapids, Mich.: Eerdmans, 1964–1977.

Serjeant, R. B. "The 'Sunnah Jāmi'ah,' Pacts with the Yat̲h̲rib Jews, and the 'Taḥrīm' of Yat̲h̲rib: Analysis and Translation of the Documents Comprised in the So-Called 'Constitution of Medina.'" *Bulletin of the School of Oriental and African Studies, University of London* 41 (1978): 1–42.

Seznec, Jean. *The Survival of the Pagan Gods: The Mythological Tradition and Its Place in Renaissance Humanism and Art.* Translated by Barbara F. Sessions. New York: Pantheon, 1953 [French ed. 1940].

Shaki, Mansour. "*dēn*." Pages 279–81 in *Encyclopaedia Iranica*, Vol. 7. Edited by Ehsan Yarshater. Costa Mesa, Calif.: Mazda, 1996.

Sharf, Robert H. "Experience." Pages 94–115 in *Critical Terms for Religious Studies*. Edited by Mark C. Taylor. Chicago: University of Chicago Press, 1998.

Sharpe, Eric J. *Understanding Religion*. New York: St. Martin's, 1983.

———. *Comparative Religion: A History*. 2nd ed. La Salle, Ill.: Open Court, 1986 [1975].

Sidwell, Paul. *Classifying the Austroasiatic Languages: History and State of the Art*. Munich: Lincom Europa, 2009.

Simon, I. M. "The Khāsi Language: Its Development and Present Status." *Contributions to Asian Studies* 11 (1978): 167–80.

Singer, Dorthea Waley. *Giordano Bruno: His Life and Thought*. Reprint ed. New York: Greenwood, 1968 [1950].

Skinner, Quentin. *The Foundations of Modern Political Thought*. 2 vols. Cambridge: Cambridge University Press, 1978.

Smith, Huston. *The Religions of Man*. New York: Harper, 1958.

———. *The World's Religions: Our Great Wisdom Traditions*. San Francisco: Harper SanFrancisco, 1991.

Smith, Jonathan Z. "Bible and Religion." *Bulletin of the Council of Societies for the Study of Religion* 29 (2000): 87–93. Reprinted in Jonathan Z. Smith, *Relating Religion*, 197–214.

———. "God Save This Honourable Court: Religion and Civic Discourse." Pages 375–90 in Jonathan Z. Smith, *Relating Religion*.

———. "A Matter of Class: Taxonomies of Religion." *Harvard Theological Review* 89 (1996): 387–403. Reprinted in Jonathan Z. Smith, *Relating Religion*, 160–78.

———. *Relating Religion: Essays in the Study of Religion*. Chicago: University of Chicago Press, 2004.

———. "Religion, Religions, Religious." Pages 269–84 in *Critical Terms for Religious Studies*. Edited by Mark C. Taylor. Chicago: University of Chicago Press, 1998. Reprinted in Jonathan Z. Smith, *Relating Religion*, 179–96.

———. "Tillich['s] Remains." *Journal of the American Academy of Religion* 78 (2010): 1139–70.

Smith, Wilfred Cantwell. *The Meaning and End of Religion: A New Approach to the Religious Traditions of Mankind*. Reprint ed. Minneapolis: Fortress, 1991 [1963].

Smith, William Robertson. *Lectures on the Religion of the Semites*. Edinburgh: A. and C. Black, 1889.

Solmsen, Friedrich. "Wilamowitz in His Last Ten Years." *Greek, Roman, and Byzantine Studies* 20 (1979): 89–122.

Southern, R. W. *Western Society and the Church in the Middle Ages*. New York: Penguin, 1978.

———. *Western Views of Islam in the Middle Ages*. Cambridge, Mass.: Harvard University Press, 1962.

Stambaugh, John E. "The Functions of Roman Temples." *Aufstieg und Niedergang der römischen Welt* 2.16.1 (1978): 554–608.

Stopford, Joshua. *Pagano-papismus, Or, An Exact Parallel between Rome-pagan, and Rome-Christian, in their Doctrines and Ceremonies*. London: Printed by A. Maxwell for R. Clavel, 1675.

Stowers, Stanley. "The Ontology of Religion." Pages 434–49 in *Introducing Religion: Essays in Honor of Jonathan Z. Smith*. Edited by Willi Braun and Russell T. McCutcheon. London: Equinox, 2008.

———. "Theorizing the Religion of Ancient Households and Families." Pages 5–19 in *Household and Family Religion in Antiquity*. Edited by John Bodel and Saul M. Olyan. Oxford: Blackwell, 2008.

Stroumsa, Guy G. *A New Science: The Discovery of Religion in the Age of Reason*. Cambridge, Mass.: Harvard University Press, 2010.

Suda. *Suidae Lexicon*. Edited by Ada Adler. 5 vols. Leipzig: Teubner, 1928–1938.

Sullivan, Robert E. *John Toland and the Deist Controversy*. Cambridge, Mass.: Harvard University Press, 1982.

Sundermann, Werner. *Mitteliranische manichäische Texte kirchengeschichtlichen Inhalts*. Berlin: Akademie-Verlag, 1981.

Sweetman, Will. *A Discovery of the Banian Religion and the Religion of the Persees: A Critical Edition of Two Early Works on Indian Religions*. Lewiston, N.Y.: Edwin Mellen, 1999.

Tanner, Kathryn. *Theories of Culture: A New Agenda for Theology*. Minneapolis: Fortress, 1997.

Tcherikover, Victor. *Hellenistic Civilization and the Jews*. Reprint ed. Peabody, Mass.: Hendrickson, 1999 [1959].

Teeuwen, Mark. "From *Jindō* to Shinto: A Concept Takes Shape." *Japanese Journal of Religious Studies* 29 (2002): 233–63.

Teeuwen, Mark, and Fabio Rambelli, eds. *Buddhas and Kami in Japan: honji suijaku as a Combinatory Paradigm*. London: RoutledgeCurzon, 2003.

Terence. *Terence.* Edited by John Barsby. 2 vols. Cambridge, Mass.: Harvard University Press, 2001.

Tertullian. *Quinti Septimi Florentis Tertulliani Opera.* Edited by E. Dekkers, J. G. P. Borleffs, R. Willems, R. F. Refoulé, G. F. Diercks, E. Kroymann, A. Gerlo, J. H. Waszink, A. Reifferscheid, G. Wissowa, J. J. Thierry, E. Evans, and A. Harnack. 2 vols. Turnhout: Brepols, 1954.

Thal, Sarah. "A Religion That Was Not a Religion: The Creation of Modern Shinto in Nineteenth-Century Japan." Pages 100–14 in *The Invention of Religion: Rethinking Belief in Politics and History.* Edited by Derek R. Petersen and Darren R. Walhof. New Brunswick, N.J.: Rutgers University Press, 2002.

Thomas Aquinas. *An Apology for the Religious Orders: Being a Translation from the Latin of Two of the Minor Works of the Saint.* Translated by John Procter. London: Sands, 1902.

———. *S. Thomae Aquinatis: Opera omnia 2.* Edited by Roberto Busa. Stuttgart: Frommann-Holzboog, 1980.

Tiele, Cornelis P. *De godsdienst van Zarathustra van haar ontstaan in Baktrië tot den val van het Oud-Perzische Rijk.* Haarlem: A. C. Kruseman, 1864.

———. *Outlines of the History of Religion to the Spread of the Universal Religions.* Translated by J. Estlin Carpenter. Boston: James R. Osgood, 1877 [Dutch ed. 1876].

———. "Religions." Pages 358–71 in *Encyclopaedia Britannica: A Dictionary of Arts, Sciences, and General Literature,* Vol. 20. 9th ed. Boston: Little, Brown, 1886.

Tindal, Matthew. *Christianity as Old as the Creation: Or, the Gospel, a Republication of the Religion of Nature.* London: n.p., 1730.

Tolan, John V. "Peter the Venerable on the 'Diabolical Heresy of the Saracens.'" Pages 345–67 in *The Devil, Heresy, and Witchcraft in the Middle Ages: Essays in Honor of Jeffrey B. Russell.* Edited by Alberto Ferreiro. Leiden: Brill, 1998.

———. *Saracens: Islam in the Medieval European Imagination.* New York: Columbia University Press, 2002.

Toland, John. *Nazarenus: Or, Jewish, Gentile, and Mahometan Christianity. Containing the history of the antient Gospel of Barnabas, and the modern Gospel of the Mahometans, attributed to the same Apostle: this last Gospel being now first made known among Christians.* 2nd revised ed. London: J. Brotherton, J. Roberts, and A. Dodd, 1718.

———. *The Reasons for Naturalising the Jews in Great Britain and Ireland: On the Same Foot with All Other Nations: Containing also a Defence of the Jews against all Vulgar Prejudices in all Countries.* London: Printed for J. Roberts, 1714.

Tooley, M. J. "Introduction." Pages vii–xxxix in *Six Books of the Commonwealth: Abridged and Translated by M. J. Tooley.* Oxford: Blackwell, 1955.

Toropov, Brandon, and Luke Buckles. *The Complete Idiot's Guide to World Religions.* 3rd ed. Indianapolis: Alpha, 2002.

Turner, Frank M. "Why the Greeks and Not the Romans in Victorian Britain?" Pages 61–81 in *Rediscovering Hellenism: The Hellenic Inheritance and the English Imagination.* Edited by G. W. Clarke. Cambridge: Cambridge University Press, 1989.

Van Herten, Joseph Christiaan Antonius. thrēskeia eulabeia hiketēs. *Bijdrage tot de kennis der religieuze terminologie in het Grieksch.* Amsterdam: H. J. Paris, 1934.

Vega, Garcilaso de la. *The Royal Commentaries of Peru, in Two Parts.* Translated by Paul Rycaut. London: Miles Flesher for Jacob Tonson, 1688.

Veldhuis, Niek. *Religion, Literature, and Scholarship: The Sumerian Composition Nanše and the Birds, with a Catalogue of Sumerian Bird Names.* Leiden: Brill/Styx, 2004.

Waardenburg, Jacques. *Muslims and Others: Relations in Context.* Berlin: de Gruyter, 2003.

Wagner, Henry Raup, and Helen Rand Parish. *The Life and Writings of Bartolome de las Casas.* Albuquerque: University of New Mexico Press, 1967.

Waldron, Jeremy. *God, Locke, and Equality: Christian Foundations in Locke's Political Thought.* Cambridge: Cambridge University Press, 2002.

———. "Locke: Toleration and the Rationality of Persecution." Pages 61–86 in *Justifying Toleration: Conceptual and Historical Perspectives.* Edited by Susan Mendus. Cambridge: Cambridge University Press, 1988.

Walker, Daniel Pickering. *The Ancient Theology: Studies in Christian Platonism from the Fifteenth to the Eighteenth Century.* Ithaca, N.Y.: Cornell University Press, 1972.

Wallace-Hadrill, Andrew. *Rome's Cultural Revolution.* Cambridge: Cambridge University Press, 2008.

Wansbrough, John. *Quranic Studies: Sources and Methods of Scriptural Interpretation.* Revised ed. by Andrew Rippin. Amherst, N.Y.: Prometheus, 2004 [1977].

Wasserstrom, Steven. *Religion after Religion: Gershom Scholem, Mircea Eliade, and Henry Corbin at Eranos.* Princeton, N.J.: Princeton University Press, 1999.

Watson, Alan, trans. *The Digest of Justinian*. Revised ed. 2 vols. Philadelphia: University of Pennsylvania Press, 1998 [1985].

Watson, Richard. *An Apology for Christianity: In a Series of Letters Addressed to Edward Gibbon, Esq., Author of the Decline and Fall of the Roman Empire.* Cambridge: F. Archdeacon for T. and J. Merrill et al., 1776.

West, E. W. *Pahlavi Texts Part I: The Bundahis, Bahman Yast, and Shâyast Lâ-Shâyast.* Oxford: Clarendon, 1880.

Whitney, William D. "On the So-Called Science of Religion." *Princeton Review* 57 (1881): 429–52.

Wilamowitz-Moellendorff, Ulrich von. *Der Glaube der Hellenen.* 2 vols. Berlin: Wiedmannsche Buchhandlung, 1931–1932.

Willey, Basil. *The Seventeenth Century Background: Studies in the Thought of the Age in Relation to Poetry and Religion.* Reprint ed. New York: Columbia University Press, 1977 [1934].

Wissowa, Georg. *Religion und Kultus der Römer.* Munich: C. H. Beck, 1902.

Wittgenstein, Ludwig. *Philosophical Investigations: The German Text with a Revised English Translation.* Translated by G. E. M. Anscombe. 3rd ed. Oxford: Blackwell, 2001 [1953].

———. *Tractatus Logico-Philosophicus.* Translated by C. K. Ogden. London: Keegan Paul, Trench, and Trubner, 1922.

Wolf, Kenneth Baxter. "Christian Views of Islam in Early Medieval Spain." Pages 85–108 in *Medieval Christian Perceptions of Islam.* Edited by John V. Tolan. New York: Routledge, 2000.

———. "The Earliest Spanish Christian Views of Islam." *Church History* 55 (1986): 281–93.

Wolff, Robert Lee. "Barlaam and Ioasaph." *Harvard Theological Review* 32 (1939): 131–39.

Womersley, David. *Gibbon and the 'Watchmen of the Holy City': The Historian and His Reputation 1776–1815.* Oxford: Clarendon, 2002.

Woodard, William P. *The Allied Occupation of Japan 1945–1952 and Japanese Religions.* Leiden: Brill, 1972.

Wootton, David. "Pseudo-Bodin's *Colloquium heptaplomeres* and Bodin's *Démonomanie.*" Pages 175–225 in *Magie, Religion und Wissenschaften im Colloquium heptaplomeres: Ergebnisse der Tagungen in Paris 1994 und in der Villa Vigoni 1999.* Edited by Karl Friedrich Faltenbacher. Darmstadt: Wissenschaftliche Buchgesellschaft, 2002.

Yang, C. K. *Religion in Chinese Society: A Study of Contemporary Social Functions of Religion and Some of Their Historical Factors.* Reprint ed. Berkeley: University of California Press, 1967 [1961].

Yates, Frances A. *Giordano Bruno and the Hermetic Tradition.* Chicago: University of Chicago Press, 1964.

———. "The Mystery of Jean Bodin." *New York Review of Books* (23) 1976. http://www.nybooks.com/articles/8723 (accessed 23 October 2011).

Young, Katherine K. "World Religions: A Category in the Making?" Pages 111–30 in *Religion in History: The Word, the Idea, the Reality.* Edited by Michel Despland and Gérard Vallée. Waterloo, Ontario: Wilfred Laurier University Press, 1992.

Zaehner, R. C. *Zurvan: A Zoroastrian Dilemma.* Oxford: Clarendon, 1955.

Zaidman, Louise Bruit, and Pauline Schmitt Pantel. *Religion in the Ancient Greek City.* Translated by Paul Cartledge. Cambridge: Cambridge University Press, 1992 [French ed. 1989].

Zilkha, Avraham. *Modern English-Hebrew Dictionary.* New Haven, Conn.: Yale University Press, 2002.

Zivie-Coche, Christiane. "Preface" to *Gods and Men in Egypt: 3000 BCE to 395 CE* by Françoise Dunand and Christiane Zivie-Coche. Translated by David Lorton. Ithaca, N.Y.: Cornell University Press, 2004 [French ed. 1991].

Zwingli, Ulrich. *Commentary on True and False Religion.* Edited and translated by Samuel Macauley Jackson and Clarence Nevin Heller. Durham, N.C.: Labyrinth, 1981.

———. *Opera D. Huldrychi Zuinglii.* Edited by Rudolf Gwalther and Leo Jud. Zurich: Christoph Froschauer, 1545.

INDEX

Abraham: as ancestor of Brah-
mins, 111; as ancestor of
Christians, 55–57, 74; as
ancestor of Jews, 74; as ancestor
of Khoikhoi, 115; as ancestor of
Muslims, 62–64, 74; in the
Qur'an, 43–44; *thrēskeia* of, 35
"Abrahamic religions," 128
Ackerman, Robert, 222n31
Acosta, José de, 134–36
Adler, Joseph A., 167n1
African religions, 113–16
Al-Biruni, 70
Albright, William F., 202n53
Alexander of Lycopolis, 187n10
Ali, Abdullah Yusuf, 184n53
Allan, David, 213n57
Allen, Michael J. B., 195n9,
195n10, 196n12
Almond, Philip C., 192n53,
193n61, 209n22
Ambrose of Milan, 162n11,
205n80
Americas, discovery of, 107
anachronism, 158, 227n69
ancient religion, 8, 10, 16, 84, 113,
132–53
Ancient Theology (*prisca
theologia*), 87–95
Ando, Clifford, 27, 229–30n13
Andreas, F. C., 187n11
Antichrist, 190n35
Aquilecchia, Giovanni, 198n24

Arberry, Arthur J., 59
archeology, 11, 23, 133–34,
144–45
Aristotle, 136
Arius, 74
Armstrong, Karen, 18–19, 130
Arnobius of Sicca, 29
Arnold, Edwin, 112
art, 140, 222n32
Artapanus, 196n14
Asad, Talal, 4–5, 54, 162n8, 164n8
Ashley, Lord Anthony, First Earl
of Shaftesbury, 101, 104
Ashoka, 162n7
Aśvaghoṣa, 83, 192n55
Auffarth, Christoph, 165–66n19
augury, 51
Augustine of Hippo: as follower
and critic of Mani, 67, 71–72;
as source for early colonial
authors, 135; on Hermes
Trismegistus, 195n5; on Roman
gods as demons, 133; use of
religio by, 30–31, 33, 86–87, 89
authenticity, 111, 113

Balagangadhara, S. N., 163n13
Banians, 110–12
Barlaam and Ioasaph, story of, 9,
38, 66, 77–84
Barnes, Timothy D., 170n21
Baronius, Caesar, 77
Baynes, Norman H., 176n73

263